# THE
# PSYCHOLOGY
# OF DYSLEXIA

## A HANDBOOK
## FOR
## TEACHERS

# THE
# PSYCHOLOGY
## OF DYSLEXIA

## A HANDBOOK
## FOR
## TEACHERS

### SECOND EDITION

*With Case Studies CD-ROM*

## Michael Thomson

A John Wiley & Sons, Ltd., Publication

This second edition first published 2009
© 2009 John Wiley & Sons Ltd.

Edition history: Whurr Publishers Ltd (1e, 2001)

Wiley-Blackwell is an imprint of John Wiley & Sons, formed by the merger of Wiley's global Scientific, Technical, and Medical business with Blackwell Publishing.

*Registered Office*
John Wiley & Sons Ltd, The Atrium, Southern Gate, Chichester, West Sussex, PO19 8SQ, UK

*Editorial Offices*
The Atrium, Southern Gate, Chichester, West Sussex, PO19 8SQ, UK
9600 Garsington Road, Oxford, OX4 2DQ, UK
350 Main Street, Malden, MA 02148-5020, USA

For details of our global editorial offices, for customer services, and for information about how to apply for permission to reuse the copyright material in this book please see our website at www.wiley.com/wiley-blackwell.

The right of the author to be identified as the author of this work has been asserted in accordance with the Copyright, Designs and Patents Act 1988.

Wiley also publishes its books in a variety of electronic formats. Some content that appears in print may not be available in electronic books.

Designations used by companies to distinguish their products are often claimed as trademarks. All brand names and product names used in this book are trade names, service marks, trademarks or registered trademarks of their respective owners. The publisher is not associated with any product or vendor mentioned in this book. This publication is designed to provide accurate and authoritative information in regard to the subject matter covered. It is sold on the understanding that the publisher is not engaged in rendering professional services. If professional advice or other expert assistance is required, the services of a competent professional should be sought.

*Library of Congress Cataloging-in-Publication Data has been applied for*

ISBN 978-0-470-74096-5 (hbk)   978-0-470-69954-6 (pbk)

A catalogue record for this book is available from the British Library.

Set in 10.5/13 pt Palatino by SNP Best-set Typesetter Ltd., Hong Kong
Printed in Singapore by Fabulous Printers Pte Ltd

1   2009

# Contents

# Preface

The need for a second edition has arisen out of the fact that *The Psychology of Dyslexia* is often used as a textbook for some of the teacher training courses – teachers undertaking diplomas or certificates for specific learning difficulties/dyslexia. The book has been out since 2001, and inevitably, there has been further research and new developments.

However the substantial descriptions of dyslexia and the psychology background remain the same and the descriptions of how to use the book and my general approach to dyslexia as outlined below remain the same.

The following are the major changes:

- The book has been extensively updated and expanded.
- The chapters on the recognition of dyslexia and the current Special Educational Need policies have been updated.
- The chapter on the assessment of dyslexia has been completely rewritten, taking into account the recent assessment developments, such as the Wechsler Intelligence Scale IV.
- As an adjunct to this second edition, a CD-ROM is being made available. This contains over 25 case histories of children who have been assessed using cognitive, attainment and diagnostic tests. These are educational psychologist's reports looking at children who are typically dyslexic, but include those where there is some overlap between dyslexia and, for example, attention deficits, motor development (dyspraxia), mathematical difficulties and those with high or low intelligence IQ.
- The chapter on models of reading, writing and spelling, working memory and phonological skills in dyslexia have all been

updated, taking into account recent research, as well as further information on neuropsychology of dyslexia, including recent studies on brain scans.

- There is a completely new chapter on the social psychology of dyslexia, which looks at the social background, as well as issues such as bullying and secondary behavioural reactions to specific learning difficulties.
- Finally, the CD-ROM not only includes the case histories, as mentioned earlier, but also some guides to help with teaching children, hearing them read, aspects of their working memory and processing speeds, but also examples of Graded Phonic Tests (reading and spelling), which have been produced by East Court School and are available for teachers and others to use.

As a result the book has grown in size, not only due to the additional social psychology chapter, but also the addition of the CD-ROM on case histories, which accompanies this book.

In particular, I would draw teacher's attention to the East Court Graded Phonic (reading and spelling) Tests which, provided they are appropriately acknowledged, are available for use.

## The structure of this book and how to use it

Please read this!

The purpose of this book is to present the underlying psychology of dyslexia to, mainly, teachers who may be undertaking a training course on teaching children with dyslexia. The book will also be of interest to parents of dyslexic children, teachers who are already trained and want to brush up current knowledge and teachers who have dyslexic children in their class.

The book grew out of the once-weekly lectures on psychology that I gave to the Dyslexia Institute's Diploma in Specific Learning Difficulties in the 1999–2000 academic year. I have tried to make the style accessible, with tables and diagrams wherever possible. Inevitably, there are references and complex arguments to be taken into account, but I have tried to provide an overview of the essentials, with further reading suggested.

*Content and structure*

The content broadly follows the psychology syllabus of 'Dyslexia Teaching' diplomas and certificates. The following topics are specifically covered.

Chapter 1:    The nature of dyslexia as a syndrome and its histori-
              cal context: descriptions, education acts.
Chapter 2:    Basic psychometrics: how psychological and educa-
              tional tests are constructed; standard scores, valid-
              ity, what the tests measure.
Chapter 3:    How dyslexia is assessed: ability, attainment and
              diagnostic tests given by psychologists; how to
              interpret reports; what tests teachers can use; case
              history, examples.
Chapter 4:    Current issues on diagnosis of discrepancies
              between intelligence, attainment, phonological
              skills and assessment.
Chapter 5:    Basic neuropsychology: brain function/language
              areas; auditory and visual processing; hemisphere
              function.
Chapter 6:    Neuropsychology of dyslexia: genetic predisposi-
              tion; cerebral dominance; laterality; electroencepha-
              lograph, brain imaging; dichotic listening; written
              language functions, cerebellar and visual transient
              theories.
Chapter 7:    Models of reading and spelling: nature of written
              language; stage models of development; skills
              needed to acquire written language.
Chapter 8:    Models of memory, particularly working memory
              and its relationship to reading skills.
Chapter 9:    Phonological and memory skills in dyslexia: notion
              of core phonological deficit; memory difficulties.
Chapter 10:   The social psychology of dyslexia

*How to use the book*

The reader will note from the above that some chapters are basic psychology topics whereas others focus on dyslexia. Unless the reader is familiar with psychology, it is suggested that the basic knowledge chapters are read first, followed by the 'dyslexia' chapters.

As it is unlikely that the reader will take in the whole book at one sitting, I have deliberately sandwiched dyslexia chapters between the basic psychology. Each chapter forms a coherent (I hope!) whole, equivalent to two or more lectures. Each chapter could be read independently, but here are two suggestions for reading the book.

1.  Reading individual subject basics followed by the relevant 'dyslexia' section. This follows the order of the chapters in the book, that is, Chapter 1, then 2, 3, 4 (assessment), 5, 6 (neuropsychology), 7, 8 and 9 (cognitive).
2.  Reading all 'basics' followed by all 'dyslexia': Chapter 1, then 2, 5, 7 and 8 (basics), then 3, 4, 6 and 9.

Alternatively, completely ignore the above and read from page 1 to the end or any other way you want!

*Why have I organized the book like this*

It seems to me that the first stage of understanding dyslexia is to recognize children who have dyslexic difficulties. This implies observation and, crucially, assessment. Before reading the psychologists' reports and undertaking your own assessments, it is important to understand the assessment process, hence the first four chapters.

I have then divided the aetiology of dyslexia into two broad areas: its biology and the cognitive expression of the underlying neuropsychology. This division essentially follows the model given in Figure 1. This is my adaptation to dyslexia of a developmental model put forward by Frith (1992). She has since extended this to look at different theories of aetiology and these are the 'models of deficit' in the dyslexia chapters.

At the bottom of Figure 1 are the observable characteristics of dyslexia entitled 'behavioural manifestations'. The features listed here are examples of those typically observed in dyslexic children. We examine and list these in more detail in Chapter 1.

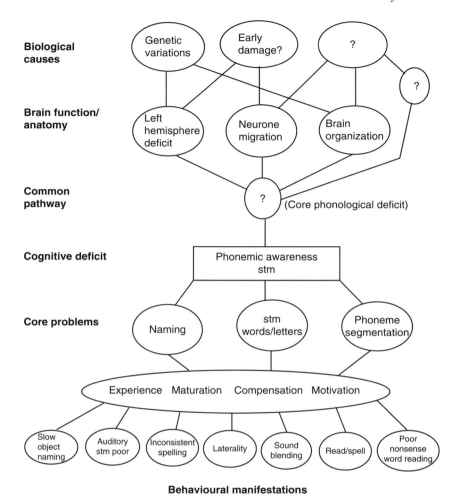

**Behavioural manifestations**

**Figure 1** Model of developmental disorders. (Adapted from Frith, 1992.) (stm, short-term memory).

Although there are some commonalities, each child brings his or her own experience, particular received teaching, level of difficulty and so on.

However, there is a common pathway to the syndrome. If we start at the top of Figure 1, you can see suggestions of biological causes linked to brain function and anatomy. These issues are discussed in Chapters 5 and 6. There is then a hypothesized common pathway. These result in cognitive deficits and core problems which are discussed in Chapters 7, 8 and 9. The cognitive builds on the biological basis, hence the position of the neuropsychology chapters first.

# Acknowledgements

Firstly, I would like to acknowledge the hard work of Sharon Wilson in translating my ramblings into early first drafts and subsequently into proper working drafts. Sharon has also been superb at scanning in and creating new diagrams, particularly on neuropyschology and brain function.

Acknowledgements are also due to Nanette Bech-Nielsen (psychology student on placement) and Amy Richardson (Assistant Psychologist) for their early trawl of the literature and providing me with a pile of books and papers with comments! This was above and beyond the call of duty and very much appreciated. Thanks are also due to Nanette for re-analysis of our current data on Wechsler Intelligence Scale for Children (WISC-IV) profiles and index scores from both school and assessment service sources.

Thanks are also due to Alexea Stevens (Assistant Psychologist) for her technical work in re-calibrating test scores from the WISC-IV, but mainly for her sterling efforts in initial choice and collation of the case histories, which are on the CD-ROM.

Thanks are due to Wendy Goldup at the Dyslexia Institute (DI) who was the organizer of the Tonbridge DI Diploma course 1999–2000. Thanks also to the teachers on that course who gave valuable feedback on the quality of my overheads and handouts upon which this book is based, and to Martin Turner, Head of Psychology at the DI, for encouraging me to use my lectures as a basis for a book.

Finally, thank you to my partner Amanda for her patience and support, when I was burning the midnight oil and getting anxious about deadlines!

# 1

# The Nature of Dyslexia

## Emergence of a syndrome

Although many books and papers refer to the case histories of Hinshelwood (1900) and Morgan (1896) describing word-blind children and the recognition of acquired dyslexias from the beginning of the century, it was not really until the 1970s that dyslexia has been recognized as a specific learning difficulty in this country. Similar developments have taken place in other parts of the world, particularly in the United States.

In the United Kingdom, in the early 1970s, the 1944 Education Act was still in force. Basically, this argued for a number of categories of handicap, in which dyslexia and specific learning difficulties were not included. If you did not fall into one of these categories, you officially did not exist, and therefore, the notion of dyslexia did not exist.

What we might call 'barriers to learning', that is, factors that were seen to prevent children from acquiring literacy, fell into broad categories of problems, which were seen to be either extrinsic to the child, for example, to do with society and school teaching, or intrinsic, that is, within the child, which were to do with intelligence and gross neurological problems.

A typical child guidance centre at the time, to which children were referred if they had a variety of educational difficulties including problems with reading, included a psychiatrist, an educational psychologist, a social worker and a teacher. Problems were very

*The Psychology of Dyslexia – A Handbook for Teachers,* by Michael Thomson
© 2009 John Wiley & Sons Ltd

broadly viewed within social background and intellectual and emotional spheres.

As far as social background was concerned, Table 1.1 shows the typical finding (Eisenberg, 1966) of the relationship between presented reading difficulties and socio-economic class.

The fact that children of a lower socio-economic status background had more difficulties in reading and spelling was seen to be the result of factors such as linguistic background, perceptual experience, attitudes from home towards school and so on. For example, it was felt that, if parents had fewer educational qualifications, the implication was that they discouraged their children from seeing school work as important and the children picked up that view. If there was a restricted use of language or less richness of environmental experience at home, this might prevent a child from being ready to acquire written language learning. Programmes such as Head Start (which gave us Sesame Street and the Muppets!) and others were all geared towards making a child ready to acquire reading, writing and spelling.

As far as the intellectual sphere was concerned, it was recognized that there was a good correlation between intelligence and reading ability. Children were categorized, based on intelligence test scores, into those who might fall into the 'educationally subnormal' or the 'severely subnormal' categories, which reflected the Education Act categories of handicap. Children typically falling within these cut-offs might be referred for education in special schools. In later chapters, we examine in great detail this relationship between intelligence and reading and discrepancy models of dyslexia.

If there were no explanations to be found within the child's social background (social worker) or his or her intellectual profile (educational psychologist), then an explanation was sought within the emotional sphere. Here, children might be perceived to be

**Table 1.1** Percentages of children with reading difficulties in different occupational classes.

| Class | Percentage |
|-------|-----------|
| 1 and 2 | 7 |
| 3 | 19 |
| 4 and 5 | 27 |

emotionally disturbed, which was preventing them from acquiring written language learning. The response to this might be either drug therapy or, if the child was perceived to have particular psychiatric problems, through play therapy at the child guidance centre.

There was, therefore, a reasonable set-up for the identification of children in the described areas. However, many teachers were still commenting on children who, despite not showing any of the mentioned so-called barriers to learning, were still not acquiring reading, writing and spelling. Early identification of dyslexia was therefore based on the descriptions by teachers and others working in this area, as well as exclusionary definitions. In other words, if a child was intelligent, came from a well-supported home background and did not have a primary emotional problem but was still failing to read, write and spell, he or she might be described as dyslexic.

There were, at the time, a number of these descriptions or symptomatologies and these are still produced. The British Dyslexia Association, the Dyslexia Institute, the Hornsby Centre and many other well-known organizations working in dyslexia all produced their own lists of 'symptoms'. A typical example of this is given in Table 1.2.

**Table 1.2** Features of dyslexia.

---

A puzzling gap between written language skills and intelligence

Delayed and poor reading and spelling, often with persistent reversals and disordering of letters, syllables and words (d/b, was/saw, place/palace)

'Bizarre' spelling (raul/urchins, kss/snake, tars/trumpet) and others that are more recognizable (wayt/wait, pant/paint, boll/doll)

Confusion of left/right direction

Sequencing difficulties such as saying the months of the year in order; poor directional scan in reading; weak sequential memory

Poor short-term memory skills (repeating digits; following complex instructions)

Problems in acquiring arithmetical tables

Problems in repeating polysyllabic words (sas'tis'ti'cal for statistical, per'rim'min'ery for preliminary)

Difficulties in expressing ideas in written form

---

Source: from a booklet produced by East Court School (1983, 2000).

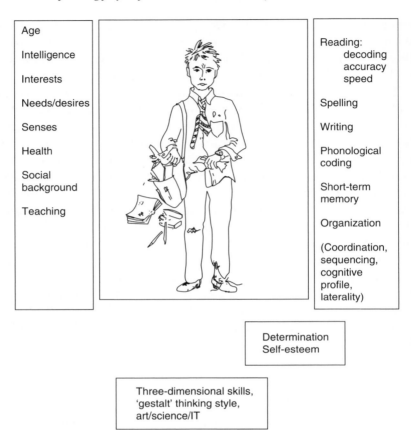

| Age | | Reading: |
|---|---|---|
| Intelligence | | decoding |
| | | accuracy |
| Interests | | speed |
| Needs/desires | | Spelling |
| Senses | | Writing |
| Health | | Phonological |
| | | coding |
| Social | | |
| background | | Short-term |
| | | memory |
| Teaching | | Organization |
| | | (Coordination, |
| | | sequencing, |
| | | cognitive |
| | | profile, |
| | | laterality) |

Determination
Self-esteem

Three-dimensional skills,
'gestalt' thinking style,
art/science/IT

**Figure 1.1** 'Charlie', a dyslexic 11-year-old.

Other associated factors may include late language development and continued pronunciation difficulties; ambidexterity or mixed-handedness; similar problems in other members of the family; clumsiness; poor graphic (writing) skills; and dyspraxia.

We can make this a little more concrete by looking at case histories and examples of actual and hypothetical children. Let us look at 'Charlie', shown in Figure 1.1.

Charlie is a young man aged 11 years who has just started his secondary school and is dyslexic. On the left-hand side are a number of characteristics that are similar to those in other children of his age, and on the right-hand side and the bottom are a number of characteristics that are different from those of other children. The right-hand side shows those skills that Charlie does less well than his peers, and at the bottom are those items that he might do rather better than his peer group.

If we look at Charlie himself, we get some clues about some aspects of dyslexia. He is looking rather worried and anxious. He has not been sleeping very much. This results partly from the fact of starting a new school where he is rather lost. Children with dyslexia sometimes have difficulty with orientation, and he finds it very difficult to know where he is at any given time. Particularly important, he finds it difficult to read his timetable. This is a very long and complicated document. He is not sure whether he is supposed to be reading it across the top or down the side, and does not understand the abbreviations. He also finds it difficult to read some of these. As a result of this, he not only has problems in finding out where he is supposed to be, but he also does not know what lessons he is having either in the morning or in the afternoon on a given day. To solve the problem, he takes all the books he needs for all of his classes around with him! This results in a huge bag full of all the books and papers that he needs. Inevitably, as a result of his weak organizational skills, a lot of the contents fall out. You will notice that he is carrying lots of pencils because he forgets them and does not want to get into trouble for losing them. He often gets shouted at by teachers or told off for not having the right materials or equipment at any given time. As he has weaknesses in short-term memory, this forgetfulness is inevitable.

Many, but not all, children with dyslexia are somewhat more clumsy than their peers, and therefore, he has problems in doing up his tie and his shoelaces even at the age of 11. At the present time, he is looking at his watch, not just to see what time it is but actually to work out which direction is left and which right, as he has been told to go down the left-hand corridor, followed by the right-hand corridor, straight along for two or three doors, and go up the stairs and turn left towards the science block where he will find his next lesson! He has problems in processing all this information as well as, of course, remembering it. It is not surprising that he is looking worried and lost!

On the left-hand side are things in which he is similar to other children. He is the same age as the other children and he is of the same general intellectual background. It is a misnomer to say that all dyslexic children are intelligent – sometimes reported erroneously in the media. It is obviously easier to spot a dyslexic child if his attainment skills are well below his intelligence. Nevertheless, people with dyslexia have just as wide a range of intelligence as the rest of the population. He may be bright, he may be less able on intelligence tests or he may be of average ability. Charlie's interests are the same as those of other children. Currently, as I write, these are scooters and 'yo-yoing' at my school, but there will be something different next term, I am sure. He has the same needs and desires – he wants to be successful; he needs to be loved; he needs to be secure; he needs to have all those things that make a child of 11 feel comfortable and happy in his environment and school.

By and large, his senses are the same as those of other children – he can see (he might have glasses, he might not) and on the whole, he can hear well. There may have been some slight hearing losses when he was younger – grommets and such like – which are often more common in dyslexic children. Charlie's health, social background and the received teaching he has had are all the same as for other children, and yet he has problems in reading and spelling.

On the right-hand side are the things with which he has difficulty. Obviously dyslexic children are seen to have problems with reading, but we should note here that this is not all aspects of reading. If we are able to help the dyslexic child work out what the words are in reading, his comprehension can be quite good. The problem is not in higher order skills – we shall be looking in some detail at these later – but in decoding the words; so decoding, accuracy and speed of reading are all weak, as are spelling, writing, phonological or sound coding, short-term memory and the other items listed. We look at all of these in more detail later Chapters 3 and 9. Sometimes, dyslexic children will have problems with coordination, sequencing, language and laterality. Again, we examine all of these in greater detail (Chapter 6).

At the bottom of the diagram are areas that some people with dyslexia do well on. My clinical, research and teaching experience suggest that many people with dyslexia are rather better at three-dimensional skills, that is, they have what we might term 'gestalt' thinking. Within families, one gets good skills in engineering, architecture, dentistry, medicine, art, design and so on. At school, they tend to do rather better at science (the experimental part, not the copying from board and writing!), art and Information Communication Technology (ICT). An anecdote that I have written elsewhere illustrates this point. Some time ago, we had a craze for remote-controlled cars at the school, and I bought a kit for one of my own children (but, in reality, to make for myself!). I tend to be a very linear thinker and I like to read the instructions and follow step 1, step 2 and so on. After months of trying to construct this model, burning the midnight oil, I still could not make it work. One day, I brought it over to the school and the children looked at the cogs and gears and said, 'You've got them all the wrong way round, sir!' and like magic rearranged the whole of the gearing so that it worked. They were able to look at the exploded diagram, understand the spatial relationships involved and how the whole thing worked, and construct it in that way – a much more relevant skill than mine. Of course, I am lucky that linear/verbal skills tend to be tapped in the early part of a child's school career as opposed to those skills that many people with dyslexia have, which tend to be in the visualization and three-dimensional area.

You will notice that Figure 1.1 talks about self-esteem and determination. Children with dyslexia who are not given help have very low self-esteem and we also look at this in a little more detail later. However, given the right sort of help, they can build up a strong determination to succeed. If they can overcome the 'I am dyslexic and I can't do it' approach, they can do very well. Again, our experience is that many of our children who go on to their senior schools can do rather better at 'A' levels than their nondyslexic peers. This is because, if you have never had a problem with reading and spelling in education, you sail through your GCSEs with no problem. There is a big gap between GCSE and 'A' level standard. Some students find it very hard work and are not sure how to deal with it. The child with dyslexia who has been given good study skills and knows how to work, metaphorically says, 'Oh, more hard work – no problem' at 'A' level and just gets on with it.

Although this is not a book about how to recognize dyslexia as such and we are focussing on the psychological background, it is

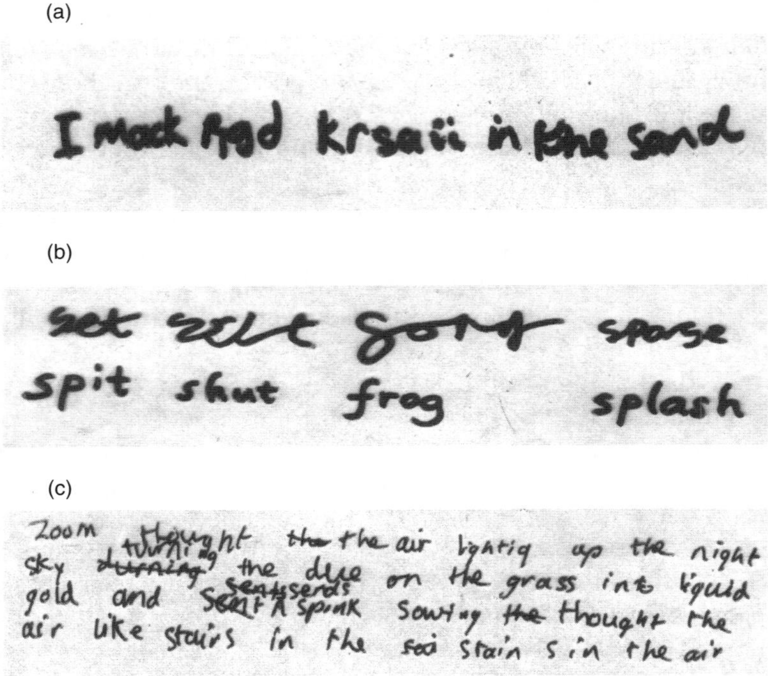

(a)

(b)

(c)

**Figure 1.2** Examples of dyslexics' writing.

always useful just to note a few examples of writing, particularly in the context of describing dyslexia.

If the reader is interested in more detailed case histories, there is an example in Chapter 3 and also the CD-ROM accompanying this book has many examples of different case histories including background, detailed breakdown of reading and spelling errors and so on.

There are three examples of writing detailed here (Figure 1.2).

Dyslexia used to be defined very much in terms of a child's reading, writing and spelling difficulties, rather than a more systematic diagnostic approach as is used nowadays. The first piece of writing (Figure 1.2a) says, 'I made sandcastles in the sand.' Secondly (Figure 1.2b), there are examples of spellings of single words. There are obvious errors, such as omissions of consonants, confusion of vowels, letter order errors, repetition of words, approximations to sounds and all of the other errors that are typically associated with dyslexia. These two examples were by a 10-year-old boy with reading levels of approximately a six-year-old.

The third example (Figure 1.2c) not only illustrates difficulties, but also demonstrates the tremendous difference between the imagery and the, sometimes, rich use of language that dyslexics have in contrast to their ability to express it in writing. This says, 'Zoom! Through the air, lighting up the night sky, turning the dew on the grass to liquid gold and sending a spark soaring through the air like stars in the satin stained (the) air.' Although overwritten for a modern taste, do bear in mind this is an 11-year-old, trying to express his observations of the firework display at the school!

While there is evidence that dyslexia is a broad language disorder, particularly in the phonological area, one should not forget that this does not necessarily apply to vocabulary and the semantic component of language, and indeed, many children have produced wonderful poetry at my school.

To return to the main theme of this first chapter, the general realization of dyslexic problems tended to be based on descriptions of children such as Charlie and symptomatologies as listed in Table 1.2. I do not propose to present a whole series of case histories here. There is a psychometric case history in the next chapter, which will be referred to when we look at the assessment, but many books give case histories, my own (Thomson, 1990) and many others included. I would assume that the reader will be familiar with such books; the purpose of this book is to look at the underlying psychological constructs of dyslexia.

The next development in recognition of the dyslexia syndrome was the Government Green Paper, the Tizard Report, Department of Education and Science (1972). This was based on the Isle of Wight study of Rutter, Tizard and Whitmore (1970). The Isle of Wight was taken as a representative sample of the social background of the United Kingdom, and a number of educational, social and medical details were looked at. A brief technical digression is needed here. This study, along with that of Yule (1967) and Yule *et al.* (1974), examined the relationship between intelligence and reading in the general population, using regression equations. Regression here refers to the interrelationship of variables, in this case, between intelligence and reading, and what they were able to do was to make a prediction of what a child's reading and spelling should be like, based not only on his or her chronological age but also on his or her intelligence. The reader should not confuse 'regression' as a correlation with 'regression to the mean'. This is the tendency for population characteristics (e.g. height or intelligence) to tend towards the average of that population. We shall be examining this later when discussing discrepancy models, but there is this potential confusion based on the technical terms used in statistics and psychometrics.

The following is an example of a regression equation, looking at the relationship between reading and intelligence, which predicts reading accuracy for a child of a given age:

Reading accuracy $= 3.87 + (0.93 \times IQ) + (0.68 \times CA)$.

Here, the IQ refers to the sum of the scaled scores from the short form of Wechsler's Intelligence Scale for Children (range 4–76, average 40) (Wechsler, 1992), and the reading is the Neale Analysis Accuracy score in months (Neale, 1997). (The chronological age or CA is also in months.) The other figures were derived from the way in which reading and intelligence were correlated in that particular population. For any individual child in the Isle of Wight, therefore, and also when they undertook similar work looking at the effects of lead on IQ in the then Inner London Education Authority, we can look at what their expected reading should be. On the basis of this, they found that children could be divided into those who had a general reading difficulty (e.g. a 10-year-old who had an IQ of around 80 and who might be reading at the eight-year-old level) and those who had a specific difficulty (e.g. a 10-year-old who had an IQ of 115 and would be expected to be reading at, say, the 10.5-year-old level but who was only reading at the 8.5-year-old level). We look at this issue in more detail when we look at criticisms of the notion of discrepancy and its actual use in educational psychology practice nowadays (see p. 47). However, Rutter, Tizard and Whitmore (1970) presented data that showed the differences between those children with general reading difficulties and those who had specific reading difficulties. These are presented in Table 1.3.

**Table 1.3** Children with general and specific retardation.

| General | Specific |
| --- | --- |
| Mean IQ 80 | Mean IQ 102 |
| General development delays | Speech/language delays |
| 54% male | 76% male |
| Better prognosis | Very poor prognosis |
| Overt neurological deficits: for example, 11% cerebral palsy | No organic, fewer neurological deficits |
| High incidence of large families | Lower incidence of large families |
| High number of low status homes | Low number of low status homes |

It may be seen that those with a general reading difficulty had general developmental delays, that is, late in walking and talking, came from social backgrounds that might be expected to cause problems in literacy learning and had more neurological dysfunctions that were organic. However, the children with specific difficulties had only language/speech delays; there were many more boys than girls, and their problems have much more to do with reading and spelling rather than general educational failure. The children with specific difficulties were also more difficult to help, despite, on average, being brighter; in other words, they make less progress in reading.

Based on this, the Green Paper identified children who had 'specific reading retardation'. Those of us working in dyslexia at the time said, 'These are the dyslexic children.' We also argued that, because dyslexia was not just about reading but included spelling, difficulties in writing and a number of other things, some of which we have delineated in Charlie and some of which are tabled later in this chapter, there was a considerable overlap between these groups. However, at least this was the first official recognition that there were children who had specific difficulties, and it laid the foundation for an acceptance of dyslexia as a learning problem.

Moving on very rapidly in the development of dyslexia as a concept, we pass the Warnock Report, and to date with the abolition of the 1948 Education Act and the introduction of the Special Educational Needs Acts of 1981, 1983 and 1994. Here, statutory assessments can take place, giving rise to a Statement. Special educational needs (SENs) are defined as a learning difficulty requiring special educational provision. This involves a learning difficulty, which can be defined as the following:

1.  There is significantly greater difficulty in learning than for others of the same age.
2.  The disability prevents or hinders the use of educational facilities for children of the same age in local education authority (LEA) schools.
3.  If a child is aged under 5 years, (1) and (2) would apply if the child was at school.

There are a number of key features in this list that should be examined. One is that these are essentially normative assumptions – in other words, there is some recognition that a child is being compared with his or her peer group, and there should be some expectations of what 'normal' children should be doing at a given age. This is important because it implies some form of psychometric analysis and comparing children across norms, something that is very variably applied in schools and by educational psychology practice. Also, there is an implication for some developmental context, that is, we are looking at children changing and developing over time – a key feature – as children learn and grow. Finally, there is an underlying assumption that these learning difficulties are preventing a child from accessing the curriculum. Table 1.4 shows how the Special Educational Need Act applies to a dyslexic child.

We now have a situation in which children are defined as having SENs, and if we look at the Code of Practice, specific learning difficulties are one of these.

The current Code of Practice is rather vaguer than the early pronouncements from the 1982 (and following) Education Acts. Table 1.5 illustrates the position of specific learning difficulties in relation to all the other various 'barriers to learning' that are given in the current Special Needs Code of Practice. 'Specific learning difficulties' are under the speech and language and cognition and learning categories and are highlighted.

I wish that I could now say that we now have a clear historical development of the emergence of dyslexia as a syndrome from the

**Table 1.4** Code of Practice with regard to a specific learning difficulty.

| | |
|---|---|
| i. | There are extreme discrepancies between attainment in different core subjects of the National Curriculum or within one core subject, particularly English/Welsh. LEAs should be especially alert if there is evidence that, within the core subject of English/Welsh, a child has attained average or high levels in Attainment Target (AT) 1, speaking and listening (oral in Welsh) but significantly lower levels in AT2, reading, and/or AT3, writing. |
| ii. | Expectations of the child, as indicated by a consensus among those who have taught and closely observed him or her, supported, as appropriate, by appropriately administered standardized tests of cognitive ability or oral comprehension, are significantly above his or her attainments in National Curriculum assessments and tests and/or the results of appropriately administered standardized reading, spelling or mathematics tests. |
| iii. | There is clear, recorded evidence of clumsiness; significant difficulties of sequencing or visual perception; deficiencies in working memory; or significant delays in language functioning. |
| iv. | There is evidence of problems sometimes associated with specific learning difficulties, such as severe emotional and behavioural difficulties, as indicated by clear, recorded examples of withdrawn or disruptive behaviour, an inability to concentrate or signs that the child experiences considerable frustration or distress in relation to his or her learning difficulties. LEAs should be particularly alert if there is evidence of such difficulties in some classes or tasks such as reading or writing but not in others. |

LEAs, local education authorities.

early 1970s to the twenty-first century. Unfortunately, some have attempted to turn the clock backwards to nonrecognition of dyslexia. So, despite the British Psychology Society's Division of Educational Child Psychology recognizing dyslexia in their working party report of 1999 (see more details of this in Chapter 4), we have Elliott (2005) commenting at conferences and a Channel 4 documentary discussing the so-called 'Myth of Dyslexia', stating that not only did dyslexia not exist and was a myth, but also that identifying dyslexics took resources away from other children.

Ironically, the television programme actually presented some of the current research findings, which we will review later, on

**Table 1.5** Special educational needs in the United Kingdom.

Communication and interaction (speech, language and communication):
- language delay
- **specific learning difficulties**
- sensory impairment
- general learning difficulties
- autistic spectrum disorders

Cognition and learning:
- moderate, severe or profound learning difficulties
- **specific learning difficulties**
- (sensory impairment, autistic spectrum)

Behavioural, emotional and social development:
- withdrawn/isolated
- disruptive/challenging
- hyperactive (attention deficit disorder/attention deficit hyperactivity disorder)

Sensory and/or physical needs:
- visual/auditory impairment
- physical/physiological
- multi-sensory (medical conditions)

phonological deficits in children and magnetic resonance imaging brain scans indicating differential brain processing in children with specific learning difficulties, that is, dyslexia, and then carried on to rubbish the concept. We shall return to this issue of resources in a little bit more detail in Chapter 4, when we talk about definitions and discrepancies. I can do no better than to quote from Snowling (2005) in reaction to the Channel 4 programme.

No one in the field of education would deny that there are myths surrounding dyslexia. But this does not mean that dyslexia is a myth. On the contrary, there is strong scientific evidence concerning the nature, causes and consequences of dyslexia. Thus, dyslexia can be readily identified by educational professionals and its potentially negative effects can be ameliorated.

A crucial questions therefore is whether, if appropriate procedures for the identification, assessment and intervention of children at risk of reading problems were put in place in all schools, would dyslexia go away? The answer is quite simply no. Dyslexia is a brain-based disorder with consequences that persist from the pre-school years through to adulthood. (*From There are myths about dyslexia, but dyslexia is not a myth*)

I include these rather depressing controversies just to illustrate that, as always, recognition of special needs in education is not static and to further illustrate the point that dyslexia will not go away. Later in the chapter, I share with you some data on the lack of progress made by children with dyslexic difficulties, if not given the appropriate help.

Before finishing this section, it is useful to look at some of the other features of dyslexia that are not subsumed by the LEA notion of 'specific learning difficulty'. Tables 1.5 and 1.6 show some comments that reflect a dyslexic child's difficulties, both at home and at school.

Most of the features mentioned in Tables 1.6 and 1.7 are self-explanatory, but some comments may be helpful. Children with dyslexia will often miss out on assignments, resulting partly from short-term memory difficulties because the teacher quickly says, at the end of the lesson as the children are leaving, something like, 'Oh yes, homework on Wednesday, Chapter 6, pages 29 to 35. Don't bother with question 3, and by the way use last week's notes for question 2 and don't forget I want at least a page of summary at the end.'

There will be similar problems in copying from the board and speed of work as a result of difficulties with visual memory (board to book) and speed of processing. Children with dyslexia may be still on an earlier piece of work when the teacher is moving on or giving out instructions! Note the comment about parents. It is easy to blame parents for not helping children to organize themselves, but they may also be dyslexic – in fact, this is highly likely, given the genetic predisposition that occurs.

In Table 1.7, there is a reference to attitude to others. This can refer to taking it out on a younger sibling who can read, as well as other secondary reactions to a primary learning difficulty that I explore in Chapter 10 on the social psychology of dyslexia.

Before leaving this introduction, it is worth spending a little time looking at other SENs that overlap with dyslexia.

**Table 1.6** Some difficulties facing children with dyslexia around the school.

Organization
- timetables; homework and assignments; completion of work
- finding the way around school
- personal organization
- (parents' organization!)

Coordination
- ball games: cricket/squash, and so on, for some (see below)
- fine motor versus gross motor skills

Note taking
- from blackboard
- from dictation

Project work
- extraction of information from source
- time to complete assignment

Positive features
  Good skills in:
- work effort and determination
- global 'gestalt' thinking; logically applied, sometimes maths
- computer studies
- CDT, including technology/design/art skills/engineering
- games ability, namely 'balance', three-dimensional skills
- science, especially experimental laboratory skills, but see note taking!

**Table 1.7** Difficulties shown by the dyslexic child around the house.

Disorganization
  Bedroom – tidiness
  Planning life – events, times, activities
  Out and about on own – buses, finding way
  Time keeping!

Memory
  Homework
  Objects/clothes
  Events/time keeping!
  Instructions

Personal
  Hair/teeth/dressing!
  Attitude to others
  Homework!

The notion of related specific difficulties or a 'dys-' constellation is described by Habib (2003). The notion is that many different learning difficulties are interrelated and are sometimes described by the rather clumsy term 'comorbidities'.

## Overlapping SENs or comorbidities

The term comorbidity in this context is sometimes used to describe the overlap between dyslexia and other SENs and learning difficulties. Often, this just gives children additional labels to dyslexia, when a lot of the behaviour is actually part of the dyslexia problem or maybe a secondary reaction to that. You will know from my earlier comments and throughout the book that I feel that 'dyslexia' is a useful label to describe a syndrome or pattern of learning difficulties that affects children. The label is useful diagnostically as it implies certain treatment programmes and, in my experience, very helpful indeed to the child and their families (see comments earlier and in Chapters 3, 4 and 10).

However, it is certainly the case that behaviours or aspects of this dyslexia syndrome overlap into other areas, which are sometimes also given labels. Table 1.8 gives examples of particular SENs that are described and recognized in literature and in educational contexts.

While it is clear that the descriptions in the table refer to SENs in their own right, you can see that some dyslexics do show some of these features. It is almost a truism to say that dyslexic children have difficulties with tables and certainly problems with arithmetic (as opposed to mathematical concepts, for example) are very common to dyslexics. However, not all dyslexics, by any means, have what one might describe as dyscalculia. Indeed, some teachers find the concept of dyscalculia rather daunting in the implication that the child will never learn to do arithmetic – rather like some of the objections to the term 'word blind' in the past.

In relation to dyspraxia, some, but not all, dyslexics do also have difficulties with fine motor control and can be clumsy. As you will see in later chapters, there is a specific theory of dyslexia relating to cerebellum function, which does argue that most dyslexics' difficulties have their origins in motor development function. I certainly do not have any concerns about describing both 'dyscalculia' or

**Table 1.8** Summary description of special educational need categories overlapping with dyslexia.

Dyscalculia
This can describe a discrepancy between a person's cognitive ability and maths ability, rather like dyslexia and literacy or a total inability to process abstract concepts and numbers.

 Dyscalculia can include difficulties in learning to count by rote, poor mental maths, sometimes problems with remembering concepts, rules and formulae, problems with time and sequence and sometimes poor sense of direction and difficulty with layouts, as well as, of course, with basic mathematical computational difficulties.

Dyspraxia
This is sometimes known as developmental coordination disorder. This is a weakness in motor functions. It can affect speech and language as in verbal dyspraxia, where words are formed poorly with the mouth. It could also be in gross motor movements, such as walking, balance or gym. It can be in fine motor movements, such as writing or tying laces. In addition, there can be problems in visual perceptual difficulties such as jigsaws, spatial concepts, getting dressed and in other gross motor aspects of games.

Attention deficit hyperactivity disorder (ADHD)
This includes attention deficit disorder (ADD) and ADHD. It is important to distinguish the two in a practical situation. The former is being easily distracted and forgetful, often difficulties in following instructions and sticking to an activity, whereas ADHD will also include being restless, not being able to sit still, interrupting others, not being able to stop talking, being impulsive and not thinking about the consequences. Other problems include the inability to wait your turn, being distracted by external stimuli, not listening or oppositional behaviour.

Asperger's syndrome
This is seen as a mild form of autistic spectrum disorder. The main characteristics are difficulties with communication, social relationships and imaginative ability. The notion is that this is a problem with taking notice of other people's reactions and being over literal in your jokes, for example. In relationships, difficulties include picking up the cues that other people do and sometimes there is a high level of skills in learning facts, but finding it hard to think in abstract ways.

**Table 1.8** *Continued*

---

The severely autistic child really has a very large overlap with severe learning difficulties, whereas Asperger's is seen to be more of a difficulty in forming relationships and in language processing. There can be avoidance of eye contact, obsessive repetitiveness routines or preoccupations, speaking in exaggerated tones or being slightly compulsive although not necessarily all features are present.

Specific language difficulty
These can include aspects of the speech apparatus such as stammering or dis-fluency, but is mainly described in terms of phonology, syntax, semantics and pragmatics. There is also a general difference between receptive or expressive language function. Each of these can be described as having a particular difficulty independent of overall intelligence. In other words, a child is not generally slow learning, but has very specific weaknesses in any of these areas.

This can affect many different aspects depending on which area is weak. There might be problems in understanding sentence structure, for example, different situations, meaning or perhaps being able to understand but not being able to express your ideas very well.

Semantic pragmatic disorder
Although this has some overlap with language impairment and Asperger's, it is seen to be mainly in the nonverbal communicative function of language, although some speech and language therapists prefer not to use the term.

This also relates to information processing, particularly in knowing what to say and when to stop talking when the listener is not listening to you, interpreting facial expressions, difficulty in giving specific information and difficulties to do with abstract concepts.

---

'dyspraxia' as difficulties within the individual dyslexic child, but again, many dyslexic children do not show such problems.

I think it becomes a little more complex with the remaining descriptions given in the table. For example, as far as attention deficits are concerned, it is very difficult to sort out the chicken and the egg. For example, any of us presented with a task that we could not do, would soon begin to develop alternative behaviours in class, such as looking out of the window, not engaging as it 'is not worth it because you cannot do it anyway' and so on. I find that many children who have a supposed severe attention or even hyperactivity difficulty soon do not display these symptoms with the right structure and support for literacy. An important observational point in the checklists used to diagnose these sorts of attention deficit conditions is not only the frequency in which the behaviours occur, but also the context in which they do so. A child who is able to focus detailed attention while doing a scientific experiment, as opposed to writing it up, does not have a primary attention deficit disorder – it is a function of the task that they are asked to do. It is unfortunate that even definitions of hyperactivity result from questionnaires that are undertaken by both teachers and parents, and behaviours in different contexts can be very different. For me, the true attention deficit disorder (ADD) or attention deficit hyperactivity disorder (ADHD) child (and in the case of the extra 'H', i.e. hyperactivity – additional impulsivity and not being able to sit still, etc.) is the inability for the child to control it and the fact that it occurs across all contexts, subjects and activities.

The other three descriptions do shade into elements of language difficulty. It is true that dyslexic children can do less well on aspects of language, particularly vocabulary development, which can be so dependent on learning to read. However, by and large, the dyslexics' difficulty focuses on the written language, albeit the phonological component; many dyslexics can have excellent verbal reasoning, comprehension or other language skills. It comes a moot point as to which is language and which is written language.

People who complain about labels of dyslexia are often, on the other hand, very happy to apply the label of Asperger's syndrome or autistic spectrum disorder (ASD), or more recently termed autistic spectrum condition on children. This seems to be used with less evidence than dyslexia, where at least you have some cognitive objective information about reading and spelling levels, and even if you do not like a discrepancy model, you can actually make some clear definitions. Autism diagnosis refers to the so-called 'triad of impairments' and can be very vague. The triad refers to (i) difficulties in social *communication* – facial expressions, jokes, literal interpretation, (ii) difficulties with social *interaction* – not recognizing others feelings, prefer to be alone, not understanding unwritten social rules, and (iii) difficulty with social *imagination* – predicting what might happen, new situations, lack of imaginative empathy.

My personal experience has found many children being labelled 'autistic' or 'Aspergers' who have come to us for an assessment or to the school, clearly have difficulties with social communication, because of their learning problems and not because of a primary communication dysfunction.

I should clarify that I am not arguing against the concept of a diagnostic category within SEN of ASD, but that one must be clear to apply careful criteria, which would include the 'triad' as well as aspects of rigidity of routines, sensory sensitivity, special interests and some times general learning difficulties. Furthermore, while aspects of dyscalculia, dyspraxia and ADD can be helped by a 'dyslexic-friendly' teaching programme, helping a genuinely autistic child requires a completely different programme.

Semantic pragmatic disorder is a label which is open to dispute. Here we have overall some generalizations about processing information, particularly as it relates to personal communication. The idea that language consists of syntax (grammar), semantics (meaning), phonology (sounds) and then additionally pragmatics, that is, the nonverbal and interactive communication aspects, is well established in language theory. On the other hand, what is one person's Asperger's syndrome or semantic pragmatic disorder, is another person's eccentric behaviour, creativeness, alternative world view or reaction to their difficulties in communicating in writing!

In summary, research shows a good deal of overlap in the so-called dyscalculia and dyspraxia among dyslexics. There are certainly language difficulties that a few dyslexic children show that shade into Asperger's, specific language difficulties and semantic pragmatic disorders, and there are also some dyslexic children who have ADHD. However, as with all ranges of learning difficulties in children, none are either mutually exclusive or all are required to be present!

A useful further review of this may be found in Brown and Rack (2004).

## Written language expectations

Finally, a comment on the severity of reading, writing and spelling difficulties in children with dyslexia should be given. Going back to Table 1.3, one of the important differences between the general

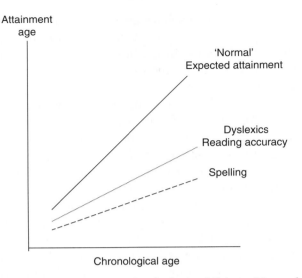

**Figure 1.3** Observed attainments in dyslexic children. Normal improvement ratio = 12 months in 12 months = 12/12 = 1.0. Improvement ratio in dyslexics not receiving help: reading = 0.40 (5 months in 12); spelling = 0.27 (3 months in 12). (Data based on 500 case studies in Aston University.)

and specific retardation was the prognosis. Despite being of generally higher intelligence, children with specific learning difficulties made less progress in reading, writing and spelling in a follow-up study undertaken in the Isle of Wight. If we look at what children with dyslexia can be expected to achieve without being given help, we find something rather like Figure 1.3.

These data are taken from the University of Aston and have been presented elsewhere (Thomson, 1990), but they are essentially from a cross-sectional study, which shows children's performances seen on assessment for the first time and at various different age levels thereafter. Obviously, one would normally expect children aged 8 years to be reading at the eight-year-old level, those aged 9 to be reading at the nine-year-old level and so on, in which case, one would get a straight graph. This is, of course, on average (children and adults do vary, and what is 'normal' can be debated at length!). Children with dyslexia who are not given help make, on average, progress of 5 months in reading per year and of 3 months in spelling. Thus, as they get older they get further and further behind in reading, writing and spelling. What may be a 1-year retardation at age 7 becomes one of 3 or 4 years at age 10 and of 5, 6 or 7 years at age 15. The whole notion of 'do not worry, children will grow out of it' is something we need to resist. Our task as educators is to stop that gap widening and ideally, to increase the rate of the reading and spelling improvement so that children get up to a competent standard of literacy.

## Further reading

For a detailed overview of the historical context of dyslexia, see the following:

Miles, T.R. and Miles, E. (1998) *Dyslexia 100 Years On*, 2nd edn, Open University Press, Buckingham.

Pumfrey, P.D. and Reason, R. (1991) *Specific Learning Difficulties*, NFER–Nelson, Windsor.

Thomson, M.E. (1990) *Developmental Dyslexia*, 3rd edn, Whurr, London.

For a general guide including some history:

Ott, P. (2007) *Teaching Children with Dyslexia: A Practical Guide*, Routledge, Oxford.

# 2

# Basic Psychometrics and Assessment

The next three chapters look at the process of assessing a child with dyslexia, from the point of view of both the educational psychologist and the teacher. The aim of these chapters is to give the reader an understanding of the way in which tests are constructed and how they are used, how educational psychologists assess children, how to interpret reports and test results given by psychologists and finally, how to assess dyslexic children themselves.

The next chapter will present a brief case history to illustrate aspects of the assessment process, and as an important addition to this second edition of the book, there are a number of case histories presented on the CD-ROM. Introductory details of these may be viewed by accessing the Introduction section on the CD-ROM.

This chapter then looks at how tests, in general, are constructed, and further chapters look in detail at tests of ability, attainment and other diagnostic tests that are relevant to dyslexia.

## Purpose of psychometrics

In assessing individuals or children in general, and this includes trying to identify children with dyslexic difficulties, there is a variety of evidence that one can draw from. In general, assessments require collecting data – taking that information from a number of sources, which will include psychometrics. We might want to obtain information by direct observations of a pupil's behaviour in class or in

*The Psychology of Dyslexia – A Handbook for Teachers*, by Michael Thomson
© 2009 John Wiley & Sons Ltd

his or her work, looking at examples of his or her work and also obtaining judgements from other people. On the other hand, we might decide to use a test to find out about a child. Salvia and Ysseldyke (2004) defined assessments as processing and collecting data for the purpose of making decisions about individuals and groups. Boyle and Fisher (2007) described assessments being carried out for a reason, for example, how do reading skills compare with other people of the same age or how good are they at phonic skills. We might also want to test a specific hypothesis about learning performance, for example, what specifically might have caused a learning difficulty, for example, dyslexia. Boyle and Fisher (2007) further commented that a test is a 'form of systematic assessment, with standardised procedures, from which numerical scores are taken.' They further went on to make the point that there is an important relationship between defining the assessment need and the test actually used and commented on the assessments in education as being four main types – entitlement, accountability, instruction and gathering information. Table 2.1 gives details of these types.

Later on in this chapter and the next chapter, we will look at the specific examples of tests, which illustrate aspects of psychometrics and also in relation to dyslexia. However, there are some general comments about the types of a test, which are helpful to look at.

One is the notion of difference between formative and summative assessments. This has become fashionable recently, particularly in evaluating teaching. A summative test essentially looks at an assessment of learning and provides a summary of what an individual knows, whether it was a child or an adult. Formative assessment (assessment for learning) would require frequent testing to examine the problems a child might have in learning. It is also a way of providing information, and the results of this test will help someone to identify the ways of making teaching and learning more effective. In other words, a formative test is aimed at trying to make a decision as how one could help a child learn, whereas the summative assessment is about finding out what a child actually knows.

There is also a broad distinction in tests of aptitude, attainment and ability. Aptitude looks at the skills that might be used, for example, music and spatial relationships – the idea is to predict a person's future performance based on that. So, for example, one

**Table 2.1** Types of assessment in education (from Boyle and Fisher, 2007).

1. Those related to *entitlement* or *eligibility* for additional support:
   - Does the pupil have a significantly more marked learning difficulty than the majority of learners of his/her age which make him/her eligible for additional support (for example, specialist teaching or special examination arrangements on account of dyslexia)? This may involve individual assessment or perhaps screening a class to identify learners with additional support needs.
   - Should a learner be referred to a specialist agency?
   - Documenting the nature and range of a learner's additional support needs.
2. Those related to *accountability*:
   - Evaluating progress of a support plan or programme;
   - Evaluating outcome from special initiatives;
   - Determining 'value added'; and
   - Monitoring standards of attainment in literacy and numeracy in a class.
3. Those related to *instruction*:
   - Identifying what pupils have learned to inform the planning of what they should be taught;
   - Identifying strategies to improve pupils' attainments;
   - Deciding how to group pupils; and
   - Testing hypotheses about the nature of a pupil's additional support needs to help in the formulation of a programme.
4. Those related to *gathering information over time from a range of specific contexts*:
   - Determining the nature and extent of a pupil's behavioural difficulties (which are often context-specific) by classroom observation;
   - Monitoring 'on-task' behaviour in class; and
   - Evaluating the effectiveness of intervention for pupils with social, emotional or behavioural difficulties.

might select for students going on a mechanical engineering course based on a test, which shows a prediction of performance.

An attainment test is used widely in education, of course, and looks at achievement, for example, in reading, spelling or number, and evaluates knowledge and understanding in curriculum areas.

An attainment test might also include diagnostic screening or tests to determine progress or evaluate effectiveness.

Finally, tests of ability are those that look at general cognitive ability, such as intelligence or specific cognitive skills such as short-term memory, or reasoning abilities and would be both diagnostic and in order to predict a person's future performance.

## Measurement in testing

Psychological testing has a background of individual differences in psychology. Essentially, tests may measure the difference among individuals or within the same individuals, for example, on different occasions. A psychological or educational test is simply a means of measurement and, as we shall see, the names given to tests are sometimes quite arbitrary and do not necessarily reflect accurately the underlying cognitive or behavioural traits that they purport to measure.

It is also important to consider what kind of level of measurement a particular test has. Traditionally, in statistics and psychometrics in psychology, there are three types of measurement – nominal (e.g. boys/girls, children with/without dyslexia), ordinal (ranking data, comparing individuals with others – fifth in class, thirtieth centile) and finally, interval (which attempts to give an absolute value, e.g. quotient of 112 or 17/25 on a test). An interval score with children usually has an implication of relative value. This is because a test that gives a quotient, centile or other score will usually have been standardized on children of different ages. This implies that a good score for a 10-year-old, for example, may be a poor score for a 13-year-old, and that individual development needs to be taken into account.

A test may be defined as an objective and standardized measure of a sample of behaviour. It is objective because the same result should be obtained every time that it is given, and it is not based on someone's subjective opinion of another person's ability. It is standardized because it is given in the same way every time. This is essentially what instructions for tests are all about and it is important to follow them carefully. It is also standardized because it may have been tried out on a large sample of individuals. Finally, the notion of a sample of behaviour is important. It is only a snapshot of a person's given behaviour at that particular time. There are many other variables that may account for this behaviour, and therefore, there is always a built-in error of measurement. This error can be quantified, as we see later (see p. 42 ff). It is very important to remember that a test is only a small sample of an individual's behaviour. It gives us a guide and no more; we return to this point later. For the teacher, it is only really a starting point in trying to evaluate a child's cognitive, educational and other skills, with the fundamental purpose of trying to teach them in a better way.

The test is usually based on a small but carefully chosen sample of individual behaviours; for example, in developing a Vocabulary Scale, we might choose a representative sample of words for different ages. These words are then tested out on many individual children and only those tests that differentiate different age groups, for example, would be chosen for the final Vocabulary Scale. A test should have diagnostic or predictive value, that is, it should indicate broad significant areas of behaviour that we are trying to tap. It should ideally be able to predict future behaviour. There is also usually a close parallel between the test itself and behaviour, for example, between the knowledge of a word list in a vocabulary test and mastery of vocabulary in language use.

There are many different uses of tests. They can simply be a description of individual differences, but they can also measure qualities of human behaviour or describe them operationally, for example, intelligence or anxiety. They are often used in making practical decisions about people or predictions. Examples include identifying mental handicap; diagnosing the reason for attainment failure in children; identifying variables in an experiment and describing the effect of 'treatments'; in vocational guidance, selection or assessment and many other uses in occupational, clinical and educational psychology. Table 2.2 gives examples of different types of tests.

## Standardization of tests

There are two aspects of standardization. One is how a test is given and the second is how it is constructed. As far as the first is concerned, it is important to produce uniformity of procedure in the administration of the test. In other words, the same test should be

**Table 2.2** Examples of different types of tests.

| | |
|---|---|
| Achievement/attainment (of ability, aptitude); specific/ general abilities | Reading, for example, general: Neale Analysis of Reading Ability, specific: British Ability Scales Word Reading |
| Intelligence (general mental ability) | Wechsler Intelligence Scale for Children |
| Special aptitudes | Phonological Abilities Battery |
| Personality (trait/projective) | Trait: Eysenck's Personality Inventory, projective: Rorshach 'Ink Blot' |

given to all individuals. The only independent variable should be the individuals being tested.

It is important, then, in learning to use tests that you become totally familiar with the materials and the oral instructions. The number of demonstrations that should be given to the person being tested are important to develop the right set or approach to the test. Another important aspect is timing – this can present quite a problem even in a relatively 'simple' test such as the Neale Analysis of Reading. Here, we need to listen to children reading (and make notes on errors and approach to reading), time them carefully and finally, ask questions at the end of each passage. Sometimes, when starting to use a test, we can easily lose track of all these different aspects, and it is important to practise the test many times before giving it to an individual, when it is 'important'.

The objective is that all examiners should give the same assessment. However, another important element that is very difficult to quantify is that of rapport. If a child is not feeling well, does not like the examiner, is unhappy, is feeling low because of a bad playground experience or any other factor, then we are not going to get a very reliable or valid test. It is very important to make a child feel relaxed, motivated and alert with the aim of maximizing an individual's performance within the constraints and standardization of the way in which the test should be administered. Spending some time chatting to children and putting them at ease is an absolute must, and a warm, friendly atmosphere is important. Children should not feel that they are being examined in a punitive way. With this in mind, a child's performance on a test is really only a basal level.

These rapport and elicitation, that is, drawing out a child's best performance without giving him the answer, are difficult for some teachers. Occasionally, teachers may find themselves wanting to tell the child the answer or help him, which of course is not allowed within a test situation. Unfortunately, some teachers are so used to dealing with children in a large group that their personal individual skills may be a little rusty and they can come across as a little formal and pedagogic. If you feel that you cannot achieve good rapport with an individual child whom you are testing, it may be wise to ask a colleague to undertake the testing for you.

However, it is my experience that, with the right practice and guidance, teachers can become excellent testers, particularly if they are going to be following up teaching that child, in the case of dyslexia, because the psychometric profile is only the start. Diagnostic teaching is a very important, if not the most important, component in the total picture of a child's learning process.

In general, tests are either norm referenced, criterion referenced, curriculum based or dynamic.

Curriculum-based approaches look at the performance within the curriculum and essentially is a version of criterion-orientated assessment, based on some definition of curriculum content. For example, a particular way of undertaking fractions to achieve success in performing a set of 'fraction' sums. The dynamic approach looks at the test–teach–retest sequence and looks at the learner's way of adapting towards the tasks that are given focussing on the learning process. Although this has a teaching focus, it also needs, in my view, to be supported by normative or criterion-oriented tests to provide objective data on, for example, attainments.

The second type of standardization refers to how the test has been developed in other populations. In general, tests are either norm referenced or criterion referenced. A norm-referenced test compares the score to that of other similar individuals, usually belonging to the same age groups in the case of children. It is not the ideal performance but depends on levels of difficulty. To take a concrete example, if we had a word reading test of 50 items, it might be a good performance for a child aged 10 years to read 15 of these, whereas if a child aged 6 reads 15 items, it might be an excellent performance; conversely, a child aged 13 reading only 15 items might be rather weak. Obviously, this means that the test items have to be standardized and tried out on large samples of children. It is important, therefore, to make sure that the tests have been standardized over appropriate groups. This also leads us to the notion of standardization samples. In other words, on what population was the test standardized? If a test is to be used widely, it should show in its manual a wide variety of social backgrounds and geographical areas.

In general, tests are constructed to be normally distributed, and later in the chapter, we look at this concept; it may, however, depend on the type of discrimination between individuals or within individuals that is described on a particular test. The idea is to compare (in the case of children – the main focus here) with the general peer group. The way in which this is done is often by standard score, Z scores or percentiles. We will look at these in detail because they are crucial to our understanding of what test results are, whether we undertook tests ourselves or interpreted other people's reports.

It is important to note in relation to standardisation, particularly in norm referencing, that sample upon which the test is "normed" is trying to reflect the whole population. For example, anyone in the British Isles or even larger, for example, the USA. It is obviously impossible to obtain scores from every single child in the whole population and, therefore, a standardisation is based on a sample. There are a lot of technical and other issues involved in deciding which is an appropriate population on which to standardise your test so that it reflects an appropriate measure of social class, ethnicity educational background, age and so on. Usually it is assumed that the test will approximate to a normal distribution (for example see Figure 2.3) and it is important for the sample not to be "skewed" or unrepresentive in any way. See Boyle & Fisher (2007), Page 38 for further discussions on this issue.

The other standardization type mentioned is the 'criterion reference'. Here, there is an absolute score rather than a relative one comparing other children. It has become more popular recently, particularly in education. The question here would be: can an individual define 20 words or not? We set a particular criterion and the question is whether the child can or cannot do it. This has often been used and developed into individual education plans in the case of dyslexia, for example, a goal could be the criterion of the child reading and spelling 10 consonant blends. This is thus an assessment and a teaching goal. Of course, the problem is specifying the so-called 'ideal performance' and whether the objectives be clearly stated and agreed on.

## Evaluation of tests

The question here is: 'how good is the test, and does it actually work?' The first component of this is reliability.

### Reliability

It is important for a test to be reliable, that is, do we achieve consistent scores? Ideally, the same individual using the same test on a different occasion should give us the same score. Obviously, individuals are not like blocks of wood to be measured exactly by physical means. People's behaviour intrinsically varies from day to day (especially children's!), and there is always some inbuilt error within the test. Psychometricians recognize this and develop an error of measurement in the individual score. This is the chance of 'irrelevant to the test' factors. The test is essentially an estimate of the so-called 'true' characteristics of the individual – their moods, day-to-day changes, personalities, testing conditions, examiner, perceived importance of the test and so on, will all affect the result and, of course, error variance. It will also depend on standardization conditions and the sample, that is, the normative sample, on which the test has been standardized. We look at the error of measurement and its relationship to the spread of scores later (see p. 42), but it is important to recognize here that the reliability or coefficient stability is the same as a general correlation coefficient, that is, it ranges from −1 to 0 to +1. Just to remind the reader, a correlation coefficient is the relationship between two variables; for example, there is a high positive correlation between people's height and the size of their feet, although there is usually a negative correlation between rainfall and temperature in the United Kingdom, that is, the higher the rainfall, the lower the temperature. Usually a high positive correlation is needed for a test to be reliable, that is, one of +0.8 or so.

There are various types of reliability as follows.

*Test–retest reliability*   This involves correlating the test over time. Of course, in children, this is difficult to do because they are learning and developing. A test–retest would therefore rarely exceed 6 months in the case of children. However, there are also problems in practice and recall effects, so simply retesting a person on the same test as a measure of reliability tends to be used less often in practice.

*Alternative form*   This usually compares two different forms of the same test, for example, the Neale Analysis of Reading has two forms. The forms are developed in parallel and measure the same thing. Reliability is thus compatibility between parallel forms.

*Internal consistency*   This looks at the correlation between test items, for example, in a vocabulary test of, say, 20 items, items 1–2, 3–4 and so on are correlated, and internal consistency is measured.

*Scorer reliability*   Here again, we should get the same score on a test for the same individual even though it was given by different people. This is more likely in simple objective tests, for example, reading individual words, but is less likely in clinical and subjective tests. Tests that require interpretation are also less reliable.

Basically, the reader needs to look at the test manual to see whether there is evidence given about the reliability of the test. Does the test produce the same results on different occasions and with different testers? It is important for there to be a high positive correlation for the test to be considered reliable.

## Validity

The other important aspect of test construction is what the test measures and how well it tests. The test name usually gives a general guide, but it is not always completely clear, for example, in reading, we could test accuracy, speed, comprehension, single-word reading, reading individual letters, understanding stories and so on.

Sometimes, factor analysis is used to give tests their labels. Factor analysis is basically a multiple correlation with different tests or different measurable behaviours. A good example of this was given in our case history at the beginning of the chapter. The Wechsler Intelligence Scale for Children IV (WISC-IV) gives us Index scores, which are given labels based on the intercorrelation between the test items. So, for example, Information, Vocabulary, Comprehension and Similarities (a verbal reasoning test) are put together as the Verbal Comprehension Index. (See Table 3.1 p. 54 for a description of these subtests.) They are linked together because they are correlated highly in objective testing of many children. However, the label was one based on what it was assumed the tests measure. It is important to recognize that sometimes test labels are only the results of correlational links and the assumed underlying cognitive processes that they measure. Intelligence is a good example of a label given to a set of behaviours that correlate well (although they do have other validities) but are open to philosophical, technical and psychological debate.

However, to return to validity, we can look at a number of different kinds of validity as follows.

*Face validity*   This is what the items appear to measure and can be important to the individual, for example, a reading test usually has words to read! This is not as fatuous as it sounds, because sometimes we may find a very high correlation between a test and later behaviour, for example, there is a good correlation between rhyming ability at 5 or 6 years and later reading and spelling development; so if we gave a rhyming test to a five-year-old, we could argue that it measured aspects of reading ability, although that would be difficult to justify to a parent who might say: 'why didn't you give a reading test?'

*Content validity*   This is 'Does the test include a representative sample of the behavioural domain?' The question, of course, is still posed in the reading example: 'what aspects of the behavioural domain?' There may be overgeneralization, for example, in spelling, should we include a multiple-choice spelling or words written down from dictation or words used in writing as the measure of spelling? All are equally valid but measure different things.

*Criterion-related validity*   This is perhaps the most important validity and it looks at whether the test is linked to the direct independent measure to which it purports, for example, if we used a test to select a person for a job, does high performance on the test predict good performance later in the job? In early occupational psychology, a well-known mistake occurred in which police officers were rejected on the grounds that they did poorly on a particular selection test. Later, the occupational psychologist tested successful policemen and found that they also did very poorly on that test; therefore, it was not a very good predictor of future performance and not valid as a selection procedure. In other words, does the test relate to real-life behaviour, that is, the criterion?

There are basically two types: predictive and concurrent or diagnostic. Predictive validity asks the question: 'does the test predict future performance?' A good example of this is when I was developing the Aston Index (Newton and Thomson, 1976). We tested children at 5 years and went back to the same children 2 or 3 years later to see which test items predicted their later reading and spelling development. This is predictive validity. For example, poor scores on sound blending linked to later reading difficulty. In addition, there was a correlation of 0.83 between sound blending at age 5 years and reading level (Schonell Reading) at 8 years.

Concurrent validity asks the question: 'does the test correlate well with present performance, or do particular groups of people score well or poorly?' Again, in the Aston Index example, we tested children aged 8–12 years and looked at those who had reading and spelling difficulties to find out whether they also scored less well on the items of the Index. There are various criteria that can be used to evaluate either predictive or concurrent validity, for example, academic achievement, performance in training, previously available tests, job performance, contrasting groups and, of course, educational success at school.

*Construct validity*   This refers to the psychological state, process or trait being measured, and looks at the relationship between the test and the theory. We should be able to predict from the theory what the test should measure.

Table 2.3 gives examples of different kinds of validation, which should make the previous discussion clearer.

**Table 2.3** Types of validation on, for example, Arithmetic Reasoning Test.

| Purpose | Example question | Type of validity |
|---|---|---|
| Achievement in primary school | How much has Fred learnt? (or what was learnt?) | Content |
| Aptitude to predict secondary school achievement | How well will Fred learn in the future? (or will he do well on Maths course) | Criterion related – predictive |
| Technique to identify/diagnose arithmetic difficulties | Is Fred 'dyscalculic'? | Criterion related – diagnostic (concurrent) |
| Measure of logical reasoning | How can we describe Fred's psychological functioning? | Construct |

## Scoring tests

We now look at another element of psychometrics, that is, the kinds of scores derived from the test. This is important because often tests have different kinds of scores, and it is essential to understand how they are derived and what they mean. Perhaps, I should mention in passing here that, as well as the establishment of rapport and getting the optimum performance from a subject, it is imperative to check one's personal accuracy using stencils and keys, and to be consistent and careful in the way that we score tests. These can be important factors in children's lives and it is essential to get it right. It is also important to respect the confidentiality of the material, as well as the fact that the test is only one element of a child's total profile.

Obviously, the raw score itself is only a numerical report of performance and has no significance unless it is compared with some standard. We cannot interpret psychological tests as we do physical measures. Differences in, for example, reasoning ability do not present true differences between individuals, unless we know their background, age and so on. The raw score is therefore converted into some kind of derived score, that is, a permanent record of the

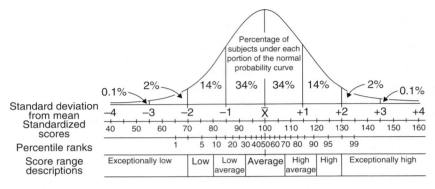

**Figure 2.1** Normal distribution and associated score system.

individual's relative position. There are two main kinds of derived scores – centiles and standard scores. It is perhaps worth presenting at this point a normal distribution and aspects of score systems that will give rise to these (Figure 2.1).

*Centile scores*

A centile or percentile score is a rank expressed in percentage terms. A percentile is a way of expressing a large number of people in a rank order score. Therefore, a percentile or centile of 88 means that an individual is better than 88% of the population and worse than 12% on that particular test. Conversely, a centile of 40 means that an individual is better than 40% of the population or worse than 60% of the population. One of the advantages of percentiles is that they are relatively easily understood and give a fairly exact interpretation with no gaps in the raw score (they are also psychometrically easy to compute in test development). One of the problems, however, is that they do magnify small differences near the mean. If we look at Figure 2.1, one can see that the average range for percentiles lies between 25 and 75. The descriptions of score range used on Figure 2.1 are similar to the Wechsler classification. They may differ slightly from test to test, but the principles and statistical range will be the same. This means that a percentile of 40 is not reliably worse than a percentile of 60. They are all within the average range, and therefore, there is no real difference between a centile of, say, 45 and 55. Centiles apparently give an indication that there is a difference here, and that is very important to understand in their interpretation. Conversely, there is a reduction in the size of large differences near the tail ends of the distribution. If we look at the normal distribution in Figure 2.1 and compare, say, the ninetieth with the ninety-ninth centile, we can see that there is only a very small percentage of the population (under the curve) scoring in that area. What this means statistically is that a small difference between 90 and 95 (or 10 and 5 at the lower levels) makes a great deal of difference in terms of the test scores for those individuals. Thus, the difference of five centile points is very significant at the extremes, whereas it is of little significance between 50 and 45 or 50 and 55. This is an important statistical point that is sometimes ignored and is one of the problems of using centiles.

*Standard score*

A standard score indicates a person's place in the frequency distribution of the test. We can look at an example of a standardized score, that is, the so-called Z score. This is computed by looking at the individual's score and looking at the standard deviation (SD) (spread) of the scores, for example, if John gets 22 for an arithmetic test and the others get 12, 14, 12, 14, 14, 17, 19, 11, 15 and 20, the mean or average score is 15.4. The SD or spread of score is 3.42 (we look at this concept later – see p. 40). Therefore, John's standard, or Z score, is:

$$\frac{X - M}{SD}, \text{ that is, } \frac{\text{his score} - \text{mean}}{SD} = \frac{22 - 15.4}{3.4} = 1.9.$$

This Z score, therefore, which has a mean of 0 and an SD of 1, can be compared from test to test. It is also important to recognize that one can transform a Z score so that the mean is 100 and the SD is 10 (Z × 10 + 100). This is essentially what has happened when, as is the case in many tests, a quotient with an average or mean of 100 is set and we look at deviation scores or quotient scores such as IQ, British Picture Vocabulary Test and some reading and spelling tests (see Chapter 3).

Before looking at the alternative standard scores, it is important to understand the concept of SD. SD is essentially the variability of a particular random score. Figure 2.2 (two normal distributions) shows two examples of populations, that is, individuals who have been given tests and the scores have been added up.

In one situation (a) with the narrow bell-shaped curve, there is a very narrow range of scores; and in the other (b), with a wide bell-shaped curve, there is a wide range of scores. Note that the same average, or mean, applies. In the first case, most of the individuals have scored at around the same level, whereas in the second case there have been a very wide variety of scores. The SD is essentially just a statistical measure of this variety or spread of score.

What test constructors do is essentially assume that their tests are normally distributed (or, better still, base them on the standardization sample on which they have developed the test). There are, therefore, a number of standard scoring systems that you will come across in your interpretation of tests, and some of these are shown in Table 2.4.

If we compare Table 2.4 with Figure 2.1 showing the normal distribution, we get an idea of the different standardization systems. In the case of the Wechsler scores given, these refer to the individual subtests (see case history on p. 49 for example). Here, the mean, or average, is set to 10 and the SD is at 3. Note that examples are given with *one* SD above the mean and *two* SDs below the mean.

This is just to show the reader the score variations – try to work out scores with 2 SD above and 1 SD below for further illustration.

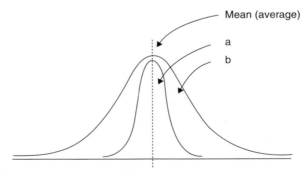

**Figure 2.2** Normal distribution of the population. See the text.

**Table 2.4** Standard score systems.

| Mean set equal to | Standard deviation (SD) set equal to | Standard score corresponding to 1 SD above mean | Standard score corresponding to 2 SD below mean | System |
|---|---|---|---|---|
| 0 | 1 | 1 | −2 | Z scores |
| 5 | 2 | 7 | 1 | Stanine score |
| 10 | 3 | 13 | 4 | Wechsler subtests |
| 50 | 10 | 60 | 30 | t Scores |
| 100 | 15 or 16 | 115 or 116 | 70 or 68 | Quotient/deviation |

Therefore, on the WISC, an individual scaled score of 13 would be *one* SD above the mean, whereas a scaled score of 4 would be *two* SDs below the mean (7 would be 1 SD below the mean). The other examples given are the *t* scores, which are used in the British Ability Scales, but the most common is the mean set to 100, the so-called deviation score, which is used for IQ and a number of other tests. Again, looking at the SDs above and below, the means will give some idea of what these scores actually mean statistically.

It may be seen, therefore, that standard scores give proportional differences to the raw scores and make more sense statistically. They can also give easy comparisons across tests and they do not have the magnification of small mean differences and reduction of large differences shown by the centiles. However, they can be difficult to understand, as may be seen from the previous discussion, and do rely on a normalized distribution.

It is worth noting that, in Figure 2.1, the 'average' range is set between 90 and 110 standard scores. Some tests use the range 85–115 as the 'average'. This is based on 1 SD either side of the mean. Many psychologists, using the Wechsler and similar cognitive tests as the model use the 90–110 as the 'average' and this would be 50% of the population.

## Attainment ages

Another common form of standardization used in education is the attainment age. This would give a reading or spelling age, which is

**Table 2.5** Examples of different reading test scores for the 10-year-old chronological age based on different raw scores on Wechsler Individual Achievement Test (WIAT) Word Reading.

| Raw score | Reading age (yr:mo) | Standard score | Percentile rank |
|---|---|---|---|
| 104 | 10:4 | 97 | 42 |
| 65 | 6:4 | 59 | 0.3 |
| 120 | 16:0 | 121 | 92 |
| 100 | 9:4 | 92 | 30 |
| 116 | 14:0 | 116 | 86 |

readily understood and easy to use to compare children with each other. However, a further word of caution here because, if we take on board all that has been said so far, it is clear that 1 or 2 months is not a significant difference in terms of test measurement. To say a child who has a reading age of 9:6 is reading better than a child with a reading age of 9:3 is not reporting a reliable difference, a point that we shall make even clearer when we look at the way in which error can be measured. Similarly, if we convert reading ages or other attainment ages into centiles or standard scores, it gives us a better idea of whether a child is within a normal distribution. Table 2.5 presents some examples of reading ages compared with other scores from the Weschler Individual Attainment Tests Word Reading to give a flavour of how important it is to understand these elements in interpreting test scores, and how ages and scores vary.

As far as age is concerned, we can also develop a quotient score by looking at mental age over chronological age, as the Stanford–Binet test did when first developing intelligence tests. We could do the same thing by dividing a reading or spelling age by chronological age to give a quotient score, but again, this should be used very cautiously and it is better to look at the standardization scores from the test itself.

## Standard error

As we have mentioned before, it is possible to measure the standard error of tests, and many tests do give this in their test manuals.

The standard error of measurement is computed by the following formula:

$$\sigma_{\text{meas}} = \sigma \sqrt{(1 - R_{11})},$$

where $\sigma$ = SD of test and $R_{11}$ = reliability, for example, IQ test SD 15 and reliability 0.89, $\sigma_{\text{meas}}$ = 5 (from $15\sqrt{(1 - 0.89)}$ = $15\sqrt{0.11}$ = 15(0.33) = 5). Thus, an IQ of 100 is in the range of 95–105.

To rephrase that, in the example of an IQ test with an SD of 15 (see Table 2.4) and the reliability of the test is 0.89, we have a standard error of measurement of 5. Therefore, if a person scores at an IQ of 100, the range of scores is between 95 and 105.

The next bit is where many teachers I have talked to hold up their hands in horror and say, 'Well, what is the purpose of giving tests at all?', and that is when we look at confidence limits. A confidence limit looks at how sure we can be that the test scores achieved are a 'real score', that is, they do actually reflect what that individual person does. Confidence levels look at what the percentage of a score is at various SDs (see Figure 2.1). We know, for example, that 68% of scores on a given test lie between +1 and −1 SD from the mean (34% below and 34% above the mean). Therefore, in the example that we looked at earlier, this gives a 0.68 probability of the measured IQ of 100 being between 95 and 105. This is derived from our standard error of measurement, which we computed at 5 (see previous discussion), and the range is 5 either side of 100. The confidence limit is computed by multiplying the SD (in this case 1) by the standard error of measurement (in this case 5). Another way of expressing this is that there is a 2 to 1 chance (68 : 32) of our score being a 'correct' one. If, on the other hand, we wanted to be 99% sure of our score, we would have to look at the 99% of scores on a normal distribution. Here, we find that 99% of the scores lie between +2.58 or −2.58 SD (again see Figure 2.1). Therefore, the confidence limits are computed by multiplying the SD by the standard error of measurement, which in this case is 2.58 × 5 = 13. So our score of 100 ranges between 87 and 113 if we are looking at a 0.99 chance of the real score being within these levels.

Therefore, our score of 100 has various ranges depending on how confident we are, in statistical terms, about the test. This is why psychologists report that average scores for intelligence lie between 90 and 110, because this is the confidence range.

Please note that we are talking about statistical confidence here, not necessarily confidence about whether the test is measuring what we want it to measure. A typical limit for reading age in a test such as the Neale Analysis of Reading in some months either side of the observed, for example, Raw Score 53, Reading Age 9.00, 68% confidence band, gives 8:7–9:11. Note that these confidence limits are based on the reliability of the test. Despite these caveats on attainment tests and confidence limits, I must reiterate that I, as well as many psychologists and teachers, still use attainment tests as a good indicator of the child's achievements. They provide a guide to attainment but, as with all tests, are a 'snapshot' of the child's skill.

We have only skated over the surface of some of the technical issues involved in psychometrics (the reader may feel that we have gone too deep!). It is now time to move on to the realities of the test situation and to describe the assessment process for dyslexia in more detail.

## Further reading

An excellent book that gives more background detail and highly recommended reading for all aspects of psychometrics is *Educational Testing: A Competence-Based Approach* by James Boyle and Steve Fisher. This is a text for the British Psychology Society Certificate of Competence in Educational Testing Level A, and I would suggest it is a key read for all those who are going to be involved in educational testing, let alone those who want to obtain the Certificate of Competence.

Anastasi, A. (1988) *Psychological Testing*, 6th edn, Macmillan, New York.
Aitkinson, R.C., Atkinson, R.C., Smith, F. and Bem, D. (1993) Assessment of mental abilities, in *Introduction to Psychology*, 11th edn, Harcourt, Brace Jovanovich, Orlando, FL.
Cronbach, L.J. (1984) *Essentials of Psychological Testing*, 4th edn, Harper Row, New York.

Murphy, K.A. and Davidshofer, O.C. (1991) *Psychological Testing. Principles and Applications*, Prentice Hall, Englewood Cliffs, NJ.

The mentioned references are basic texts that provide more detail on psychometric theory and practice. For an (slightly dated) overview of different forms of practical assessment, try:

Mittler, P. (ed.) (1976) *The Psychological Assessment of Mental and Physical Handicaps*, Methuen, London.

Examples of specific tests are given at the end of Chapter 3.

# 3

# Assessing the Dyslexic Child

In this chapter, we look at the assessment procedure for identifying children with dyslexia. I hope, by the end of this chapter, to enable readers to be more confident in interpreting an educational psychologist's report, and also in understanding what tests and what interpretations they can make from these tests in their own assessments.

The structure of this chapter is going to take the form of presenting an assessment case history with comments on the issues that arise from each section of the assessment. This is an example of a dyslexic child who was assessed at our own Psychological and Educational Assessment Centre. The case history takes the form of a psychologist's report. This serves two functions. One is to help understand an educational psychologist's report as I go into some detail, particularly about intelligence test items, which may be less familiar to teachers. I also refer, at various points, to tests that might be used by teachers to obtain similar profiles. Secondly, however, I discuss the side issues that pertain to dyslexia and expand on these issues in more detail, sometimes by referring to other parts of this book. The case history is presented in slightly smaller print to differentiate it between the comments that I make between each section.

Following suggestion from reviewers of the proposed second edition, we have included a series of case histories in an Appendix. This takes the form of a CD-ROM and is included with this book. This includes, essentially, different examples of assessments

*The Psychology of Dyslexia – A Handbook for Teachers*, by Michael Thomson
© 2009 John Wiley & Sons Ltd

illustrated by the inclusion of our own reports on the children (and in some cases adults) concerned, with some notes.

Note that the case history presented in this chapter is somewhat abbreviated, as I have added notes to make points for this chapter. The full report is given in the appendix CD-ROM in the 'Typical Dyslexics' section labelled 'James Wright', (we have changed the names of the children for the purposes of confidentiality). An introduction to these case histories may be accessed in the Introduction section on the CD.

The purpose of assessment is, of course, not only to give a diagnostic description of a child, whether in terms of 'dyslexia' or of a 'specific learning difficulty', but also partly to include a delineation of his or her particular strengths and weaknesses. The aim is to develop appropriate remedial teaching on the basis of this. As I have said, assessment is only the start because teaching also needs to be diagnostic. Observation, particularly in terms of the response that a child makes to your own teaching, is an important element of the diagnostic and assessment process.

## Example summary case history

(See 'James Wright' in 'Typical Dyslexics' example assessments given on the CD-ROM for further details – all of the tests results are listed there along with our detailed analysis and interpretation. In order to illustrate the assessment process by this example, I have just put in a brief background, a summary of our findings and then the psychometric results. In the ensuing discussion, I also quote parts of the full assessment to make specific points.)

I have also included the bar charts of the index and attainment standard scores from the Wechsler Scales as well as the subtest scores. These are referred to in the discussion.

### Brief Background

James' parents requested this assessment. James has had two previous assessments from the local education authority's Cognition and Learning Service. These identified a significant delay in his literacy skills. The current report was to ascertain if James' difficulties were a certain indication of dyslexia, and to ascertain the level of support he will require as he transfers to secondary education in September.

## Summary

In summary, the report finds James to be a boy of at least average verbal and visual intelligence with very good skills in verbal reasoning, attention to visual detail and in his understanding of verbal concepts. James achieved aged appropriate scores in general knowledge and word knowledge. He showed a lower ability in processing speed and his working memory skills are equivalent to the bottom 2% of the population. Importantly, many dyslexic students show a weakness in these two areas.

Only James' reading rate and understanding of text is at age level. In contrast, his spelling and alphabetic decoding skills are in the bottom 1% of the population. James' word reading is around 4 years below his chronological age – and text reading at around the $8\frac{1}{2}$ year level, which will prevent him from accessing the curriculum adequately.

**We conclude that James has specific learning difficulties/dyslexia; we would describe these difficulties as severe, as his reading and spelling levels are delayed by 3–5 years. James' writing skills are poor and may be an indication of some fine motor difficulties.**

The report concludes by making some suggestions as to ways in which we feel the support James requires might best be directed, both now and in the long term.

## PSYCHOMETRIC TESTING

### Intelligence and Ability
Wechsler Intelligence Scale for Children IV
*Indices: Standard Score (Average score = 100)*
*Subtests: Scaled Scores (average score = 10)*

| General Ability Index (GAI): 108 | | | |
|---|---|---|---|
| Verbal Comprehension Index | 108 | Perceptual Reasoning Index | 106 |
| Similarities | 13 | Block design | 9 |
| Vocabulary | 11 | Picture concepts | 12 |
| Comprehension | 11 | Picture completion | 12 |
| Working Memory Index | 68 | Processing Speed Index | 80 |
| Digit span | 7 | Coding | 4 |
| Letter–number sequencing | 2 | Symbol search | 9 |

**Attainments**

|  | Age-related score (yr:mo) | Actual standard score (average = 100) | Percentile equivalent (average = 50) | Predicted standard score (from GAI) | Difference |
|---|---|---|---|---|---|
| Wechsler Individual Achievment Test |  |  |  |  |  |
| Word reading | 7:8 | 76 | 5 | 106 | Significant at $p < 0.01$ |
| Spelling | 6:8 | 64 | 1 | 106 | Significant at $p < 0.01$ |
| Pseudoword reading | 5:4 | 64 | 1 | 105 | Significant at $p < 0.01$ |
| Neale Analysis of Reading Ability |  |  |  |  |  |
| Accuracy | 8:7 | 84 | 14 | n/a | n/a |
| Rate | 10:1 | 90 | 38 | n/a | n/a |
| Comprehension | 12:8+ | 108+ | 70 | n/a | n/a |

**East Court Phonic Reading Test:** James read correctly 59 of the 85 given words. He read a variety of words but misread six words at the CCVC and CCVVC level – including *'spot'* as *'sport'*, *'strap'* as *'srip'* and *'slump'* as *'slub'*.

James' writing includes weak letter formation. Clearly writing is not easy for him and he is currently unable to demonstrate his ideas and good intellectual ability. Speed of writing is around three words per minute – and places James in the bottom 0.2% of the population.

**CTOPP: Sound Ellison –** 8/13. The tester presents the child with a word and the child is asked to respond by saying what is left if you take a particular sound out, for example, *bus* without the [b] says [us] or *bag* without the [g] says [bae].

**Aston Index:** sequencing skills – sound-blending score 6/10 – James' performance is equivalent to the $9\frac{1}{2}$ year level. The tester presents the child with the component sounds which make up a word. The child is then required to blend sounds together to make the complete word, for example, /c/ /a/ /t/ = 'cat'.

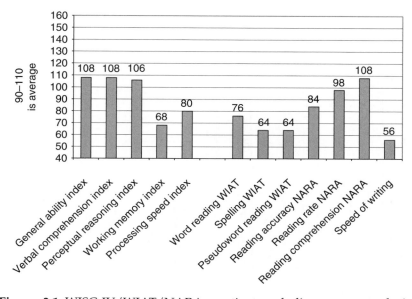

**Figure 3.1** WISC-IV/WIAT/NARA quotient and discrepancy analysis. WISC-IV, Wechsler Intelligence Scale for Children; WIAT, Wechsler Individual Achievement Test; NARA, Neale Analysis of Reading Ability.

Figures 3.1 and 3.2 show the given scores in bar chart form. The reader may wish to refer to these from time to time when reading the text.

In general terms, the case history presented has been divided into three types of test: firstly, the intelligence or ability tests, secondly, the attainment tests and finally, the diagnostic tests.

## Intelligence tests

I think that the evaluation of intelligence is an important element of the assessment of dyslexia and I have gone into this in some detail elsewhere (see Thomson, 1990), but let us look here at the specific examples given in the case history (see Table 2.1).

The first aspect is the general, overall IQ. If a teacher is looking at a quotient obtained by an educational psychologist, or not obtained by yourself using alternative tests, it is important to recognize the variability of performance within individual children.

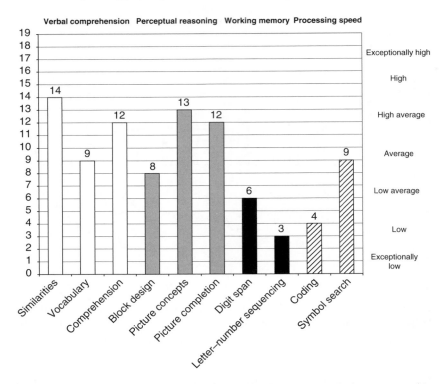

**Figure 3.2** Wechsler Intelligence Scale for Children-IV-scaled scores profile analysis.

The previous chapter examined standard errors of measurement and aspects of the reliability and validity of tests.

You will notice that in this case, there is an overall IQ called the General Ability Index (GAI). This is given as 108 and very broadly indicates a boy of at least average ability. I say at least average because some scores are low and some scores are higher, and we shall look at the implications of this later.

In other words, the reading and spelling difficulties of the child do not appear to result from a slow learning potential but, more importantly in this context, they are used as a baseline to evaluate the relationship between his reading and spelling performance and that predicted on the basis of intelligence. This is an important issue that I have examined in Chapter 4, because there are some quite detailed arguments to take into account.

The previous Wechsler Scales (III) looked at the overall IQ and 'Verbal' and 'Performance' subtests. In the WISC-III case, verbal subtests would have been those under Verbal Comprehension (VC) in WISC-IV, but also including aspects of Working Memory (WM), for example, Digit Span. The performance items of WISC-III would include those items under Perceptual Reasoning (PR) in WISC-IV, including Coding and (when given by the tester) Symbol Search under the Processing Speed (PS) index.

The point I wish to make here is that the new structure of the WISC-IV looks in more detail at different aspects of cognitive ability. A description of WISC-IV and its subtests is given in Figure 3.3 and Table 3.1.

The Wechsler IV, which is the current assessment used by many educational psychologists, looks at four Index scores. Sometimes, the individual subtests can be used to give an overall IQ or a full-scale IQ. In the case described, if all of the individual subtests were used, this would give a full-scale IQ of 92. This is an important issue, that is, which is the so-called 'true' IQ of the child. We have discussed this issue in the previous chapter under reliability and

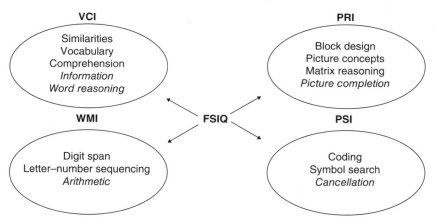

**Figure 3.3** Structure of WISC-IV. There are 10 core tests that make up the full-scale IQ. The structure is given below:
This structure will enable a detailed comparison of cognitive ability (sub-tests) as well as an analysis of types of intelligence (index scores). Note: supplemental subtests are shown in italics; core tests are in plain type. VCI, Verbal Comprehension Index; PRI, Perceptual Reasoning Index; WMI, Working Memory Index; PSI, Processing Speed Index; FSIQ, Full Scale IQ.

**Table 3.1** Description of Wechsler Intelligence Scale for Children (WISC-IV).

Subtest rationales

Below are detailed descriptions of the subtests:

*Similarities:* the child is presented with two words that represent common objects or concepts and describes how they are similar. Designed to measure verbal reasoning and concept formation. It also involves auditory comprehension, memory, distinction between nonessential and essential features, and verbal expression.

*Vocabulary:* for picture items, the child names pictures that are displayed in the Stimulus Book. For verbal items, the child gives definitions for words that the examiner reads aloud. Designed to measure a child's word knowledge and verbal concept formation. It also measures a child's fund of knowledge, learning ability, long-term memory and degree of language development. Other abilities that may be used by the child during this task include auditory perception and comprehension, verbal conceptualization, abstract thinking and verbal expression.

*Comprehension:* the child answers questions based on his/her understanding of general principles and social situations. Designed to measure verbal reasoning and conceptualization, verbal comprehension and expression, the ability to evaluate and use past experience, and the ability to demonstrate practical information. It also involves knowledge of conventional standards of behaviour, social judgement and maturity, and common sense.

*Information:* the child answers questions that address a broad range of general knowledge topics. Designed to measure a child's ability to acquire, retain and retrieve general factual knowledge. It involves crystallized intelligence, long-term memory, and the ability to retain and retrieve information from school and the environment. Other skills that may be used by the child include auditory perception and comprehension, and verbal expressive ability.

*Word reasoning:* the child identifies the common concept being described in a series of clues. Designed to measure verbal comprehension, analogical and general reasoning ability, verbal abstraction, domain knowledge, the ability to integrate and synthesize different types of information, and the ability to generate alternative concepts.

**Table 3.1** *Continued.*

Subtest rationales

*Block design:* while viewing a constructed model or a picture in the Stimulus Book, the child uses red-and-white blocks to recreate the design within a specified time limit. Designed to measure the ability to analyse and synthesize abstract visual stimuli. It also involves nonverbal concept information, visual perception and organization, simultaneous processing, visual-motor coordination, learning and the ability to separate Figure and ground in visual stimuli. It may also involve visual observation and matching abilities for younger children, as well as the ability to integrate visual and motor processes.

*Picture concepts:* the child is presented with two or three rows of pictures and chooses one picture from each row to form a group with a common characteristic. Designed to measure abstract, categorical reasoning ability. Items are sequenced to reflect increasing demands on abstract reasoning ability.

*Matrix reasoning:* the child looks at an incomplete matrix and selects the missing portion from five response options. It has long been recognized that matrix analogy tasks are good measures of fluid intelligence, and reliable estimates of general intellectual ability. Matrix reasoning tasks are also relatively culture-fair and language-free and require no hand manipulation. The four types of matrices are: continuous and discrete pattern completion, classification, analogical reasoning and serial reasoning.

*Picture completion:* the items require the child to view a picture and then point to or name the important part missing within a specified time limit. It is designed to measure visual perception and organization, concentration and visual recognition of essential details of objects.

*Digit span:* for digit span forwards, the child repeats numbers in the same order as presented aloud by the examiner. For digit span backwards, the child repeats numbers in the reverse order from that presented aloud by the examiner. Designed as a measure of auditory short-term memory, sequencing skills, attention and concentration. It involves rote learning and memory, attention, encoding and auditory processing. Digit span backward involves working memory, transformation of information, mental manipulation and visuospatial imaging. The shift from the digit span forward task to the digit span backward task requires cognitive flexibility and mental alertness.

**Table 3.1** *Continued.*

---

Subtest rationales

---

*Letter–number sequencing:* the child is read a sequence of numbers and letters and recalls the numbers in ascending order and the letters in alphabetical order. Involves sequencing, mental manipulation, attention, short-term auditory memory, visuospatial imaging and processing speed.

*Arithmetic:* the child mentally solves a series of orally presented arithmetic problems within a specified time limit. Involves mental manipulation, concentration, attention, short- and long-term memory, numerical reasoning ability and mental alertness. It may also involve sequencing, fluid reasoning and logical reasoning. Note that the memory loading on this test has been increased since WISC-III.

*Coding:* the child copies symbols that are paired with simple geometric shapes or numbers. Using a key, the child draws each symbol in its corresponding shape or box within a specified time limit. In addition to processing speed, the subtest measures short-term memory, learning ability, visual perception, visual-motor coordination, visual scanning ability, cognitive flexibility, attention and motivation. It may also involve visual and sequential processing.

*Symbol search:* the child scans a search group and indicates whether the target symbol(s) matches any of the symbols in the search group within a specified time limit. In addition to processing speed, the subtest also involves short-term visual memory, visual-motor coordination, cognitive flexibility, visual discrimination and concentration. It may also tap auditory comprehension, perceptual organization and planning and learning ability.

*Cancellation:* the child scans both a random and a structured arrangement of pictures and marks target pictures within a specified time limit. The test is similar to previously developed cancellation tasks designed to measure processing speed, visual selective attention, vigilance and visual neglect.

---

validity of tests, but here, it becomes particularly crucial as expectations can be changed markedly on the basis of what teachers and others think is the overall ability of a child. The Wechsler IV not only suggests the psychologist to focus on the Index scores, but also specifically argues that if there are discrepancies among Index scores, the full-scale IQ should not be used. Here, we have very little difference between the VC and the PR indices. If there was a discrepancy between VC and PR, we might reach some very general conclusions. For example, if the VC was weak, we might refer the child to a speech and language therapist for more complex language assessment, or if the PR was weak, we might suspect some potential motor problems and maybe ask an occupational therapist or others to look at the possibility of dyspraxic difficulties.

However, you will note in this case that the WM and PS indices are much weaker than the others. If these two subtests are significantly weaker than the others, the WISC-IV manual indicates that one should use the GAI. The GAI is an IQ form that uses six subtests from the VC and PR indices. This represents an estimate of general cognitive ability and is less sensitive of the influence of PS and WM. It is also argued for example that these alternative IQ calculations are appropriate, as WM and PS are both similar and separate from the VC and PR. This is due to:

- higher factor loadings on other tests compared with WM and PS;
- increased use of WM and PS tests for IQ computation compared with WISC-III;
- might underestimate IQ, especially in high IQ and as WM/PS is diagnostic/dyslexia loaded.

See, for example Ralford *et al.* (2006) and the WISC-IV manual for further discussion of this issue.

Here, as mentioned earlier, we find that using all the subtests gives a full-scale equivalent of 92. However, as both WM and PS index scores are significantly weaker than the other two index scores, we need to use the GAI. This is the figure shown in the test results discussed earlier.

In fact, around 70% of dyslexic children do show weaknesses in these two Index scores, and Table 3.2 shows the summary of the

**Table 3.2** Mean WISC-IV index scores and % discrepancies between indices of dyslexic children (assessed at East Court School, $n$ = 180, ages 7–16).

| | |
|---|---:|
| Mean index scores | |
|     Verbal comprehension (VC) | 107 |
|     Perceptual reasoning (PR) | 110 |
|     Working memory (WM) | 90 |
|     Processing speed (PS) | 92 |
| % Significantly different scores – WM and PS lower | |
|     VC against WM | 72% |
|     VC against PS | 56% |
|     PR against WM | 81% |
|     PR against PS | 79% |

index scores taken from a large population of dyslexic children (Thomson, 2003; Bech-Nielsen, 2008) – and it can be used as an element of the diagnostic process.

The use of the GAI overcomes the difficulty that I mentioned and described in the first edition of this book. That is, what is the true IQ of a child with dyslexia? For example, in this case history, if we average out all the scores as given earlier, is it an appropriate way of dealing with the IQ? If there are some very specific weaknesses, which there often are in dyslexic children, is it fair to include these as part of the IQ? For example, poor, Digit Span is often and fundamentally linked to dyslexic difficulties. It is rather like evaluating a dyslexic child's intelligence on the basis of whether not he or she can read or not.

However, the use of the GAI has made this debate less crucial. It allows an overall estimate of intelligence as it takes into account the specific difficulties that dyslexics may have.

Looking at the subtests, you may recall as we saw in Chapter 2 that the Wechsler Scale scores have a mean of 10. If a child obtained a scale score of 10 on all the items, that would be equivalent to an IQ or index quotient or standard score of around 100. You can see in this particular case that Digit Span, Letter–Number Sequencing and Coding are particularly weak. Some educational psychologists describe four subtests on the previous Wechsler III Scales as being particularly weak as the 'SCAD' profile. The SCAD profile consists of Symbol Search, Coding, Arithmetic and Digit span items. Arithmetic was a test given on the previous Wechsler III and came under the heading of Freedom from Distractibility, which is now relabelled WM. Prior to the idea of a SCAD profile, there was a so-called Arithmetic, Coding Information and Digit span profile. The evidence for this is reviewed elsewhere (Thomson, 1990). Again, recent research has shown that dyslexics can have a characteristic profile (Thomson, 2003; Bech-Nielsen 2008).

Figure 3.4 shows a profile based on Z scores . Here, one can look at the deviation from the mean or expected scores in a sample of children. In this case, this sample is of over 300 dyslexics and one can see that Digit Span, Letter–Number Sequencing, Coding and Symbol Search are poorer than the other scores and go in the left-hand direction, that is, negative, whereas other subtests are actually rather higher. This is due to the fact that the overall sample is of high average intelligence. One can see how the Z scores show a pattern of four weak subtests and six stronger subtests. Of course, not every child displays this particular pattern, and indeed, our case history in this chapter has a Symbol Search score that is rather higher. Our experience is that the Symbol Search is the most likely

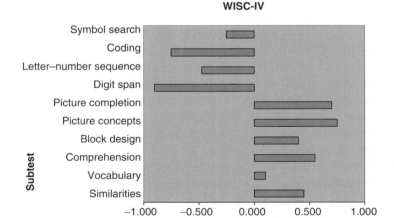

**Figure 3.4** Z score of the Wechsler Intelligence Scale for Children-IV subtest for dyslexic children assessed at East Court School.

not to be weak followed by the Letter–Number Sequencing, whereas Digit span and Coding are the most likely to be the weakest sub-tests. Do look at the descriptions of these subtests in Table 3.1 and you can see how they might be difficult for the dyslexic. You can see our own interpretation of these weaknesses in the case in the full case history. Indeed, the reader might care to print out or peruse Case History 'James Wright' in the 'Typical Dyslexics' file from the CD-ROM at this stage. You can then follow through our own descriptions of the child's cognitive performance in detail in our report, based on the data given earlier.

The subtests from the Working Memory (WM) Index reflect two different aspects of WM skills (which are described in detail in Chapter 8). Digit span is a test of auditory sequential memory or particular aspects of phonological WM. The phonological loop in WM has been shown to be very important in aspects of the aetiology of dyslexia, but obviously links to remembering spelling patterns. Letter–Number Sequencing, a new test in the Wechsler IV, looks at remembering sounds, but also the so-called executive function of memory. This is monitoring of WM skills, for example, taking 9 away from 27, where you have to remember addends and procedures.

As far as Speed of Processing (PS) is concerned, the lower score on Coding is related to the elements of visual processing, not so much visual recognition and identification as such but, serial scanning, short-term memory, graphic skills and PS, all of which tend to mitigate against dyslexic children.

The Symbol Search, which you can see in this particular profile is not as weak as the Coding, involves serial scanning, that is, deciding whether a given symbol or two symbols appear in another array of them, and is less prone to the graphic output and memory component difficulties that the Coding text reflects. Nevertheless, dyslexic children do suffer with this and some do less well with this test. Where there are elements of three-dimensional skills or other tests, dyslexic children may do rather better in my experience. It is important for us not just to look at the comparison between dyslexics and the general population, but also at the individual's performance.

In the case history, we are discussing here, the child is in the top end of the average range for the skills typically associated with school learning but weak in areas linked to dyslexic difficulties. The poor WM and PS problems related to classroom learning are mentioned in many case histories on the CD-ROM and there are also some guides to classroom procedures on the CD. The following is the summary of this cases' cognitive skills taken from our reports:

> In summary, therefore, James is a boy with at least average verbal and visual intelligence. He has particular strengths in verbal and nonverbal reasoning and attention to visual detail. James' vocabulary and general knowledge are age appropriate. He was less able on a task of three-dimensional construction, which may be linked to some motor-type difficulties. In contrast, James has a weaker ability in processing information at speed and a low ability in working memory. He achieved low scores on tasks of processing with the production of simultaneous output at speed, and in the rehearsal and manipulation of short-term information.

It is hoped that this gives some insight into the most commonly used individually administered intelligence test by educational psychologists, the Wechsler Scales. The British Ability Scales is another test that is widely used, and that will also have weak scores in speed of processing and short-term memory skills. The important point really is to look at the details and, if you are only given a general IQ score, ask your educational psychologist for the breakdown of the subtests. This enables you to examine the mentioned issues in terms of the child's actual cognitive profile and whether the IQ is a good reflection of that, as well as some of the issues about what it tells us in respect of underlying cognitive processes.

As the Wechsler and other individually given tests are closed and available only to educational or chartered psychologists, the teacher will need to choose some other tests of ability as a substitute.

NFER–Nelson produce a number of verbal reasoning tests, but of course the problem for dyslexic children is that, these very often involve reading questions. I recently undertook an analysis of a verbal reasoning test and found that 49% of the items were essentially spelling or letter manipulation with minimal verbal reasoning, and a further 11% were biased against dyslexics. I concluded that many items seriously underestimated the ability or intelligence of dyslexics, even those who are good readers, as the test tapped mainly spelling. Dyslexics that are poor readers will be further penalized.

For example one question might be: write in the empty boxes **one** letter that will complete the first word and begin the second word. The same letter must fit into both empty boxes.

| question | | | answer | |
|---|---|---|---|---|
| tear | not | | tar | note |

The reader can see that this item is to do with the manipulation of letters. In addition, phonemic awareness is tested as the sound letter links need to be placed at the beginning or end of words let alone use of vowel-consonant-e rules and sound changes involved in changing tear to tar! This kind of skill is notoriously weak in dyslexics and I personally do not see how this relates to conceptual understanding or reasoning or even verbal intelligence.

'Reasoning' is, essentially, drawing conclusions or inferences from observations, facts, evidence or hypothesis. It also includes arguments towards these conclusions. Verbal reasoning in general would include verbal concept formation, development of vocabulary, verbal understanding, conceptualization and evaluation for verbal inferences. However, I am beginning to go off the subject and get carried away, so we need to return to the assessment of a dyslexic child, as in the case history illustration! I have included the full critique of the 'reasoning' test for the interested reader in the CD-Rom.

As far as the verbal scale given is concerned, I would suggest that the British Picture Vocabulary Scale (BPVS) is used. The second edition looks at receptive or comprehension vocabulary in English and has an age range from 3 to 18 years. There are also alternative norms for pupils for whom English is not their mother tongue.

I would suggest that, as far as a nonverbal test is concerned, there are two possibilities. One is the Matrix Analogies Test (MAT) (Naglieri, 1985), which is a test of visuospatial reasoning. This involves various forms, including pattern completion, and is very similar to the other test that I would recommend, which is Raven's Matrices (see Appendix). This comes in two forms – one, standard, for a wide variety of age ranges, including adults, and the Coloured Raven's, which is also a test of visuospatial reasoning for younger children. Additional measures of verbal ability might include the

Mill Hill Vocabulary Scale or the Crichton Vocabulary Scale. See the list of tests at the end of this chapter for other examples and the publishers.

Another test that is available for teachers is the Wide Range Intelligence Test (WRIT). This test is particularly recommended by the Dyslexia Action, and the use of it is part of the Certificate and Diploma course that they run. This test involves four subtests enabling a general IQ with verbal and visual IQs. The verbal component consists of verbal analogies – similar to fire is to hot as ice is to … – and vocabulary – defining words. The visual component consists of matrix tests similar to many others that are currently used – completing patterns and also a diamonds test. The diamonds test involves two-dimensional diamond square shapes, which are used to create three-dimensional block-type shapes. This test gives standard scores and IQ equivalents. It is also claimed that the verbal component is crystallized intelligence and the visual component is fluid intelligence. This has been touched on before, but perhaps a little more detail here might be helpful to the reader.

Cattell (1963) and Horn (1967) proposed that crystallized intelligence relates mostly to verbal information acquired in the context of formal schooling. It develops largely as a function of exposure to structure and academic settings and is organized by learning in traditional educational environments. On the other hand, fluid abilities represent a broader base capability not dependent on formal school learning and is better acquired from exposure to more general and novel learning experiences. Fluid abilities seem to be a more abstract aspect of intelligence and more easily reflected in nonlanguage tasks, where novelty and flexible thinking are essential. It is argued that fluid ability is a less culturally bound than crystallized ability. In addition, fluid intelligence is described as being more sensitive to the effects of age, whereas crystallized ability is more influenced by culture and development.

The authors of the WRIT have attempted to choose two verbal subtests representative of crystallized intelligence and two visual subtests to represent the fluid ability.

Certainly, the WRIT is a very helpful addition to the specialist teachers' armoury. However, similar to the Wide Range Achievement Test (WRAT), it is, unfortunately, very much a US-based test. The actual items themselves have not been 'anglicized' to represent a British child population. For example, the use of the word 'gasoline' in the vocabulary test. More importantly, the norms are based on US standardization and population samples and are not strictly applicable to UK samples. The Wechsler Scales, on the other hand, have not only been anglicized in terms of the actual test items but are standardized on UK populations.

Teachers using these tests will be able to obtain a quotient or centile, which will give some general guide to overall ability. They will also be able to look at any discrepancies that there might be between verbal and nonverbal abilities, and form a basis for looking at the relationship between ability and reading and spelling levels. This can be done by developing a graphic display similar to that in Figure 3.1. Here, we can include, for example, the BPVS and Raven's Matrices scores expressed as quotients instead of the WISC scores, and instead of the Wechsler Individual Attainment Test scores, we can use other forms of reading and spelling tests. A further example of this is given later in the chapter (see p. 48).

## Attainment tests

We now turn to attainment tests, and in the case history given, there are a variety of reading and spelling tests given here, including tests taken from the Wechsler Individual Achievement Test (WIAT), which are the written language tests associated with the Wechsler Scales. They are often used by educational psychologists because they enable one to produce a predicted standard score based on IQ. This in turn enables one to look at the statistically significant difference between the predicted score and that which is actually observed. In the case given, one can see that the predicted scores based on the GAI of 108 are around 106 or 105, depending on the particular attainment examined. The actual standard scores are also shown, which are lower at quotients of 64. The differences between predicted and observed scores are statistically significant at the $p < 0.001$ level. Basically, this means that the differences between the observed and the expected reading scores are only likely to result from chance once in 1000 times. This discrepancy analysis is, in my opinion, a crucial first stage in the identification of specific learning difficulties because it points to a specific underachievement. Other parts of the assessment are trying to tease out the cause of this particular underachievement.

These are issues that are discussed by the recent British Psychological Society Working Party on the assessment of dyslexia, where there have been suggestions that this discrepancy analysis, taking into account intelligence, is not the most important facet of assessment. These are important issues, which are taken up in Chapter 4 in some detail, because these are areas of potential controversy, and it is important for the reader to understand the issues involved (as well as hearing my own particular view, of course!).

To return to the case, we have a discrepancy between the child's actual reading and spelling performance based on the standardization sample given in the WISC and WIAT. More simply, we can look at the reading and spelling ages and note that the child's word reading is some 4 years behind his chronological age. Word reading on the WIAT is an individual word recognition test. Spelling is at least 5 years behind chronological age.

Further information of reading is given from the Neale Analysis of Reading Ability Test. Accuracy involves reading a series of graded passages and looking at the errors made. Comprehension is slightly different from some other tests in the sense that, if an accuracy error is made, the word is supplied to the child. Questions are asked at the end so that there is less of the word-decoding element. Finally, the rate is simply the speed of reading.

Whatever reading tests are given, the first stage of the attainment process is to look at the general levels of performance and how these might relate to overall ability. Figure 3.5 shows how this can be done using the matrices, BPVS, the WRAT reading (individual word decoding), spelling and arithmetic. It is taken from examples given at the Dyslexia Institute (now Action) by Martin Turner. I have included this example because it illustrates some elements of the error of measurement that we discussed in Chapter 2.

In Figure 3.5, the top and bottom of each of these shapes represent the range or error of measurement for the particular test. Obviously, if there is a great deal of overlap between them, there is not much discrepancy between ability and attainment. On the other hand, if, as in the example showing BPVS/MAT and WRAT reading, there is little or no overlap, we can be pretty sure that there is a significant discrepancy between ability and attainment.

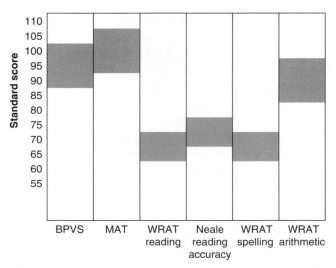

**Test adminstered**

**Figure 3.5** Graph showing standardized tests expressed in confidence bands. Reproduced with the permission of Martin Turner, the Dyslexia Institute. All the above results, except for the Matrix Analogies Test (MAT), are expressed at the 68% confidence level, that is, one can be sure, about $\frac{2}{3}$ of the time, that the subjects' 'perfect' or 'true' score would lie within the upper and lower limits indicated. The MAT gives confidence of 85%. The results above represent a graphical display of the table below. Example: CA 8:4

| Test | Raw score | Standard score | Standard error of measurement | Range | Confidence level (%) |
|------|-----------|----------------|-------------------------------|-------|----------------------|
| BPVS | 80 | 95 | ±6 | 89–101 | 68 |
| MAT | 27 | 101 | ±6 | 95–107 | 85 |
| WRAT reading | 17 | 67 | ±5 | 62–72 | 68 |
| Neale Reading Accuracy | 12 | 72 | +5 | 67–77 | 68 |
| WRAT spelling | 12 | 67 | +5 | 62–72 | 68 |
| WRAT arithmetic | 21 | 90 | +6 | 84–96 | 68 |

CA, chronological age; BPVS, British Picture Vocabulary Scale; WRAT, Wide Range Achievement Test.

This graphic representation is particularly useful because we do not have a statistical interpretation of the attainment/intelligence discrepancy as is given on the Wechsler Scales, for example. It also enables a wide variety of different tests to be used in order to compare the child's attainments (assuming they give standardized scores with a mean of 100).

Of course, looking at a child's reading and spelling age and stating that there is a significant weakness is just the start of the story. This emphasizes the underachievement, and once again, the reader is referred to Chapter 4 for details of the evaluation of this discrepancy exercise. What is also equally important is to look at the reading and spelling errors and the way in which the child undertakes the reading process. Some examples of reading and spelling errors are given in the case histories on the CD-ROM, and one can see problems of letter order, omissions of vowels, difficulties with end sounds and so on. A very important part of the diagnostic procedure is to write down errors and see how these relate to the way that the child operates in his or her reading or spelling task, for example, *gup* for *jump* is a reasonable error because the child is using the 'g' as a soft 'g' for the 'j' in jump. On the other hand, he or she is omitting the nasal blend, and we can relate that to some of the diagnostic tests that might be undertaken as well as there could be some phoneme awareness problems.

There are many other important aspects of looking at a child's reading performance, for example, where does a child start on the page? Does he or she need to follow a line when he or she is reading? Does he or she ignore punctuation? What is his or her knowledge about text in general? A detailed analysis of reading and spelling errors is of fundamental importance to plan help with reading and spelling. Of course, sometimes this is difficult to interpret, for example, is *aminal* for *animal* a result of misreading caused by sequencing or 'jumping' of letters, or is it the result of the child recognizing the word correctly and mispronouncing the word *animal*? There are obviously basic factors to observe, such as difficulties with vowel combinations or consonant blends, but it is also worth looking in some detail or asking the children themselves, as well as listening to the way in which they go about reading and spelling to give clues about where the learning difficulty lies.

In many of the case histories, including this one, you will note the inclusion in the attainment of 'East Court Phonic Reading'. There is often a very steep graduation into irregular words in most published reading and spelling tests. This does not always reflect the children's written language development and, indeed, their teaching programme. There are some tests to overcome this, for example, the Phonic Reading Tests (see list of tests at the end of this chapter), which has, similar to the Neale, passages of increasing difficulty. The difference here is, however, the passages have 'cvc' words, consonant blends, vowel combinations and so on.

We have devised our own tests called 'East Court Graded Phonic Reading and Spelling' tests. I have included both those tests on the CD with the case histories. They are unpublished and unstandardized. They are a criterion-orientated test but give some idea of where the children are breaking down in their attainments. Some preliminary research by students on placement with us show that there are good correlations between these tests and reading and spelling ages. Readers are free to use these texts provided that they are acknowledged – further details are given in the CD-ROM under 'East Court Graded Phonic Tests'.

The words follow the written language structure as taught by a specialist teacher CVC, CCVC, two-syllable regular vowel combinations and so on.

In our case history, we have used the psuedoword reading from the WIAT. There are other versions of nonword reading as well. For example, Graded Nonword Reading test (e.g. text list).

As well as formal reading and spelling tests, we also need some form of measure of writing. This can include free writing, where we ask a child to write about anything he or she likes or to make up a story, or it might be a more formal assessment in which, for example, we give 10 words and the child has to write 10 sentences using each word, and then we look at the writing rate.

It is often difficult to evaluate writing. We attempted to do it in the Aston Index (Newton and Thomson, 1976) by providing a series of categories such as grammar, writing style and so on, under which teachers could rate the child's performance. We need to just look at it qualitatively and make some comments as has been shown briefly in that case history. It will be seen a speed of three words per minute is given – there are norms produced by Hedderly (1995) which I find useful for this.

A summary of our comments on this particular child's attainments are given here, but again, the reader is referred to the CD-ROM for the full text of our analysis of the child's reading and spelling difficulties.

> As we have discussed, James' attainment test results show him to be experiencing written language difficulties. His alphabetic decoding, spelling and quality of writing is very low and dramatically delayed. Importantly, spelling mistakes do not yet have a consistent phonemic basis. James is more able in reading (of text and single words) but this remains delayed by around 4 years. Only the understanding of text and reading rate are average and at an age-appropriate level.

I would add a further comment to this particular case. While it is common for dyslexic children to do rather better at the comprehension aspect of the Neale Analysis of Reading Ability as words incorrectly read are provided by the tester, it is unusual for them to score so highly. This is because they make so many errors in a given paragraph of text or a page of text, that they do not go on to the next level. This particular boy had a wide variety of reading errors, making some mistakes on very simple words, but also managed to get some more difficult words correct; therefore, he managed to get on to higher levels of the Accuracy test on Neale. Also, it is unusual for the Rate of reading to be so high.

I would also refer the reader to page 71 for a discussion on 'phonemic' spelling errors and what that means in the context of phonological skills.

As far as attainments are concerned, teachers have a much wider variety of tests to choose from than intelligence tests. The reader will have his or her own favourites, but I think there needs to be at least a word recognition test involving individual graded words, similarly with spelling, and at least a test involving the reading of text or some sort of comprehension. Individual word-reading tests include the WIAT reading given and the British Ability Scales

Word Reading; Schonell is another one as is the WRAT. As far as reading from text is concerned, there are the Neale Analysis of Reading Ability, Individual Reading Analysis, the Salford Sentence Reading and many others. In spelling, there are the Vernon Spelling Test, British Ability Scales, WIAT and WRAT tests. As far as writing is concerned, there is the Sentence Completion Test by Hedderly (see Hedderly, 1995). There are many other tests. Most of the mentioned tests are available from NFER–Nelson or, in the case of the WRAT, from Wide Range in Delaware. (See the Appendix for the tests mentioned.)

## Diagnostic tests

Finally, we turn to diagnostic tests. Very broadly, these lie within two types, one of which includes diagnostic screening tests for dyslexia. As the purpose of these is to be a full assessment of them, it is not my purpose to review them here. They include the Bangor Dyslexia Test, the Aston Index, Dyslexia Screening Test and, recently the Dyslexia Portfolio tests. (See Tests pages 73–76). (See Appendix), the second kind of diagnostic tests are those specifically trying to tap a particular element associated with specific learning difficulties or a particular aspect of reading, writing and spelling problems.

In our case history (see p. 14), there are two tests quoted. One is the Phonological Abilities Battery and the other is the Nonword Reading Test. The latter (Snowling, Stothard and Maclean, 1996), as the name suggests, is a graded test of nonword reading, going from simple one-syllable words to two-syllable words with unusual letter–sound combinations. Nonword reading is proposed to be a measure of pure alphabetical skills or grapheme–phoneme correspondence skills, and it may be seen that our example has an equivalent age of 7 years on this particular test. This obviously indicates grapheme–phoneme correspondence difficulties, again common to many children with dyslexia. The other test, the Phonological Abilities Battery (Frederickson, Frith and Reason, 1997), indicates problems with both beginning and end deletion, that is, the removal of a phoneme or a sound in a word, for example, '*sand* without "n"

**Table 3.3** Examples of assessing phonological skills.

---

1. Segmentation tasks
   - Counting syllables and phonemes. Tapping tasks (syllables or phonemes)
   - Identifying syllables and phonemes, for example, first part of 'carpet'
   - Supplying missing syllables and phonemes, for example, ca(t) or (c) at
2. Blending tasks
   - Blending syllables – car'pet
   - Blending onset and rimes – c'at or tr'ip
   - Blending phonemes – c'a't
   - Single syllable and multi-syllable phoneme blending
   - Nonword blending, for example, v'u'm or t'e'k'o
3. Rhyming tasks
   - Rhyme detection, for example, picking a word that rhymes with a picture
   - Rhyme production – day, say, pay, jay and so on
   - Odd one out tasks – mad, cap, tap, sap
4. Manipulation tasks
   - Deleting phonemes – cat without (c) = at
   - Adding phonemes – mee + t = meet
   - Substituting –'c' for 'p' in 'pat' to make 'cat'
   - Transposing – John Lennon = Lohn Jennon

---

Adapted from Muter (1997), paper at the British Dyslexia Association Conference, York.

becomes sad.' As would be expected from the reading and spelling errors, this child has problems with both, but not with other elements of this particular test battery.

At this stage, it is worth looking at elements of phonological skills because they are seen to be very important in the aetiology of dyslexia (see Chapter 9 for details). There are a number of tests that have tried to look at this. Table 3.3 gives some examples of how phonological skills could be examined. This shows four kinds of tasks. Under each of these four tasks are different levels. From (a) upwards, the tasks become increasingly difficult. In other ways, I think the table is fairly self-explanatory.

These and other approaches have, therefore, given rise to a number of tests that purport to measure phonological skills. Nonword reading, which attempts to measure alphabetical decoding without lexical (word meaning) knowledge, appears in the Phonological Abilities Battery, and there are the NFER–Nelson Children's Test of Nonword Repetition (Psychological Corporation), the Hatcher Sound Linkage Test of Phonological Awareness, the Posner Test of Auditory Analysis Skills and so on.

In addition to these, there are a number of tests that also look at short-term memory skills, information-processing skills and so on. These include tests from the Aston Index such as the sound-blending, sound discrimination, auditory sequential memory and visual sequential memory tests, which are all linked to written language learning difficulties. Auditory short-term memory is also part of the WISC (digit span) and tests such as coding from the WISC can also be considered diagnostic. The Dyslexia Portfolio (Turner 2008) consists of a battery of short, diagnostic tests that help identify areas of difficulty in literacy learning. Attainment tests are Single Word Reading and Spelling, Reading Fluency and Rate of Writing. Diagnostic tests are Phoneme Deletion, Non-word Reading and Rapid Picture Naming. The latter tests include elements that have been shown by research (see reviews later in the book) to be associated with dyslexia.

The purpose of diagnostic tests is to delineate specific difficulties that the child has and link these to developmental remediation. This is beyond the scope of this book but see, for example, Thomson and Watkins (1999). Dyslexia Action (Institute) also has a number of tests that it has developed for teachers, many of which are reported in *Dyslexia Review*, the journal of the Dyslexia Institute. However, in this case history, please look that the CD-ROM to look at our own suggestions and recommendations, including an individual educational plan for this particular assessment.

I hope the reader now has a feel for the psychological background, particularly testing psychometric aspects of assessing a dyslexic. I also hope that the detailed case histories given on the CD-ROM will give a greater detail in to the sorts of difficulties and variations within the dyslexic syndrome.

# Further reading

The following references give more detail on assessing the dyslexic child:

Miles, T.R. (1993) *Dyslexia: The Pattern of Difficulties*, Whurr, London.

Reid, G. (1998) Chapters 3 and 4, in *Dyslexia: A Practitioner's Manual*, John Wiley & Sons, Ltd, Chichester.

Thomson, M.E. (1990) Chapter 5, in *Developmental Dyslexia*, Whurr, London.

Thomson, P. and Gilchrist, P. (ed.) (1997) Chapters 2 and 3, in *Dyslexia*, Chapman & Hall, London.

Turner, M. (1997) *Psychological Assessment of Dyslexia*, Whurr, London.

# Tests

The following are examples of tests under four headings of 'Ability', 'Attainment', 'Diagnostic' and 'Screening'. Three reflect the categories of assessments from Chapter 3, but I have also included examples of screening tests for dyslexia as a separate category. Some of these also include ability, attainment and diagnostic sections. I have made some comments in italic, where appropriate, often the name is self-explanatory. It is not an exhaustive list and readers will find many more examples in the publishers' catalogues and reviewed in, for example, Reid (1998) and Boyle and Fisher (2007).

Note that the Wechsler and British Ability Scales are available only for psychologists with specific training and some of the tests require special educational need teacher training. The publishers can give further information.

# Ability tests

Dunn, L.M., Dunn, L.M., Whetton, C. and Burley, J. (1997) *British Picture Vocabulary Scale*, 2nd edn (BPVS-II), GL Assessment, Windsor. *A measure of receptive vocabulary across a wide age range.*

Glutting, J., Adams, W. and Sheslow, D. (2000) *Wide Range Intelligence Test*, Psychological Assessment Resources Inc, Florida. *Ability test recommended for teachers by Dyslexia Action (Institute).*

Elliott, C.D., Smith, P. and McCulloch, K. (1996) *British Ability Scales*, 2nd edn (BASII), GL Assessment, Windsor. *Individually given intelligence test.*

Naglieri, J.A. (1985) *Matrix Analogies Test (MAT)*, Harcourt, The Psychological Corporation, London. *Nonverbal cognitive (intelligence) measure.*

Naglieri, J.A. (1996) *Naglieri Non-Verbal Ability Test (NNAT)*, Harcourt, The Psychological Corporation, London. *Nonverbal cognitive (intelligence) measure – used various matrices formats.*

Raven, J. (1995) *Raven's Progressive Matrices Standard and Coloured*, 2nd edn, GL Assessment, Windsor. *Nonverbal cognitive (intelligence) .*

Vincent, D. and Crumpler, M. (2002) *Non-Verbal Abilities Test 6-10*, Hodder Test.

Vincent, D. and Crumpler, M. (2002) *Verbal Abilities Tests 8-13*, Hodder Tests.

Wechsler, D. (1992) *Wechsler Intelligence Scale for Children IV*, 3rd edn (WISC-III), Pearson Assessment. *Individually given intelligence test.*

## Attainment tests

Neale, M.D. (1997) *Neale Analysis of Reading Ability – Revised* (NARA-II; 2nd revised British edn standardization by C. Whetton, L. Caspall and K. McCulloch), GL Assessment, Windsor. *Prose reading giving accuracy, rate (speed) and comprehension (questions on text after it has been read) scores.*

Peters, M.L. and Smith B. (1990) *Spelling in Context*, GL Assessment, Windsor. *Passages for dictation.*

Robertson, G.L. (2000) *Wide Range Achievement Test – Expanded Edition (WRAT Expanded)*, Harcourt.

Rust, J., Golombok, S. and Trickey, G. (1993) *WORD: Wechsler Objective Reading Dimension*, Pearson Assessment. *Three attainment tests: basic reading (individual word reading), spelling (graded individual words) and reading comprehension (graded texts with questions).*

Torgesen, J.K., Wagner, R. and Rashotte, C. (1999) *Test of Word Reading Efficiency (TOWRE)*, Pro-Ed, Austin, TX.

University of Edinburgh (2002) *Edinburgh Reading Tests 1-4*, Hodder Tests.

Vernon, M. (1976) *Vernon Graded Word Spelling Test*, Hodder & Stoughton, London. *Graded individual word spelling.*

Vernon, P.E. (1998) *Graded Word Spelling Test*, Hodder Tests.

Vernon, P.E. and Miller, K.M. (1998) *Graded Arithmetic – Mathematics Test*, Hodder Tests.

Vincent, D. and Claydon, J. (1982) *Diagnostic Spelling Test*, GL Assessment, Windsor.

Vincent, D. and Crumpler, M. (undated) *British Spelling Test Series*, GL Assessment.

Vincent, D. and Crumpler, M. (2002) *Salford Sentence Reading Test (Revised)*, 3rd edn, Bookbinder GE, Hodder Tests.

Vincent, D. and De La Mare, M. (1990) *Individual Reading Analysis*, GL Assessment, Windsor. *Prose reading* .

Wechsler, D. (2005) *Wechsler Individual Achievement Test – Second UK Edition (WIAT-II)*, Harcourt. *This is a variety of attainment tests including word reading and spelling as well as a number of comprehension measures.*

Wilkinson, G.S. (1993) *The Wide Range Achievement Test*, 3rd edn (WRAT-3), Pearson Assessment. *Test of graded individual word reading and spelling (also arithmetic).*

Wilkinson, G.S. and Robertson G.J. (2006) *Wide Range Achievement Test 4 (WRAT4)*, Psychological Assessment Resources, Florida Graded Word Reading and Spelling Tests.

Young, D. (2002) *Cloze Reading Tests 1-3*, Hodder Tests.

## Diagnostic tests

Crumpler, M. and McCarty, C. (2004) *Non-Word Reading Test*, Pearson Assessment.

Frederickson, N., Frith, U. and Reason, R. (1997) *Phonological Assessment Battery (PhAB)*, GL Assessment, Windsor. *A number of phonological tests including nonword reading, rhyming, spoonerisms and so on.*

Gathercole, S. and Baddeley, A. (1996) *Children's Test of Non-Word Repetition (CN-REP)*, GL Assessment.

Muter, V., Hulme, C. and Snowling, M. (1997) *Phonological Abilities Test (PAT)*, Psychological Corporation. *Similar to the PhAB but for younger children.*

Pickering, S. and Gathercole, S. (2001) *Working Memory Test Battery for Children (WMTB-C)*, Harcourt.

Snowling, M.J., Stothard, S.E. and McLean, J. (1996) *Graded Non-Word Reading Test*, Thames Valley Trust Co., Bury St. Edmunds. *Graded individual nonword reading test.*

Torgesen, J.K. and Bryant, B.R. (2004) *Test of Phonological Awareness – Second Edition: PLUS (TOPA-2+)*, Pro-Ed, Austin, TX.

Wagner, R., Torgesen, J. and Rashotte, C. (1999) *Comprehension Test of Phonological Processing (CTOPP)*, Harcourt.

## Screening tests

Butterworth, B. (2003) *Dyscalculia Screener*, GL Assessment.

Fawcett, A. and Nicolson, R. (1997 onwards) *Dyslexia Screening Tests (DEST, DST, DAST)*, LDA Learning. *Screening for pre-school, child and adult. Phonological items as well as motor development.*

Fawcett, A. and Nicolson, R. (1998) *Dyslexia Adult Screening Test (DAST)*, Harcourt.

Fawcett, A. and Nicolson, R. (2004) *Dyslexia Screening Test – Junior (DST-J)*, Harcourt.

Fawcett, A. and Nicolson, R. (2004) *Dyslexia Screening Test – Secondary (DST-S)*, Harcourt.

Miles, T. (undated) *Bangor Dyslexia Test*, LDA Learning.

Miles, T.R. (1983) *The Bangor Dyslexia Test*, LDA Learning, Wisbech. *Criterion-oriented screen for dyslexia.*

Newton, M. and Thomson, M.E. (1976) *The Aston Index*, LDA Learning, Wisbech. *Ability measures including a vocabulary scale, attainments (Schonell Graded Word Reading and Spelling) and diagnostic items such as digit span, sound blending and so on.*

Nicolson, R. and Fawcett, A. (2004) *Dyslexia Early Screening Test – Second Edition (DEST-2)*, Harcourt.

Turner, M. (2008) *Dyslexia Portfolio* GL Assessment Windsor *A battery of diagnostic tests including word reading and spelling, non-word reading, rapid picture naming and digit span.*

Turner, M. and Smith, P. (2003) *Dyslexia Screener*, LDA Learning.

Further details can be obtained from the following web sites:

- http://www.gl-assessment.co.uk
- http://www.harcourt-uk.com
- http://www.hoddertests.co.uk
- http://www.ldalearning.com

For more information on teaching, the following are useful (the second book mentioned also has a chapter on building a teaching programme from an assessment):

Thomson, M.E. and Watkins, E.J. (1999) *Dyslexia: A Teaching Handbook*, Whurr, London.

Townend, J. and Turner, M. (eds) (2000) *Dyslexia in Practice: A Guide for Teachers*, Kluwer/Plenum, New York.

# 4

# Definition and Discrepancies

## Introduction and context

There has been an increasing tendency over the last few years for a return to the notion of dyslexia as part of a general continuum of poor readers. In the 1970s, the thinking, particularly favoured by educational psychologists, was that dyslexic learning difficulties were a result of overanxious parents or perhaps those 'middle-class parents with thick children'. In other words, that parents were reluctant to accept that their child was a slow learner, and used the word dyslexia to describe his or her difficulties. There were particularly hostile reactions from many in the educational world re the notion of a syndrome of dyslexia, and you can imagine the relief in dyslexia circles when specific learning difficulties/dyslexia was recognized by the 1982 and subsequent Education Acts.

However, there has been a suggestion of a return to the 'dyslexia does not exist' notion by some academics, for example, Stanovich (1994), or 'dyslexics are just poor readers', for example, the report of the working party of the Division of Educational and Child Psychology of the British Psychological Society. The following is their working definition of dyslexia:

> Dyslexia is evident when accurate and fluent word reading and/or spelling develops very incompletely or with great difficulty. This focuses on literacy learning at the 'word level', and implies that the problem is severe and persistent despite appropriate learning opportunities. It provides a basis for a staged process of assessment through teaching.

*The Psychology of Dyslexia – A Handbook for Teachers*, by Michael Thomson
© 2009 John Wiley & Sons Ltd

This definition has been rightly criticized by the British Dyslexia Association and others as being far too general, and might be applied to all children who are poor readers and spellers. However, the crucial element of this working party is the rejection of the notion of the relationship between reading (and written language) and intelligence as an important element of the diagnostic process in dyslexia. The notion of the discrepancy model in dyslexia has been questioned by some researchers such as Stanovich (1994), following on from Siegal (1989) as well as this working party. There are very important implications for diagnosis, policy and remediation from these questions, which have been fuelled in particular by the idea that there is a core phonological deficit, which is the descriptive definition of dyslexia, and not a discrepancy between observed reading, writing and spelling and that expected based on intelligence and chronological age.

This is ironic, considering the history of the concept of dyslexia and its interrelationship with educational psychology theory and practice. In the early 1970s, dyslexia was described as essentially a syndrome by identifying particular features that were associated with dyslexia, for example, see Miles (1974) and Newton (1970). These features included not only weak auditory and visual short-term memory (particularly sequencing), but also sound blending, sound discrimination, naming and labelling skills, all of which have been described as being associated with a phonological deficit in more recent years (see also Chapter 1).

The idea of describing a particular learning difficulty in terms of its observed deficits was rejected by the educational psychology establishment at that time. However, the key epidemiological studies, for example, Rutter, Tizard and Whitmore (1970) and Yule *et al.* (1974), established 'specific reading difficulties' and dyslexia became accepted. This was on the basis of the proposal by Yule *et al.* (1974) that there were groups of children who could be divided into those who had general reading retardation and those who had a specific reading retardation. This was on the basis of the relationship between IQ and reading. A high correlation was found (around 0.6) between reading and intelligence, and Yule *et al.* were able to demonstrate that children whose reading was 2 or more years behind their chronological age alone, showed a different pattern of learning difficulties from those children whose reading was 2 or more years behind that based on chronological age *and* intelligence. (See Chapter 1, p. 11, for a summary of the differences and for further details.) Taking into account the notion that reading is not perfectly correlated with intelligence, they developed regression equations – which enabled them to predict what reading should be in a given population – early on in the Isle of Wight and later in the Inner London Education Authority, based on four subtests of the WISC, giving a short-form IQ, and using the Neale Analysis of Reading Ability.

This study was widely accepted as 'proving' that there was indeed a dyslexia syndrome, and this was based on the discrepancy model very widely accepted by educational psychologists since then. Over the last few years there have been criticisms of both a technical and a theoretical nature (see Thomson, 1990, for a review). However, it is ironic that the Division of Education and Child Psychology is now rejecting the notion of a discrepancy model in favour of describing various characteristics of the learning process (mainly involving phonological skills) that describe dyslexia, when it was educational psychologists who rejected characteristic descriptions in favour of discrepancy models.

## IQ/reading relationships

The critical examination of this relationship by Stanovich (1994) is based on points made by Siegal (1989). She argued that intelligence tests do not truly measure intelligence, and that some of the items measured by such tests are, in effect, measures of achievement, not of intelligence. The implication is that an intelligence test needs to have predictive and concurrent validity; that is, it correlates with future academic performance and current achievements. Well-validated tests such as the WISC do this, and to argue about the construct of intelligence and what the tests measure is rather sterile. Concerns over the construct of intelligence and what items should be included in intelligence testing do not, it seems to me, preclude examining the relationship between reading ability, for example, and an intelligence test score. Of course, it is the case that children who are, as she put it, 'from minority backgrounds, lower social class families and/or different ethnic groups' may be disadvantaged, but essentially, an IQ score is useful for its guide to what a child might do at school later on and in defining certain cognitive skills. This still seems to be a valid construct if we look at the standardization manuals for both British Ability Scales and the Wechsler Scales. Of course, we must be careful not to label as slow learners those children who are not; this is part of the educational psychologist's training and clinical experience, although this does not mean to say that we can use the recognized impreciseness of psychometric testing to throw out the concept altogether.

Siegal (1989) also went on to comment that 'calculating a discrepancy … seems an illogical way of calculating whether or not there is a learning disability.' I would argue to the contrary, because it is quite clear that it is possible to examine the relationship between intelligence, however imprecisely measured, and reading (also, it should be noted, imprecisely measured as reading involves many different kinds of skills and most reading tests measure these only inaccurately). The Yule and Rutter studies demonstrated how it was possible in a given population to look specifically at the relationship between attainment and IQ skills (or, if arguing about the constructs, Wechsler IQ scores and Neale Analysis of Reading Scores), whatever they measure. The most recent additions to the British Ability Scales and the Wechsler Scales include discrepancy tables that have been standardized on US and British samples (and in other countries where the scales are used). The data from these large samples are sufficient evidence that there is a relationship between attainment tests and IQ. Table 4.1 shows examples of the predicted attainments based on IQ on the WISC-IV and Wechsler Individual Attainment Test Word Reading. It shows that, for a given IQ, on the left, we can predict the quotient on basic reading, spelling and reading comprehension following on from the standardization samples in the Wechsler Scales, in this case the British sample. One should also note that this takes into account the so-called regression to the mean effect, which has also been a criticism about attainment/IQ discrepancy analysis. In other words, the correlation between reading and intelligence as measured by intelligence tests is not perfect. There is a regression to a mean, that is, children with lower IQs will tend to have higher predicted scores for attainments, and children with higher IQs will tend to have lower predicted scores for their attainments. This deals with the statistical criticisms concerning IQ/reading correlations. Note that regression to the

**Table 4.1** Predicted Wechsler Individual Achievement Test attainments for WISC IQ.

| Full-scale IQ | Predicted attainments | | |
|---|---|---|---|
| | Basic reading | Spelling | Reading comprehension |
| 75 | 84 | 86 | 83 |
| 105 | 103 | 103 | 103 |
| 125 | 116 | 114 | 117 |

mean is not the same as the regression equations used to predict reading level from age and IQ. Table 4.1 illustrates how the regression to the mean occurs based on predictions of attainments from IQ in the standardization.

There are, according to Proctor and Prevatt (2003) about four different ways of looking at discrepancies. These include simple discrepancies, intra-individual, intellectual ability, achievements and underachievement models. They argued that the individual and intellectual ability models were the most agreed on and that these were also essentially based on regression-based discrepancies as mentioned earlier. Measurement, error and reliability estimates for discrepancy scores are also important factors which are function of the reliability of the test used. The Wechsler Scales, which provides a form of discrepancy analysis by predicting a reading standard score from an IQ standard score, has good reliability. Chapter 2 discusses the reliability and error of measurement.

We can now look at some specific examples of how this discrepancy can be analysed using recent psychometrics. The tests shown also enable us to see whether differences in profile are the result of chance variation or statistically significant differences.

Table 4.2 gives typical examples of a current method of examining the difference between predicted reading quotients and observed (actual) attainments. From this, the traditionally 'discrepant model' child with dyslexia, case 1, is over 3 years behind chronological age in reading, but the difference between predicted reading and observed reading quotients is also significant at the $p < 0.001$ level. (The difference is statistically likely to be caused by chance only 1 in 1000 times.)

This sort of analysis indicates that it is quite possible to look at the relationship between attainment and intelligence in a

**Table 4.2** Predicted and observed reading quotients, ages and percentiles based on WISC-IV/WIAT Reading IQ.

| | | | |
|---|---|---|---|
| 'Dyslexic child', IQ 107, CA 10:5 | | | |
| Predicted reading quotient | Observed reading quotient | Difference | Statistically significant |
| 104 | 70 | 34 | $p < 0.01$ |
| 11:8 | 7:0 | | |
| 60st centile | 2nd centile | | |
| 'Slow-learning child', IQ 78, CA 11:5 | | | |
| Predicted reading quotient | Observed reading quotient | Difference | Statistically nonsignificant |
| 86 | 91 | 5 | |
| 9:4 | 10:4 | | |
| 18th centile | 27th centile | | |
| 'Slower-learning and dyslexic child', IQ 82, CA 9:11 | | | |
| Predicted reading quotient | Observed reading quotient | Difference | Statistically significant |
| 89 | 63 | 26 | $p < 0.01$ |
| 8:4 | 6:4 | | |
| 23rd centile | 1st centile | | |
| 'Bright dyslexic child', IQ 120, CA 10:7 | | | |
| Predicted reading quotient | Observed reading quotient | Difference | Statistically significant |
| 113 | 88 | 24 | $p < 0.01$ |
| 14:0 | 8:8 | | |
| 81st centile | 21st centile | | |

CA, chronological age.

statistically and conceptually valid manner, despite Siegal's contention that it is illogical. It is interesting to note that the dyslexic child described would fall at the second centile, which is the (arbitrary) cut-off point used by some local authorities to provide full-time specialist support for children with specific learning difficulties. The 'slow-learning' child (case 2) – or certainly the child who does less well on intelligence tests, whatever that might mean conceptually and operationally – has an expected reading level broadly within the average range (between the twenty-fifth and seventy-fifth centiles), even though his or her reading skills are weak and some 2 years behind chronological age.

The final argument that Siegal puts forward and which Stanovich, in particular, has taken up, is that poor readers with average or higher IQs are no different from poor readers with lower IQs. I do not think that anyone who is working seriously in the area of dyslexia has ever argued that all dyslexic children are intelligent. However most teachers argue that there is a great deal of difference between teaching a child who is a poor reader due to low ability and a dyslexic child.

Turner (2006) is eloquent on this issue. He pointed out that Stanovich's (1996) argument is that a phonological deficit is the sole explanation or dimension in literacy learning difficulties and an IQ is just another variable. Turner argued that both of these are wrong and that phonological deficits alone do not address the whole range of diagnostic criteria seen on a daily basis by those working in dyslexia, for example, visual-motor memory difficulties, attention problems, organizational difficulties and so on. Secondly, an IQ is not just another variable and quoted from Neisser *et al.* (1996) that 'the relationship between (intelligence test) scores and school performance tests seems to be ubiquitous' and 'whenever it has been studied children with high scores on tests of intelligence tend to learn more of what is taught in school than lower scoring peers ... intelligence tests ... are never the only influence on outcomes, though in the case of school performance it may well be the strongest.'

Given this summary by Neisser *et al.* (1996), a review of research by highly respected psychologists, it is surprising that Stanovich would say (1996, p. 155) that 'there is no logically or empirically interpretable sense that we can say that low intelligence (intelligence being a panoply of cognitive processes) causes poor reading.' Turner goes on to make the point that children with general literacy difficulties do not show different diagnostic features, for example, neuroanatomical differences according to whether they have lower or higher IQ and but that this is found in dyslexic children. The fact that dyslexia is not correlated with IQ is why we are measuring it. The fact that intelligence is such an important factor in many different aspects of our behaviour is why psychologists control it, that is, parcel it out as a variable in research looking at other aspects of learning – this is particularly important when working with children. In the case of dyslexia, we want to look at the whole cognitive profile. He made the point, of course, that intelligence can 'cause learning, learning includes language skills, language includes reading.'

Indeed, Neisser *et al.* (1996) commented that there is a correlation of around 0.5 between intelligence and many aspects of learning in school, including literacy. It is commonly accepted statistically that when looking at variation and performance in given tasks, that a correlation gives some account of how much of the variation is linked to the behaviour in question by multiplying the correlation coefficient by itself. So, in this case, a 0.5 correlation gives a 25% account of the variance or that 25% of variation in children's performance is linked to intelligence. This means, of course, that 75% of learning at school is not accounted for by intelligence or at least not linked to intelligence. Nevertheless, these researchers found no other individual correlation (even if we assume that intelligence is a panoply of different cognitive skills) showing such a high account of variance. In other words, intelligence, while not the only factor by any means, is a very important one in learning success. This statement is hardly news to any experienced teacher, but at least, it is backed up by a thorough research review.

Turner's (2006) article is worth perusing as it does point out some of the flaws in the 'dyslexia is not a syndrome' reasoning.

A key feature in defining dyslexia is to examine those particular aspects of the child's learning difficulties and skills that are independent of intelligence, or at least the results of the IQ produced by an intelligence test. Simply, this means that there are just as likely to be dyslexic children who score less well on IQ tests as those who score very well on IQ tests. Intelligence would be just one aspect of a child's psychometric profile. The 'slow-learning dyslexic child' (case 3) shown in Table 4.2 illustrates this point. Here, we have an individual who does less well on IQ tests, but his reading is still well below that based on the prediction on both IQ and chronological age. So, we can see an individual with low average IQ who, even with discrepancy analysis, we would describe as dyslexic. Of course, no one would pretend that just the discrepancy analysis on its own is a sufficient reason for describing an individual as dyslexic – we have to look at a whole number of other factors discussed in Chapter 3.

It is of interest to note in passing, before we go on to examine this issue further, that Stanovich (1994) himself proposed a kind of discrepancy notion in his identification of 'dyslexia'. This is that there should be a discrepancy between decoding and reading comprehension. This is less practical and begs a lot more questions than the IQ/reading discrepancy. The reason for this is that most comprehension tests in reading rely on word reading, for example, in the Neale Analysis, the reading test is discontinued once a certain level of accuracy has been reached. Furthermore, on this particular test, if a child makes an accuracy error, whether it is mispronunciation or anything else, the correct word is supplied. On the other hand, the Wechsler Individual Achievement Comprehension involve reading a passage silently (or aloud) and then answering questions. No corrections are given, and the comprehension score is quite clearly linked to reading decoding or accuracy. Other tests include 'cloze' procedures, sentence completion tasks and so on. There is therefore a great deal of variety in what different reading comprehension tests actually measure; in most, they are heavily loaded and correlated with reading decoding skills. Furthermore, unlike the IQ/reading dimensions, we do not have standardization correlations or predictions for comprehension/decoding. If 'verbal comprehension' is used, that is, oral comprehension as has also been suggested, then this is an intelligence test item, is it not?

## The notion of a core phonological deficit

We now turn to the idea of a core phonological deficit being the main descriptor and, by implication, identifier of dyslexia. The British Psychological Society (1999) Division of Educational and Child Psychology, following Stanovich and others, argued that we should be looking at core phonological processing difficulties as the main diagnostic criteria for dyslexia. These include problems with naming, sound patterns, phonemic awareness including segmentation, whether it be at phoneme, onset/rime or syllable level, phonological recoding, that is, grapheme–phoneme correspondence and so on. There is a great deal of research indicating that these and other skills, such as early rhyming abilities, are good predictors of later reading and spelling development in the normal population, and are often weak in children with reading and spelling difficulties. We examine these in Chapter 9. Stanovich and others who wish to do away with the intelligence/reading dimension proposed that we should be examining this as a fundamental description of 'dyslexia'. The notion here is that children of both high and low IQs would show core phonological deficits. However, Stanovich himself in 1988 seems to be a little confused on this issue. In Stanovich (1988), he argued that higher-IQ poor readers show a clear cut phonological deficit, where those 'garden variety readers' would show less of a phonological deficit. This seems to suggest that there is actually a fundamental difference between the two and that they do not generally have the same problems.

Furthermore, this proposal does not quite hold up. Frith (1999) made the point that low 'g' or general intelligence can underlie the behavioural weaknesses in children with dyslexia, that is, weak nonword reading, phonemic awareness problems, slow naming speed in tests as well as difficulties with reading and spelling. Coltheart and Jackson (1998) made this point particularly well in talking about proximal and distal causes, which I have adapted and presented in relation to this issue in Figure 4.1. Here we have similar behaviour with different aetiologies.

As Figure 4.1 shows, the cause of a phonological deficit can be the result of a number of different factors. These are the 'distal' causes. The phonological deficit itself is the proximal cause (e.g. of reading difficulty). One distal cause can be low intelligence or, if you prefer, low scores on an IQ test. The evidence is that intelligence test scores, as one measure of 'g' or underlying intelligence, are correlated with many different academic achievements in all walks of life and particularly at school age. Therefore, weak phonological

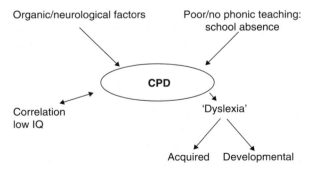

**Figure 4.1** Different 'causes' of a core phonological deficit (CPD).

skills could be caused not only by low IQ and some neurological or organic difficulty, but also, crucially, it can be the result of lack of teaching, poor phonic teaching at school or even school absence. Weakness in core phonological skills can give rise to dyslexia, whether acquired or developmental. The reason (distal cause) is the observed phonological difficulty (proximal cause).

Now, it can be argued that it could be the core phonological problems in both children with dyslexia and those who are slow learners that cause reading difficulties, but I would suggest that the different aetiologies of these are crucial in terms of the teaching programme that is undertaken. This differential teaching has been one of the main reasons for identifying individuals with a dyslexic problem as opposed to general learning difficulties. This has given rise to all the teaching programmes that are specifically used for children with dyslexia (see Thomson and Watkins, 1999, for examples). Furthermore, when we look at the reality of assessing children, it is quite common in my experience for dyslexic children to show phonological deficits (despite their high intelligence or scores on IQ tests), and for children who are slow learners or do less well on IQ tests to do quite well on phonological skills even though their reading is weak. Indeed, recent research by Johnston and Morrison (2007) found that poor readers with an IQ of 90 or below showed a more phonological approach to reading with better reading of regular than irregular words. Nonword reading skills were slow, but were as accurate as those with reading aged control. In contrast, readers with IQ scores of 110 or above showed difficulty in phonological approaches to reading and particularly impaired nonword reading accuracy for their reading ages, as well as difficulties with regular words. Here we have specific data that show children with lower IQ having better phonological skills. Of course, as mentioned earlier, no one is saying that only bright children can be diagnosed as dyslexic. One of the advantages of the discrepancy model described earlier is that one can actually delineate the difference between a child who is generally slower in all aspects of learning (see Neisser *et al.*, 1996) and those with a specific difficulty. This is illustrated in the second child mentioned in Table 4.2.

In the case histories given (see Table 4.2), the 11-year-old described as a slow learner in fact had a Graded Nonword Reading Test score (one widely agreed measure of alphabetical–grapheme–phoneme correspondence skills) at just under the fiftieth centile, whereas the dyslexic child had a score at around the tenth centile.

In addition, the whole notion of just phonological deficits as descriptors of dyslexia does not take into account many of the other problems that dyslexic children have in aspects of short-term memory, which are not specifically linked to phonemic awareness, in weak organizational skills, in arithmetic and tables skills, and in a whole variety of patterns of behaviour commonly recognized by teachers of dyslexic children.

These should give plenty of food for thought for the reader; however, is it just me being cynical by saying that doing away with discrepancy notions means that fewer 'children with dyslexia' are identified if we ignore children who are of high intelligence? By examining the centiles and discrepancies of the 'bright' dyslexic child in Table 4.2, we can see that there is a discrepancy between the predicted and observed reading ages. However, because the child's centiles are still at a relatively high level, and the child is only a year or so behind chronological age in reading, he or she would not be given any additional support. This is typical, in my experience, of a number of children attending my school whose difficulties are not recognized as being severe by the local authority because intelligence is not taken into account. Only those children who fall below the first or second centile in absolute terms are deemed to be severely dyslexic. This saves resources, but is hardly reason enough to reject a useful concept.

Elliott (2005), using the concept of a phonological deficit hypothesis, argued that the distinction between dyslexic and nondyslexic is a 'waste of resources' when the so-called 'privileged IQ' selection for dyslexics is used. Of course, the fact that we have difficulties in literacy despite universal panaceas that try to encompass the 'one fits all sizes' difficulties in literacy is important. However, even if the special educational need resources are limited, just because one group of children are recognized and get the appropriate help, does not immediately preclude other children from similar help. The current buzz word is 'synthetic phonics'. This will help many children, but some dyslexic children, particularly those dyslexic children with weak working memories and poor segmentation spans in relation to phonemic awareness, would not be able to remember individual phonemes blended together; therefore, some analytical phonics, division of words into units and syllables will be required. For the interested reader, one of the sections is our 'Guides to Reports' on the CD-ROM expands on this further entitled Synthetic/Analytic Phonics.

Duff (2008) suggests that the notion of 'Response to Intervention' could be used instead of a discrepancy model. Here children showing difficulties in relation to their peers by not responding to evidence-based methods of reading instruction (rather like the specifically retarded reader described by Rutter *et al.* (1970).)

Sometimes, academic psychologists worry that IQ tests can discriminate against individuals from minority groups; however, they go further from their data and sometimes do not understand where the educational practitioner is coming from. For example, Vellutino *et al.* (2004, p. 29) stated that 'Not only would the I.Q. achievement discrepancy to define reading disability be invalidated, there would be no role for IQ test in this enterprise.' They then went on further to suggest that the problem with 'psychometric approaches to assessing the origins of a child's reading difficulties is that they typically provide no direction for educational or remedial planning.'

I totally disagree with these statements. You can look at two or three pages of the psychologist's reports on the CD-ROM to see how useful such psychometric processes are, in both identification and remedial planning. This would include whether, for example, vocabulary, reasoning or working memory was good or poor. Do any difficulties affect written language, phonemic awareness or even classroom instructions and behaviour? In addition, the investigation of phonological skills, visual-motor processing, fine motor skills and many other key areas, is possible from the cognitive test, attainment and other standardized test scores. We have seen how this approach works in detail in Chapter 3.

Of course, no one should diagnose dyslexia just on the basis of a discrepancy – it is identifying a problem. The next question is the best estimate of what caused the problem.

# Further reading

Thomson, M.E. (1990) Chapter 1, in *Developmental Dyslexia*, Whurr, London.
Turner, M. (1997) *Psychological Assessment of Dyslexia*, Whurr, London.
Some of this chapter appeared as an article in *Dyslexia Review*, **11** (4).

# 5

# Basic Neuropsychology

As we see when we look at proposed causes of dyslexia, a number of theories focus on the neurology or neuropsychology of written language processing, where variations or 'deficits' are seen. I have always viewed explanations for dyslexic difficulties at a number of levels. As far back as the 1970s (e.g. Thomson, 1977, 1979), I was arguing that there was a neurological and cognitive level of explanation and that dyslexia was an individual difference in learning style. The neurological differences would result in cognitive differences, which would, in turn, result in specific skills that were weak in people with dyslexia, which then interacted with the written language system. In other words, we can examine what procedures are needed to learn reading, writing and spelling, how they develop and how they match with what an individual child might have.

These concepts are expressed more elegantly nowadays by, for example, Uta Frith (e.g. Frith, 1999), who talked about the biological, the cognitive and the behavioural level. An example of this general approach is given in Figure 5.1. These and further figures are a development of the outline given in the Preface. Readers may like to refresh their memory about the concepts briefly discussed there.

Here, the notion is that a developmental disorder has a primary biological cause. This might be genetic, which in turn might have to do with brain function or neurology. There is then a resulting cognitive deficit, and finally behavioural signs and observations that can be made. Interacting with all of this is the environment,

*The Psychology of Dyslexia – A Handbook for Teachers,* by Michael Thomson
© 2009 John Wiley & Sons Ltd

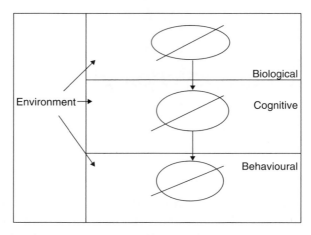

**Figure 5.1** Deficit model: general causal model of neurocognitive origin. From Frith (1999), *Paradoxes in Developmental Dyslexia*, John Wiley and Sons. Reproduced with permission.

which would be aspects of received teaching, experiences at home, other difficulties, psychosocial problems and so on, which might affect a child's learning and hence, the behavioural observations, that is, reading and spelling difficulties that might be seen.

We go into more detail in later chapters, examining different models of such a general causal framework and examining in detail the neuropsychological deficits, phonological coding deficits, cerebellar problems and so on. The reader should not forget that dyslexia is a disorder of written language. We look at models of how written language develops in children and what its characteristics are in Chapter 8. As I have argued elsewhere (Thomson, 1990), we need to look at the task demands of the written language based system and see whether the skills possessed by an individual child match those task demands.

## Neuropsychology and dyslexia

Frith (2008) commented that 'eventually education should be based on evidence from research and cognitive neuro-science.' It is almost a truism that all that we do in the end comes from our brain function, and indeed, literacy is no exception. For example, Petersson *et al.* (2000), using brain imaging compared individuals who never went to school and are illiterate to those that were literate and did go to school, and found differences in brain function. See Figure 5.2.

For example, the literate individuals showed activation patterns in the left hemisphere, particularly the areas we shall see are linked to written language. However, the individuals who could not read only had a small activation in the right hemisphere. In other words, by learning to read, the connections are formed in the brain and, in turn, brain function links to reading ability. It is the failure to make connections in the dyslexics' brain, despite the same teaching input that is 'programming' the brain in the literate individual. This could be the result of a genetic predisposition and, as we shall see, is in very specific parts of the brain that are involved in literacy. The 'illiterate' brains in Figure 5.2 result from the lack of school and teaching in this group. The dyslexic exposed to the normal school experience is a different case.

So, the purpose of this chapter is, very briefly, to outline some key elements of brain function that we need to know before we examine specific theories of how brain organization might result in dyslexic difficulties.

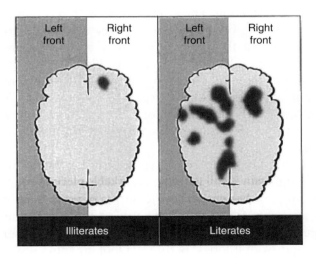

**Figure 5.2** 'Literate and nonliterate brains' from Petersson *et al.* (2000).

Although the reader should not look upon this as a potted version of the biological basis of psychology, it does provide an overview of areas of the brain and sensory function that are relevant to dyslexia. These are picked up later in Chapters 6 and 7.

## Brain function and anatomy

In general terms, we might describe the relevant aspects of neuropsychology that we wish to consider as (i) the sensory/perceptual and (ii) the linguistic/cognitive. The sensory/perceptual domain includes the sensory pathways, that is, the sense organs, the eye and ear being the most obvious and important ones in the case of reading and spelling, although, of course, motor function is also important. As well as sensory pathways, this would include aspects of the brainstem, that is, the underlying, older parts of the brain that undertake a number of functions. This includes the cerebellum, which we examine in more detail in a later chapter. Also important are 'relays', including the thalamic relays where information is passed on from the sensory organs to the brain. An example is shown later in the visual system in particular. The sensory/perceptual information that comes from our sense organs goes to various parts of the cerebral cortex. The cerebral cortices are the higher centres of brain function. Those associated with receiving information from the senses are called the primary cortices, including the primary visual and the primary auditory cortex (situated in the occipital and temporal lobes, respectively). Finally, we could include the association areas of the brain as important elements of the sensory/perceptual function. Perception, as opposed to sensory input, implies that the brain is, to some extent, constructing a model of the world, but that is perhaps taking us into other realms of psychology.

The so-called linguistic/cognitive approaches have much more to do with higher-order functions. Those parts of the brain responsible for language are particularly important when it comes to dyslexia, as we see later (p. 105). These include part of the cerebral hemispheres – involving the anterior temporal cortex, inferior parietal lobes and frontal lobes. Before we look at some of these functions, a brief simplified overview of brain anatomy is required.

Figure 5.3 shows a very crude model looking at the four major lobes of the brain from the left point of view. Note that the dotted lines are arbitrary.

Figure 5.4 shows examples of the relationship between the cerebrum in humans and some examples of the brainstem structures such as the midbrain, hindbrain, cerebrum, cerebellum and spinal cord. The functions of these are outlined in Table 5.1.

Figure 5.5 shows a diagram of the left hemisphere with various language functions highlighted. Some descriptions of the functions are also given.

Note, especially for Figure 5.5, that these areas do not have exact delineations in the brain matter. Although there is obviously agreement as to location, different books have different style diagrams and the labelled sites are indicative of general areas.

There now follows some additional comment on some of the key areas from Figure 5.5. The auditory association area has obvious implications for spoken to written language, but note the

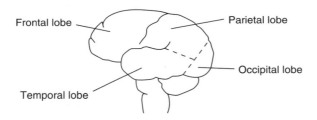

**Figure 5.3** Major lobes of the cerebral cortex.

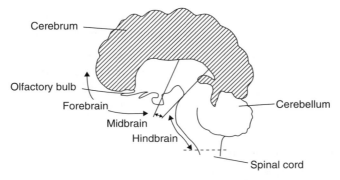

**Figure 5.4** Cerebrum and brainstem.

**Table 5.1** Parts of the brain and their associated language functions.

Cortex: concerned with the receipt and recognition of others' speech, as well as the formulation, initiation and control of own

| | |
|---|---|
| Cortical lobes with speech areas | All the lobes are important in the speech processes since any sensory impulse may make connection with the speech association areas. |

Subcortical structures: concerned with the organization and relay of sensory and motor impulses to and from the cortex

| | |
|---|---|
| Basal ganglia | Involved in the control of the muscles of the face, larynx, tongue and pharynx. Damage to them may lead to lack of coordination in articulation, gesture and facial expression. |
| Thalamus | Organizes and relays sensory data on the way to the cortex. Sensory concepts, which affect speech, may be organized here, as well as the emotional qualities of the voice. |
| Midbrain | On the sensory side, it contains relay stations concerned with sight and hearing. Similarly, on the motor side, it carries the pyramidal and extrapyramidal tracts. |
| Medulla oblongata | Contains motor nuclei for controlling basic body functions, such as breathing, together with the motor and sensory tracts connecting with the midbrain. |
| Cerebellum | The control centre for continuous muscular movements and coordination. Damage to it results in speech which is jerky, thick and slurred. |

description of the planum temporale (temporal plane) because we shall be looking at anatomical differences between children with and those without dyslexia in this area in our later discussions on causes.

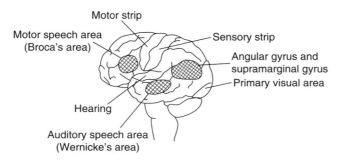

**Figure 5.5** Left cortical hemisphere showing language areas. These are:

- Auditory association areas (first temporal convolution). This area is essential for the recognition and analysis of spoken language. This area lies adjacent to the 'planum temporale'. Wernike's area lies between this and the angular gyrus.
- Broca's area. This area, which lies just anterior to the motor area that controls the movements of the face and mouth, is essential for the production of coordinated speech sound.
- Motor area for writing.
- Supramarginal gyrus. Within this area, the sounds of the words become associated with their meaning.
- Angular gyrus. Within this area, the patterns of written symbols become associated with there verbal counterparts and with the concept they represent.

Broca's area is also important, because there is an integration here between the production of speech sounds, which is important in early articulation difficulties, phonemic awareness and the relationship between phonological knowledge and later reading, writing and spelling. These are key skills, as we shall see on our later descriptions of the reading and spelling processes, and we also re-examine these concepts in terms of cerebellar and other theories of dyslexia.

The angular gyrus is also of particular interest. One of the earlier notions of dyslexia used to be the concept of 'soft neurological signs' or 'minimal neurological dysfunction', and typically, the description of Gerstmann's syndrome was used here. This was a syndrome involving four key difficulties: loss of written language, acalculia, left/right discrimination and finger agnosia. These problems were suggestive for individuals with dyslexia, although the finger agnosia perhaps was not so commonly observed. 'Finger agnosia' is based on a test where the subject closes his or her eyes and two fingers are touched by the examiner. The subject has to decide which the two fingers are, and those with finger agnosia find this difficult.

## Cerebral dominance and bilateral function

The parts of the brain described are important for dyslexia, but the notion of 'cerebral dominance' is also important. The cerebral cortex, as is widely known, is split into two halves – not totally because there are connections between the two lobes – but these are differential functions. The left cerebral hemisphere, for most people, is not only responsible for language functions, but also for serial order, sequencing and coding sorts of tasks. The right hemisphere, on the other hand, has greater facility with three-dimensional, spatial or 'gestalt' kinds of task.

The notion of a dominant hemisphere refers to the idea that spoken language is one of the 'higher-order' or evolutionarily more sophisticated skills, and therefore, the hemisphere that is primarily responsible for this kind of task is the 'dominant' one. The term was coined by early neurologists who observed how damage to various parts of the brain gave rise to particular difficulties. The notions of how the cerebral cortices are organized for this language dominance have important implications for dyslexia. We examine this in detail in Chapter 6.

Moving to a consideration of some of the sense organs and the way in which information comes into the brain, it is worth looking at some examples of the sensory perceptual pathways, in particular, examining the way in which sensory and motor mechanisms are crossed, because these have implications for cerebral dominance. If we look at the motor and sensory paths concerning handedness, a topic we also consider later (see p. 113), we can see that these are completely crossed. This is shown in Figure 5.6.

Thus, if there is damage to the motor area connected to the hands on the right hemisphere, the ability to use the left hand is lost. Similarly, if there is a stroke in the language functions of the left

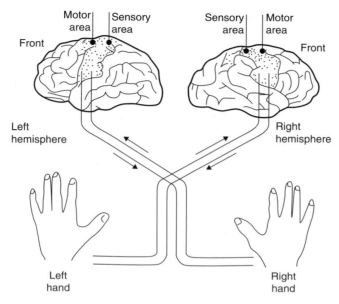

**Figure 5.6** Motor and sensory pathways to the hands.

hemisphere, particularly Broca's area, there would tend to be a loss of motor function in relation to speech. This is well known to most readers.

There is also some information on the visual route to the cerebral cortex. This is important for another reason – to illustrate the fact that the visual system is not as simply contralateral as the motor and sensory systems of, for example, a hand or foot. Basically, this means that information coming into the left visual field is dealt with in the right side of the brain, and information coming into the right visual field is dealt with in the left side of the brain. This is found from studies using tachistoscopes; that is, information is presented on a screen for varying lengths of time and subjects are required to fixate on a central point. Linguistic information, including letters, words, numbers and stimuli requiring a name code, that is presented in the right visual field is perceived or remembered or dealt with cognitively much more easily than linguistic material presented in the left visual field. This would imply a left hemisphere that is better at language processing and a right hemisphere processing that is less efficient for language-based materials.

Conversely, visuospatial material, for example, shapes, figure representations and so on, that is presented in the left visual field is dealt with more easily than that presented in the right visual field, again giving evidence for this notion of the right hemisphere being spatial rather than linguistic. The visual field is quite complicated in the sense that there are various different relay bodies. Figure 5.7 shows how visual information passes from the visual fields to the optic chiasma where the inputs are divided. Left visual field input goes to the right hemisphere (dotted line) via the lateral geniculate body, and vice versa (solid line).

There are also crossover points where information is transferred from the right to the left hemispheres. It is obviously not the case that we process information only from one side of our visual field in each side of the brain, although that is where the information goes first. What happens then is that information is transferred from one side of the brain to the other via a structure called the corpus

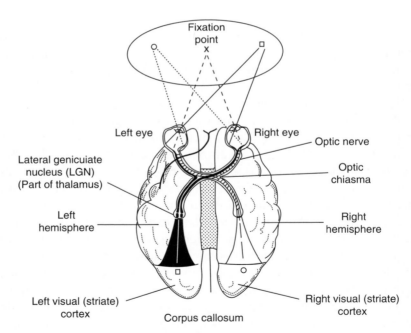

**Figure 5.7** Input of visual system to the cerebral cortex.

callosum (see Figure 5.7). The same thing happens, of course, for other sensory and motor functions.

There has been some very interesting work on what happens when people have had the corpus callosum severed. This used to be the treatment for some severe epilepsies, and often people might, for example, be able to hold an object in their left hand and explain what it was used for but not give it a name. This was because the information about the object being held in the left hand was transferred to the right hemisphere and the access point for the name of the object, which was located in the left hemisphere, for example, supramarginal gyrus (see Figure 5.5), could not be accessed because the information was not transferred across by the corpus callosum.

Interesting work has also been done on 'divided visual field studies', where people with dyslexia are asked to look at information in the left and right visual fields and the implications that might have for cerebral function, which we look at later.

The notion of the left hemisphere being responsible for serial order and symbolic skills is, of course, very interesting to those theorists who were trying to look at the written language system that appeared to be serial order, temporal and symbolic kind of functioning. The notion of two sides of the brain undertaking two different functions interested researchers as far back as the 1930s, when they were trying to develop theories about dyslexia, and we examine some of the more modern theories later.

The examination of the visual system is also important, because we shall be looking not only at theories of cerebral dominance, but also at some specific theories on the visual deficits in dyslexia, particularly the visual transient system and others in which we will need to know a little about the visual system and cerebral cortex structures.

The auditory system also has complicated contralateral connections, although it is not as complicated as the visual system in terms of its laterality and crossover. It may be seen from Figure 5.8 that the auditory pathways are partially crossed. Each hemisphere can receive input from both ears, but the neural collections from one ear to the hemisphere on the opposite side are stronger than the connections to the hemisphere on the same side. In the figure, the cochlear nucleus is part of the auditory input relay system, as is

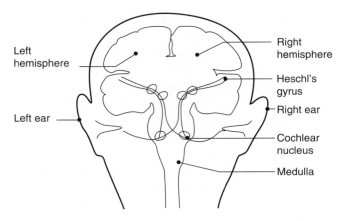

**Figure 5.8** Contralateral connections in the auditory system.

Heschl's gyrus. The medulla is simply the lower brainstem part of the midbrain.

The sort of model of brain function in terms of auditory input that has been built up is based on research such as dichotic listening, for example, auditory material that could be words, numbers, music or other acoustic phenomena is presented to both ears at the same time. If the information is verbal, such as numbers or words, individuals report or deal with or remember that information presented to the right ear rather better. This, of course, implies left hemisphere processing because there are stronger contralateral connections (from the right ear) to the left hemisphere. On the other hand, if the information is less verbal, more melodic and so on, it is much more likely to be better perceived in the left ear, although there is not quite such clear-cut evidence for this.

These sorts of neurocognitive studies, such as studies of divided visual fields and dichotic listening, were cognitive psychologists' approaches to build on the early neurologists' mapping of the cerebral hemisphere system, which is based on language in the left hemisphere and nonlanguage or three-dimensional skills in the right. These, of course, were described by the early neurologists who observed what happened in brain-damaged individuals. Thus, if a particular part of the left hemisphere had been damaged, language functions would be lost, whereas damage to the same part of the right hemisphere would not result in language loss in an individual.

## Brain function and reading

We can break down the parts of the brain that are responsible for reading functions in to more detail, but very broadly, according to Milne (2005), these relate to 'auditory' and 'visual' modules. The former is associated with phonemic awareness and some pronunciation and the latter is grapheme awareness or letter shape and word form. These have important implications when we consider models of reading and spelling process later. The auditory components contain pronunciation as well as analysis of phonemes.

Decoding, sounding out words or grapheme–phoneme conversion begins with letter identification. This is then passed to a phonemic/sound component, in other words, going from visual to auditory modules. The letters are then mapped onto corresponding sounds, so that the words can be decoded. This is also where nonword and alphabetic skills are used and essentially is a phonological stage of reading. This is obviously useful for acquiring new words.

Another circuit or module is related to word recognition and pronunciation, or if you like, direct access. These very strongly parallel theories of reading and spelling development models in cognitive psychology as we shall see later, as well as stages in the development of reading and spelling (see Chapter 7).

When we look at causes in Chapter 6, the reader may just need to refresh his or her memory on some of these basic concepts, and we examine them in the context of explanations for dyslexic difficulties.

## Further reading

Any psychology text, for example:
Atkinson, R.L., Atkinson, R.C., Smith, E.E. and Bem, D. (1993) Chapter 2, in *Introductions to Psychology*, Harcourt Brace Jovanovich, Orlando, FL.

Gross, R. (1992) Chapters 4 and 8, in *Psychology: The Science of Mind and Behaviour*, Hodder & Stoughton, London.

More specifically on written language and education:
Blakemore, S.J. and Frith, U. (2005) *The Learning Brain, Lessons for Education*, Blackwell Publishing, Oxford.
Ellis, A.W. and Young, A. (1988) *Human Cognitive Neuropsychology*, Lawrence Erlbaum, Barringstone.
Robertson, J. (2000) Chapters 1 and 2, in *Dyslexia and Reading: A Neuropsychological Approach*, Whurr, London.

# 6

# Neuropsychology of Dyslexia

This chapter examines and focuses on the biological basis of dyslexia. The assumption here is that dyslexia has a neurocognitive origin, as illustrated in Figure 5.1 (p. 92).

It may be seen from this figure that, at the biological level, there is some kind of 'brain abnormality'. This in turn gives rise to cognitive deficits and the behavioural signs. (These are also discussed in the Preface.) Of course, the environment impinges on these and this would include appropriate teaching, adaptation to learning difficulties and so on. This is an important point to make at this stage, because it is very easy to assume that a cause of neurological origin means that nothing can be done to help the child. This is akin to going back to the old notion of 'word blindness' as a description of dyslexia. The reality is that we are looking at an individual difference. This may be the result of the way in which the brain is organized and processes the information, but I personally do not like the use of the term 'abnormality' or 'deficit' in searching for neurological explanations. An individual who seems congenitally unable to hit a golf ball correctly or straight, I include myself in this syndrome, may have 'dysgolfia' (currently the children at my school are calling me 'dysjokic'!). The individual difference here is that my brain is not organized very well to strike a golf ball. We can easily examine and analyse the skills required, for example, visual focus on the ball, smooth draw back of club, timing and so on. We could then look at the particular part of the brain that undertakes these skills, finding that my brain does not have the processing skills to deal with one

*The Psychology of Dyslexia – A Handbook for Teachers,* by Michael Thomson
© 2009 John Wiley & Sons Ltd

or more elements that I need to strike the ball, and therefore, I have an 'abnormality' or a 'deficit'. However, just as I can be taught how to play golf reasonably well despite a brain not tuned to it, so we can teach a child with dyslexia to read and spell!

Before we look at brain function, however, we need to look at genetics because the implication of a biological basis is for a genetic predisposition.

## Genetic factors

It has been recognized for some time that dyslexia 'runs in families'. At East Court, we often find that fathers, mothers, siblings and other members of a family may also have dyslexia problems to a lesser or greater degree. Further evidence for genetic transmission of dyslexia in family studies has been obtained, including the study of Snowling, Muter and Carroll (2007), who found literacy difficulties in children from families who were at risk of dyslexia.

To reiterate my comments, it is worth noting that a genetic predisposition does not imply that nothing can be done to help a child with dyslexia. Dyslexic children (or adults) can learn to read fluently and spell competently. The key is to present the written language system in a way so as to meet their way of processing information.

One of the first studies in genetics was by Hallgren (1950). He believed that dyslexia was determined by an alternative form of gene, placed on a chromosome other than a sex chromosome. He drew the conclusion that the data he had obtained best fitted an autosomal dominant genetic mechanism. However, since then, there have been many researchers who have criticized Hallgren's method of analysis and questioned his conclusions. Stevenson *et al.* (1987) noted that he made no attempt to distinguish between specific and general retardation, and used language and speech delays as evidence of reading problems. It was also found that Hallgren used reports of the child's difficulties rather than an actual assessment of their performance. The concept of a non-sex-linked difficulty has also been challenged, because it appeared that a greater number of males than females were affected. It was suggested that the gene could be dominant in males, although recessive in females (Sladen,

1971; Finucci *et al.*, 1976). However, a high incidence of reading disabilities in a family may not be a sufficient indication of genetic transmission. There could be other causes of the effect, such as shared environment, particularly the educational environment created by parents for their children.

Later studies looked in more detail at the familial incidence of dyslexia. Owen *et al.* (1971) found reading difficulties in children to be particularly associated with fathers. This might have been socially determined (e.g. modelling on a parent), but it was also found that there were neurological immaturities present in both siblings (a dyslexic child and his or her sibling) that cannot be learned socially, for example, problems were found with reproducing auditory tapped patterns, distinguishing double simultaneous touch, carrying out fast alternating finger and hand movements, and making right and left discriminations. If these problems are present in siblings, it is thought to be an indication of underlying mechanisms that are acting on both children. As these aspects are not socially controlled, a familial incidence would not be related to the environment. Similar results to these were found in the Colorado Family Reading Study (1973, cited in DeFries and Decker, 1982) when whole families of dyslexics ('proband') were compared with those of control families. The greatest difference between the families was found to be that of their reading abilities, with all members of proband families performing significantly more poorly than those of the control families.

It is possible to apply Waddington's (1957) theory of canalization to the findings for dyslexia, as argued by Owen *et al.* (1971). According to this theory, the developing phenotype (observed characteristic) can be represented by a ball that rolls through valleys of varying widths and depths. At some points, a deflection can send the phenotype into different channels of development, whereas, at other points, a major deflection is required to change the course because the genetic canalization is very strong. In relation to dyslexia, this means that the impact of genetics can be stronger for different aspects of the disorder. The deep canalizations represent strong genetic influence, and it takes a lot of environmental pressure to alter the phenotype from this point. However, when the genetic effects are weaker and the channels are not so deep, the environment can effect behaviour relatively easily.

It could be the case that certain types of dyslexia are transmitted genetically, and that this may occur through multifactorial inheritance (Owen, 1979). This means that the disability may be determined by a number of genes, each of which contributes a small amount to the whole trait. The extent and expression of these genes in terms of phenotype would be a function of an interaction of a genetic predisposition, environmental experiences and changes in the effectiveness of the methods of treatment used.

## Linkage studies

Linkage studies work on the basis that, if a trait can be shown to be linked to a known genetic marker locus, then it can be inferred that a major gene for that trait is located on the same chromosome as the marker locus. Smith *et al.* (1982) looked expressly at families in which a specific reading disability appeared to be inherited through several generations in an autosomal dominant manner. A link was found to be between specific reading disability and chromosome 15. The effects of genetics can be studied by looking at families, comparing the siblings and parents of children with dyslexia with those of nondyslexic children, as was done in the studies of Hallgren (1950) and Owen *et al.* (1971). Another way of looking at genetics is to examine twins and how alike their reading patterns are. Studies conducted using this method examined both monozygotic (MZ) and dizygotic (DZ) twins, and these were separated into those raised together and those raised apart.

## Twin studies

The basis of twin studies is the difference between MZ and DZ twin pairs, based on their genetics. MZ twins have identical genes, whereas DZ twins have, on average, half of the same genes, that is, as any other sibling. It is assumed that DZ twins are brought up to share the environment to the same extent as MZ twins. This means that, if there is any greater similarity between a MZ than a DZ pair, this must reflect genetic influences. In terms of dyslexia, if both twins are affected, they are known as concordant; if not, then they are discordant. A greater MZ than DZ concordance provides evidence for a genetic aetiology.

Before 1987, Bakwin (1973) collected the largest quantity of data about twins and reading disabilities. He identified 338 twin pairs, of whom 97 children displayed difficulties with reading. Pairwise concordance was found to be 83% for MZ twins and 52% for DZ pairs. Many criticisms were aimed at these earlier studies, particularly in view of the discrepancy among the results obtained.

Stevenson *et al.* (1987) found that, when IQ was controlled for, spelling heritability was 73%. However, concordance rates for reading backwardness and specific reading retardation were found to be low in both MZ and DZ twins; the concordance was found only for spelling difficulties. They accounted for the differences between these findings and those of previous researchers by the fact that the previous studies had not used a truly representative twin sample. They also believed that there could have been an age effect; they looked at twins who were 13 years old, whereas the other studies had tended to focus on children at younger ages. They argued that genetic influences might not be as pronounced at the age of 13 as they were in younger children. Nevertheless, the apparent genetic influence on spelling disabilities seems to be more prevalent than that of the other areas.

The Colorado twin study was perhaps one of the more noteworthy studies conducted on twins with regard to reading problems (DeFries, 1985, 1991). The results of this study were that, concordance rates were 70% for MZ pairs and 48% for DZ pairs. This led DeFries to conclude that there must be at least some genetic aetiology for reading disability. Further analysis using multiple regression estimated that about half of the deficit found in dyslexics was the result of heritable influences. When Olson *et al* . (cited in DeFries, Gillis and Wadsworth, 1990) looked at different areas of reading, they found that the link between word recognition and phonological coding was significantly greater than that between word recognition and orthographic coding. They took this to mean that the genetic aetiology of deficits in word recognition may have been caused by the heritable influences on phonological coding.

The specific mechanism of genetic predisposition may be linked to phonological coding skills, in terms of the human genome and particular chromosomes and linkage methods that were reviewed above. Indeed, not only reading itself seen to be inheritable, but also verbal short-term memory and phonological awareness (Pennington and Lefly, 2001).

Using previous evidence of genetic studies of dyslexia, Pennington (1999) started with the idea that it must be genetically heterogenous and that it was likely that more than one gene was involved. He thought that possibly all reading ability is influenced by a number of genes, and that dyslexia is just one variation of these genes. He also pointed out that the locus for dyslexia is not a disease but susceptibility. A susceptibility locus, unlike a disease locus, is neither necessary nor sufficient to produce the disorder. This would explain why there does not always appear to be a genetic link, and why some children who are expected to have inherited dyslexia do not meet the criteria. If a susceptibility locus influences a continuous trait, it is called a quantitative trait locus (QTL). There are usually several QTLs required to influence a complex behavioural trait such as dyslexia.

If a small number of QTLs underlie the transmission, then traditional linkage analysis may not be applicable. In Pennington's (1999) study, he used sibling pair linkage analysis. He found evidence for a QTL on the short arm of chromosome 6; this evidence was consistent across two independent samples of sibling pairs, two sets of genetic markers and different researchers (Cardon *et al.*, 1994; Grigorenko *et al.*, 1997; Fisher, Marlow and Lamb, 1999; Gayan *et al.*, 1999). Grigorenko *et al.* (1997) also found linkage for a different phenotype, that of deficits in word recognition, with a marker on chromosome 15. This repeats the findings of Smith *et al.* (1982); there was thought to be a double dissociation between the genes influencing the two phenotypes. This led to the view that QTLs are genes that somehow lead to disruption in epigenesis and development, which in turn may eventually alter learning to read. However, the studies of Fisher, Marlow and Lamb (1999) and Gayan *et al.* (1999) both found that deficits in phonological and orthographic coding were related to the same region of chromosome 6.

The mentioned review is only a sample of some of the work on dyslexia and genetics, and although the reader may feel that it is already too technical, it can get much more so! The general conclusion we need to take away is that there is a genetic vulnerability to dyslexia in some individuals. According to Pennington, if one parent is dyslexic, 50% of the children inherit this vulnerability and

100% of children inherit it if both parents are dyslexic. Note the word vulnerability; this implies that educational and environmental input can prevent reading and spelling failure. But Snowling *et al.* (2007) also reported that a slow rate of reading and spelling development continues well into adulthood for dyslexics, as well as difficulties in increased risk of anxiety, attentional problems and conduct disorders.

Reading difficulties are commonly cited as gene/environment linked. Of course, the relationship between literacy skills and parent/child literacy levels, suggested to be a multifactorial pattern of inheritance, can be influenced by many other factors either intrinsic to the child or outside in the environment. In other words, our teaching can help!

Let us move on to how a genetic predisposition might affect brain function.

## Cerebral dominance and dyslexia

We examined notions of cerebral dominance in the human brain in general in Chapter 5, and it is particularly on this area that a good deal of research in dyslexia has focused.

The notion of a human brain that is mainly left hemisphere dominant for language, serial order and sequential skills, with the right hemisphere responsible for three-dimensional skills, has implications for dyslexic children. The former constitutes the tasks with which they have difficulty, and the latter, in terms of observations of people with dyslexia who do well at three-dimensional spatial tasks, seems to be the task that they do well.

The first person to try to relate the idea of dominant hemisphere function to dyslexia was Orton (1937). Without going into detail on his theory, he proposed that words and letters were stored as the mirror image of what was seen in the opposite hemisphere, for example, the word 'saw' was stored as 'saw' in the left hemisphere but as 'was' in the right hemisphere. This resulted in reversal and mirror imaging and the other features he observed in many people with dyslexia. The notion of mirror-image storing of 'engrams', and his rather simplistic theory of the wrong hemisphere being accessed by mistake, has since been superseded, but he was the first to draw attention to the notion that there could be some element involved.

A number of theories have proposed a relationship between cerebral dominance and dyslexia. These are presented in Table 6.1, along with my comments in the right-hand column. The detailed evidence of all of these is reviewed elsewhere (Thomson, 1990), but it is worth examining some of these issues as an historical perspective.

In the United Kingdom, Newton (1970) proposed a lack of dominance in people with dyslexia. Her early work involved the examination of electroencephalographs (EEGs), using resting records. An EEG is a measure of the electrical activity that occurs in the brain. It is measured by sticking electrodes on to people's scalp and observing what happens by means of a printout of 'brain waves'. There are various rhythms that are produced when we are alert and conscious, when in sleep, dream and so on. Early work at the University of Aston examined alpha rhythms in dyslexic and nondyslexic children. Alpha rhythm (6–10 cycles per second) occurs when people are awake in a resting state with eyes closed. It was found that the alpha rhythm from the angular gyrus region in particular (see Chapter 5 for the importance to written language) was symmetrical in children with dyslexia; that is, there was an equal amount of alpha rhythm from both hemispheres, whereas in control

**Table 6.1** Theories of aetiology relating to cerebral hemispheres.

| | |
|---|---|
| Lack of cerebral dominance. No left hemisphere dominance, or less clear cut. | Some evidence but different interpretations of data possible |
| Maturational lag or delay in left hemisphere language processing | Would expect adults to show no deficit, but they do. Some evidence, however |
| Left hemisphere deficit of some kind | Some evidence |
| Interference by right hemisphere. Right hand favoured. | Too complex, not parsimonious |
| Disassociation of auditory and visual material in different hemispheres | Some evidence |

children, there was much more alpha rhythm activity in the left hemisphere.

Also, at around this time, the notion of inconsistent laterality was put forward as evidence for a lack of dominance. As seen from our examination of the way in which our brain and brain sensory motor systems are set up, there are contralateral connections between the sides of the brain and the opposite sides of the body. This has led a number of individuals to comment on the higher incidence of left-handedness and ambidexterity among dyslexic individuals. This was an important feature of my early work on people with dyslexia (Thomson, 1975). A lot of recent work on laterality has suggested that it is largely inherited; there are some interesting theories on the way in which mixed-handedness might also be better for three-dimensional skills and less good for verbal and written language skills (see Annett, 1991).

In my experience, this tends to be very much a probabilistic observation (see Thomson, 1975, for a Bayesian statistics, a probability analysis). There are dyslexic children who are right-handed or right dominant, and there are a number of children who are not dyslexic and who are left-handed or mixed dominant. However, there seems to be a higher incidence of one than the other. This is illustrated in Table 6.2 taken from clinical studies of over 500 children at the University of Aston. Here, handedness is compared between people with dyslexia and the general population.

Sometimes the relationship between laterality and dyslexia (i.e. more mixed handers) is found in populations of children referred to clinics, whereas it is not found in general populations, when looking at overall poor reading. This, I think, results in some of the conflicting evidence and a detailed discussion is given in Thomson (1990). This relationship has not examined the concepts of cross-laterality, for example, children who are left-eye dominant and

**Table 6.2** Handedness in dyslexia children and the general population.

|  | *Right-handed* | *Mixed-handed* | *Left-handed* |
| --- | --- | --- | --- |
| General population | 68 | 28 | 4 |
| Dyslexic children | 20 | 67 | 13 |

(University of Aston).

right-handed who may have difficulty in scanning and sequencing, but is included here to provide a historical context for the development of a neuropsychological picture of dyslexia.

Moving on from laterality, at around this time, other evidence began to support the notion of a lack of hemisphere dominance, particularly in dichotic listening and divided visual field studies.

In dichotic listening, the reader will remember auditory material presented to both ears at the same time. A typical result is given in Table 6.3 from my own studies (Thomson, 1976). Here, 10-year-old children, both dyslexic and nondyslexic, were presented with numbers to the left and right ears. Table 6.3 shows the percentage of correct responses.

The point of this table is to illustrate some of the problems with interpretation of data. Initially, I interpreted the findings as suggesting a less clear-cut hemisphere dominance for children with dyslexia; that is, when comparing the left and right ears in both groups, the control group children, who are good readers, show the normal right ear effect (REA). This implies better left-hemisphere processing for verbal material, in this case numbers. Children with dyslexia do not show this better performance in the right ear, that is, no REA, and therefore one interpretation is that they do not have dominance of function for the left hemisphere. Both hemispheres perform equally at the same level. However, there is another interpretation of these data (can you suggest one without reading further?). I came to this following a discussion with Colin Wilsher, one of the research associates at Aston. If we compare children with dyslexia and controls among themselves, looking at the right ear alone rather than looking at REA, we see that children with dyslexia do less well. Therefore, the apparent lack of dominance may simply be the result of the fact that they are not as good on the right ear; that is, there is a left-hemisphere 'deficit' of some kind. When we use indirect

**Table 6.3** Percentages of correct right ear recall in children with dyslexia and controls.

|  | *Children with dyslexia* | *Nondyslexic children* |
|---|---|---|
| Right ear | 68 | 82 |
| Left ear | 65 | 68 |

measures, such as dichotic listening, it is often difficult to come to absolute conclusions. There was a plethora of research in this area during the late 1970s and early 1980s, with people reporting different results and/or different interpretations.

The same thing happened in divided visual field studies (see Chapter 5 for details) where we are looking at the right and left visual fields. I undertook a study with Graham Beaumont and Michael Rugg (Beaumont, Thomson and Rugg, 1981), well-known researchers in the area of hemisphere function, that could be interpreted as suggesting that the children with dyslexia had a normal left-hemisphere function for auditory material (they did better for auditory material on the right ear, i.e. the REA). On the other hand, they were better on the right hemisphere for visual information (they did better in the left visual field for shapes). This was not particularly conclusive because other findings contradicted this research, and indeed, the notion of children with dyslexia doing as well as controls in auditory tasks in dichotic listening had not been found in some of my own earlier research.

Fortunately, later research techniques have thrown more light on the situation, suggesting both processing and anatomical differences in the way in which children with dyslexia deal with written language information.

As well as the resting EEG record, another common technique is the evoked response. An evoked response is looking at how a particular part of the brain responds to stimuli, for example, in the visual evoked response, a strobe light flashes at, say, once per second. Electrodes are stuck on different parts of the scalp to measure activity from different parts of the brain (the way in which these electrodes are placed is based on an internationally agreed code to reflect parts of the brain). Initially, the EEGs show no reaction because there is random background activity. However, the records are passed through a 'computer of average transience', which averages out all the background activity; gradually, this builds up a response to the strobe light in that particular part of the brain that is being recorded. This can also be done with auditory evoked responses using a sound and we can look at different stimuli – words, music, shapes and so on. A typical example of this, adapted from Connors (Connors, 1970; Connors *et al.*, 1984), is shown in Figure 6.1. Interestingly, this shows both

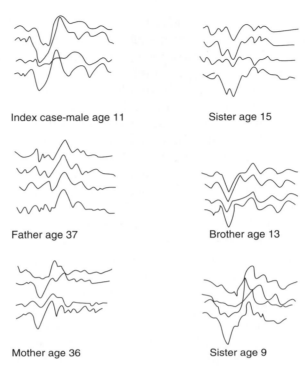

Index case-male age 11

Sister age 15

Father age 37

Brother age 13

Mother age 36

Sister age 9

**Figure 6.1** Visual evoked potentials derived from the left and right occipital, and left and right parietal regions (10–20 system) in a family of dyslexic children. Curves (top to bottom) are the left occipital, right occipital, left parietal and right parietal. Note the attenuation (weaker) of the left parietal tracing milliseconds for all siblings. Adapted from Connors (1970) and Connors *et al.* (1984).

a child of 11 with dyslexia and a father and mother, aged 37 and 36, respectively.

The evoked responses are taken from the occipital and parietal lobes. It may be seen that the third curve (from the left parietal lobe) is what is known as 'attenuated', that is, there is a reduced evoked response (in the index, i.e. case of a dyslexic boy, none at all!). This occurs both in the dyslexic child and, to a lesser extent, in the mother. This shows evidence, incidentally, of some genetic predisposition that was discussed earlier; more important is the notion that there is no evoked response in a dyslexic child in a particular area of the brain crucial for language function.

Even research, such as the ones discussed previously, was not entirely without debate, resulting, possibly, from misinterpretations. However, one important aspect is that clinic samples, that is, children referred to hospital clinics, generally in the United States, often show different patterns to children across wider populations, suggesting that there might be some other underlying neurological problem with children, in addition to dyslexia, which resulted in referral, typically, to a neuropsychology unit, for such research to be undertaken.

However, further supportive evidence of the notion of left hemisphere differences continued with Galaburda's (1989, 1999) and Galaburda, Signoret and Ronthal's (1985) anatomical studies. A typical example is given in Figure 6.2 that shows a horizontal cross-section of two brains.

As we saw when examining brain functions (see Chapter 5), the planum temporale (PT or temporal plane) is a very important area for language functions, particularly implicating sound and phonological processing, because there are close connections between this

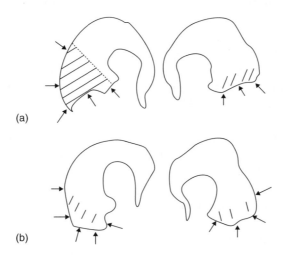

(a)

(b)

**Figure 6.2** Cross-section of the temporal plane in a person with dyslexia and a control. Superior temporal plane in (a) a control brain and (b) the brain of a person with dyslexia. The extent of the temporal plane is indicated by arrows. The dyslexic brain has an almost symmetrical plane (flat upper surfaces of the temporal lobe). Adapted from Galaburda (1989, 1999).

area and the primary auditory cortex. This provides us with a link between neuropsychology and the phonological coding and short-term memory weaknesses that people with dyslexia show (see Chapter 9).

Figure 6.2 shows that, in the control brain (rather morbidly taken from people with dyslexia *post-mortem* – there have been an increasing number of people with dyslexia who have donated their brains after death to neuropsychology research teams), the PT is larger on the left hemisphere. The dyslexic individual, however, has a symmetrical PT, which provides direct anatomical evidence for a difference in hemisphere organization between people with dyslexia and control subjects.

The notion of a macroscopic cortical 'abnormality' (i.e. the anatomical differences) is matched by deeper explanations at the microscopic level.

One of the things that happens when the young fetal brain is developing is that cells migrate or move to different parts of the body, where they begin to take up their specialized functions. This happens with brain cells and is known as neuronal migration (brain cell = neuron). According to Galaburda and others, it is possible that, at around week 24 of gestation, when the cerebral cortex forms most rapidly, cortical ectopias (warts that are 1 mm in size) can develop. Neurons migrate past the outer membranes of the developing brain to form these growths, particularly in the parietal lobes of the left hemisphere. These have been observed in people with dyslexia in some of these anatomical studies.

Therefore, there could be problems in the developing fetus that give rise to the 'deficits' in the left hemisphere, which are linked to aspects of language function and, by inference, written language functions; they are also linked to anatomical differences that may affect the way in which the brain is organized.

One final set of 'evidence' to round off our picture is the increasing use of 'imaging'. This is a technique in which pictures of the brain are taken when the individual is doing certain tasks, which could include verbal reasoning, reading, looking at shapes, jigsaw puzzles and so on.

Imaging includes positron emission tomography (PET), functional magnetic resonance imaging (FMRI), magnetic source imaging (MSI) and magnet resonance spectroscopy (MRS). All look at the changes in the brain that occur during cognitive processing. Therefore, metabolic changes reflected by using or taking up glucose from the blood or blood flowing from one part of the brain to the other can be captured by PET or FMRI showing up in different colours on 'brain maps'. Magnetic resonance imaging (MRI) came from the study of atomic particles, which, when placed in a uniform and a strong magnetic field, line up in different ways. FMRI records changes in blood flow and oxygen level as the brain goes about performing tasks or activities. It is safe to use with children and has a large magnet that allows us to know exactly where the brain differences are occurring.

MSI looks at what happens when neurons discharge, that is, changes in brain electrical activity that can be captured at the scalp by attached electrodes, a modification of what used to be called EEG. These changes occur in magnetic fields surrounding these electrical discharges at the neuron or cell level, which can be detected by MSI. MRS looks at brain chemistry in changes of state, in other words, activities occurring after the cognitive activity. Studies on PET, FMRI and MSI show that tasks requiring reading and phonological processing are associated with increased activation in the basal surface of the temporal lobe and also portions of the superior and middle temple gyri extending into the temporoparietal areas (supramarginal and angular gyri).

As you can see, therefore, these match very closely these areas are described in Chapter 5, see Figure 5.5. According to Vellutino *et al.* (2004), in children who are reading normally, there is an initial activation in the occipital areas, that is, visual processing begins. Then the basal temporal areas of both hemispheres are activated. However, there is then an almost immediate activation of three areas on the left temporal and parietal areas, corresponding to the superior temporal gyrus (Wernicke's area) and angular gyrus.

However, dyslexics using PET and FMRI (Shaywitz *et al.*, 2002) show evidence for right hemisphere activation instead of the normal left hemisphere. Other studies also reviewed by Vellutino *et al.* indicated that the angular gyrus of the left hemisphere can be poorly connected with other areas in the mediation of reading in dyslexics, compared with more proficient readers.

A number of further studies are indicative. In one study (Shaywitz, Shaywitz and Pugh, 1998), the route that information appears to take when reading is from the primary visual cortex to the visual association areas (the angular gyrus), where words and letters are linked to language, and then the temporal gyrus (i.e. Wernicke's area), where the sounds of language are translated into words or some form of semantic access. This was the 'normal' route. However, in people with dyslexia, the final path was to Broca's area, where speech is processed, rather than to Wernicke's area; this suggests that there may be a problem with lexical access, that is, finding names of words.

Figure 6.3 shows what are known as 'nonimpaired' versus dyslexic brain images. You can see dyslexics tend to activate Broca's area, more associated with the articulation word analysis system and speech production, but does not also activate word analysis and word form (parieto-temporal and occipito-temporal lobes, respectively). The only thing I would argue against here is the term 'impaired'. As argued throughout this book, I look upon dyslexia

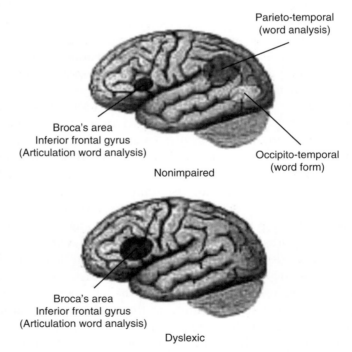

**Figure 6.3** Dyslexics and nondyslexics brain images. From Milne (2005).

as a difference in the way brains are organized or in the way in which written language is processed by different individuals, non-dyslexic or dyslexic.

Paulesu *et al.* (1996) gave people with dyslexia rhyming and verbal short-term memory tasks; there appeared to be a weak activation of the pathways that carry information from Broca's area to the superior temporal area. This also suggests a problem with translating unsegmented into segmented speech. The segmentation, or the splitting of speech sounds into individual words, is a key feature of the phonological difficulties besetting many people with dyslexia (see Chapters 8 and 9). They concluded that only a subset of brain regions normally involved in phonological processing was activated. They further concluded that the 'neuropsychological and the PET findings both point to a disconnection between different phonological codes' (Paulesu *et al.*, 1996, p. 154). This conclusion was reached because of the isolated activation of Broca's area, Wernicke's area and the supramarginal gyrus in the dyslexic subjects during the phonological tasks. Paulesu *et al.* proposed that such a disconnection can account for the difficulty experienced by dyslexic children in learning to read, and they suggested that, in learning to speak, children learn that the speech they hear maps on to the utterances that they produce. This mapping depends on connectivity between the relevant language areas in the brain. A weak connection would not only cause delays in this hearing–speech mapping, but will also cause difficulties in learning an alphabetical code that depends on mapping of graphemes, phonemes and whole word spelling and sound. Other research also suggests that the wrong information is transmitted to the parietal lobe because of the difficulties in tracking, but we look at this in more detail when we examine visual transient systems (see later).

Another interesting piece of research was by Silani *et al.* (2005), which again shared the common pattern of reduced activity or activation during reading tasks in the left hemispheres for dyslexics. However, this particular paper was more specific in that it actually argued for evidence of altered density of grey and white matters in brain regions (if you remember your GCSE Biology, the difference is that white matter in the brain tends to be axons and grey matter tends to be neurons). They argued for a reduced autoconnectivity among the phonological and reading areas in dyslexics.

Dyslexic before intervention          Dyslexic after intervention

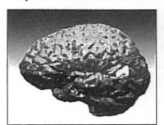 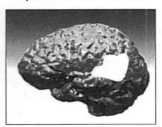

**Figure 6.4** Increased activation in the brain of a dyslexic after the intervention programme. After Milne (2005) with permission.

Some very interesting studies in functional brain imaging also look at the developmental changes in the brains of dyslexic children after a reading programme.

For example, an increase in brain activation is shown in wider areas after a reading and spelling intervention programme in Figure 6.4. Simos *et al.* (2002) and Aylward *et al.* (2003) looked at children with severe dyslexia and then again after an intensive intervention with word reading skills moved into the average range. An example is given in Figure 6.4 showing the activation of the left hemisphere after remediation. Here, one can see little activation in a child whose reading and spelling are very weak. Once intervention took place, there are activations in the left temporoparietal areas associated with the improvement of word reading. This parallels the patterns observed in proficient readers. (The right hemisphere in these studies shared normal activation in both pre- and post remediations).

So what are we to make of all this? In general, it seems that many areas of the left hemisphere may be implicated, but the puzzle is how these language areas can be affected so specifically. In other words, why are vocabulary, verbal reasoning and other higher-order language tasks robust, but written language is weak? Apart from very specific speech-to-alphabet skills, spoken language is also robust. As previously remarked, I think that we should view dyslexia as an individual difference. The evidence suggests that there is an individual difference in the way that the brains of dyslexic individuals are organized that predisposes them to being rather better at three-dimensional spatial skills and creativity but less good at language skills, particularly those involving written language. Research seems to suggest that there may be a less clear-cut dominance of function for language tasks in general, but specifically for those written language tasks that involved elements of phonological coding and aspects of the phonological loop in working memory (see Chapter 9).

The most powerful evidence comes from imaging studies, and it is here that we begin to see a relationship between what is going on at the brain level and what we observe at a cognitive and, therefore, behavioural level. The brain of a person with dyslexia is less efficient at guiding aspects of speech processing, linked to phonological and grapheme processing, to the parts of the brain that are best at processing it. Bear in mind that this is relative. So, as we have discussed, people with dyslexia communicate and function normally in everyday life, by and large. It is when we force the brain to use processes and skills linked to other tasks, for example, speech, sequential memory or temporal tracking, and apply them to written language, that we begin to see a 'system breakdown'. Our brain systems are geared up for communication, thinking and language, which are skills needed for survival, not reading. We invented written language and make our brains use systems that were evolved for other functions in order to learn to read and spell as children. Furthermore, it is only now, in the last 100 years, that reading and spelling have become a 'survival' skill for life – not surprising that some of us do not have brains as efficient for written language as they might be.

What is becoming clear from the brain imaging studies is that the very specific areas that are normally involved in reading, writing and spelling are not activated in dyslexics. So the idea, going right back to the 1970s, when I was working with Margaret Newton at Aston, of 'left-hemisphere dysfunction' or lack of cerebral dominance is now being refined into the detail of a specific part of the brain that deals with grapheme/phoneme correspondence and similar phonological skills required for reading.

There is a clear individual difference in the way in which the brain processes information in dyslexic individuals, compared with nondyslexics. It is important, particularly with the later study on what happens to the brain after teaching, that we reject the old concept of 'word blind' – that dyslexics will never learn to read.

The research suggests that instruction or literacy support can influence neural networks or brain functions, which can then mediate in word recognition and phonological skills, that is, reading.

# Further models of neuropsychological aetiology

In this section, we consider some alternative hypotheses in relation to the causes of dyslexia. Phonological decoding and working memory problems have become central in aetiology (see Chapter 9), with the assumption that these follow from neuropsychological predispositions. However, there are many different approaches, some of which focus on the wider range of difficulties presented by people with dyslexia. As we have seen, dyslexia as a syndrome is not just simply about reading; it includes many different elements. In particular, we consider two of the most well-formulated alternative theories – a cerebellum difficulty and a problem in visual processing system.

## Cerebellar difficulties

Figure 6.5 is the familiar model used by Frith (1992) and looks at the various levels of explanation – biological, cognitive and behavioural – with input from the environment. In this case, the model is used to reflect a cerebellar processing abnormality. The behavioural observations shown here, such as poor naming speed, poor time estimation and poor motor development and balance, are obviously particularly linked to this theory. A cerebellar abnormality is also linked to timing and sequential deficits which, it is argued, can lead to phonological problems, as shown in Figure 6.3.

We can look in more detail at this approach mainly as a result of the work of Nicolson and Fawcett (1999). They drew attention to the role of the cerebellum in a number of verbal tasks. They argued that a significant part of the brain is often overlooked as a result of the emphasis on cortical hemisphere function. The cerebellum (see Figure 5.3 in Chapter 5) is mainly a motor area involved with

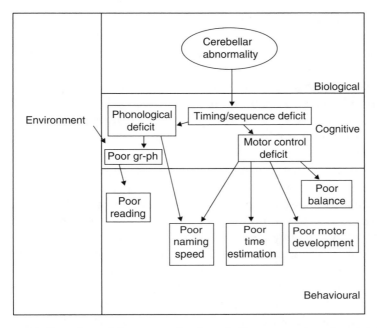

**Figure 6.5** Causal model as a result of cerebellar processing abnormality. gr-ph, grapheme–phoneme correspondence.

balance and initial motor skills learning. It is the area that is involved with enabling motor skills to become automatic, that is, to be developed without any conscious thought or analysis. A good example might be learning to ride a bike or perhaps a game such as squash. Initially, when we learn such tasks, we have to pay attention to what we are doing. Often coaching emphasizes thinking about how – for example, in squash – the racquet is held, how the arm is moved, the position of the body and so on. As this task becomes automated or 'over-learnt', we can undertake the same movement again and again without thinking about it. However, as well as motor skills learning, the cerebellum has a role in the automation of other cognitive skills. In particular, there are neurological links to the cortex, including Broca's area (see Chapter 5), which is involved in aspects of language dexterity.

It is argued that the cerebellum has a role in developing language, particularly the development of articulatory skills, where the cerebellum seems to be involved in timing and fluency. We can therefore imagine how easy it is to make the connection between articulation and phonological awareness, a link that has often been made by those who propose a phonological deficit for people with dyslexia. However, the cerebellum will also account for problems with spelling and handwriting. Disorders of the cerebellum can give rise to difficulties in posture and muscle tone (dystonia), and problems with posture or movement of the extremities (ataxia).

In addition to these observed features, the impairment of the cerebellum gives rise to difficulties in automization of skills and, in particular, immediate recognition of letters and spelling patterns. Skill performance or motor tasks rely on the expectation of smoother performance as they are 'over-learnt' or automated and require less effort after practice. Those of us who observe children struggling to learn to spell can see this lack of automation. Sometimes, a dyslexic child may spell correctly and sometimes he or she will make a mistake. The skill of spelling has not been automated in the sense of being smooth or quick, or requiring less effort with practice!

Nicolson and Fawcett (1999) have undertaken a considerable amount of research in this area, looking at both gross and fine motor skills. They found, for example, that people with dyslexia asked to do a balancing task were as good as control individuals when just simply doing the task on its own, but, if they had to undertake a dual balancing task, that is, do a secondary task involving, for example, counting, they were weaker. Similarly, using reading age controls, they found that a wider variety of tasks were weaker in people with dyslexia. These included not only spelling, segmentation and picture naming, but also balancing and bead threading. They argued that it is both phonological and motor skills that are affected, particularly involving automization and information-processing speed. It is interesting to note that the latter is a key psychometric weakness as well (see Chapter 3).

Nicolson and Fawcett developed some screening tests as a result of their theoretical formulation, the Dyslexia Screening Test (see Appendix), and Figure 6.6 presents a summary of the approach (Nicolson and Fawcett, 1999).

In Figure 6.6, the right-hand side shows writing, reading and spelling. This model accounts for weaknesses in phonological

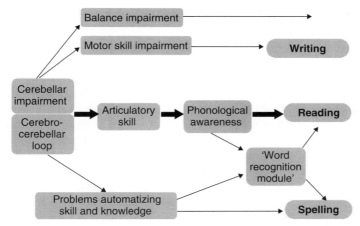

**Figure 6.6** Proposed causal chain for the cerebellum and reading. From Nicolson and Fawcett (1999).

awareness – (see Chapters 8 and 9) – but it also accounts for problems in automating skills and knowledge. It is the automization that introduces a new element to the learning process and links motor skills and skilled task learning in general to reading and spelling.

In this model, phonemic awareness difficulties result from problems in articulatory skill, which in turn come from impairment of the cerebellum, not on its own, but crucially the link between the cerebellum and the cerebral cortex. Therefore, we have a fairly formalized theory trying to account for the overall reading problems of people with dyslexia, both phonological difficulties and other areas of weakness such as reading, writing and spelling. One criticism of the theory is the question: why are there some people with dyslexia who do not appear to show motor deficiencies? I have known many children with severe dyslexia who are gifted 'sports children' and whose motor skills, balance and coordination are exceptionally good. On the other hand, quite a few children with dyslexia have overlapping difficulties in what we might call 'dyspraxia'. In general, this can refer to motor skills and movement or, in verbal dyspraxia, articulation or language problems (or both!). At my own school, for example, we can observe a number of difficulties in these areas.

The following is an extract from a description given by Sue Flory, the specialist 'motor development' teacher at East Court:

> He will lack coordination to such an extent that, even when walking, will give the appearance of being held together loosely with string. He will bump into furniture and people. This is because he lacks awareness of his own body and himself in space; he may not receive the information he needs from the environment around him through his senses, and, if he does, he may not be able to interpret, order and use it. He will fall over and fall off his chair more often; and fidget and be unable to stay still like other pupils. He may lack control in the use of his voice, speak too loudly, interrupt and have unusual intonation and breathing patterns when talking. Games and play-ground play are difficult; because he does not have the skill and coordination to join in successfully, he invades others' space and touches too heavily because he has insufficient muscular control or feedback (the problem is compounded if this is perceived by others as aggression).
>
> Organization of himself and his belongings is a constant problem, particularly if he has to move around school from class to class. Things are forgotten or dropped, and progress is slow. He usually looks untidy, shirt out, socks on inside-out, shoes undone, even on the wrong feet; trousers can occasionally be on inside-out or back to front! Food is invariably down his front and all around his mouth.

The 'skills learning approach' has personal resonance for me. When I was doing my doctorate way back in the 1970s, I was taking the view that we should look on language learning as a skill-based system. It made a lot of sense to look at reading, writing and spelling in terms of skills analysis, and subsequently to look at the kinds of task demands made by the system in terms of what a young child needed in order to meet the requirements of that task. Written language is an artificial system, and what we are trying to do is use a series of cognitive and other systems that we happen to have in our 'learning armoury', in order to learn a task that we are not evolutionarily prepared for. We are geared up for spoken language, but devised the written language as a second symbol system.

## Visual difficulties

The next alternative theory is the role of the visual system. It has been received wisdom that people with dyslexia do not have difficulty with seeing as such; that is, although some might complain that the letters jump around or that they lose their place, the problem is not in the primary visual system. It is assumed that any difficulty connected with the visual system is at the level of perception, that is, how the brain builds up a picture of the world.

It would, however, be foolish not to comment on the primary role of eyes in relation to receiving information from the world and, in particular, reading. There has been a good deal of work showing that people with dyslexia have erratic eye movements. I have reviewed this work in some detail elsewhere (Thomson, 1990), but some of it is worth reiterating. Figure 6.7 shows examples of typical eye movement patterns of a person with dyslexia. The first part (a) of Figure 6.7 shows the typical saccadic movement that results when a fluent reader is reading text; that is, the eyes move across the page in a series of saccades or sweeps, fixating on a word, then moving on. The labels are fairly self-explanatory and the bottom

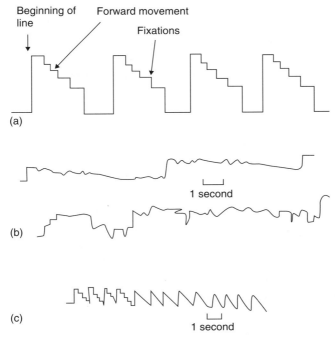

**Figure 6.7** Normal and erratic eye movements. (a, c) Typical saccadic movement when a fluent reader is reading text. (b) Saccadic patterns of two people with dyslexia. From Thomson (1990) after Pavlides (1981).

part of the figure (c) shows the typical saccadic pattern on a different scale. The other two examples (b) are from dyslexics (Pavlides, 1981). We can see how erratic these are, involving, as they do, moving backward and forward over the page, regressive eye movements and disordered movement.

Most psychologists believe that erratic eye movements are a secondary factor in dyslexics; that is, they are a result of dyslexia and not its cause. This is a good example of the interrelationship between reading and proposed cause. Later we discuss the role of appropriate research groups in dyslexia, and here is an illustrative example. The eye movements are the result of the difficulty of that test for that individual, for example, a fluent reader might be presented with an obscure legal text, which is usually dense and difficult for the nonlawyer to understand. Here, the reader's eye movements might well be erratic with a regressive pattern and eyes going back to check over the text to try to make sense of it. It may be reread again and again. There might also be attentional focus difficulties! This is not because the reader has dyslexia, but because of the difficulty of the text. Thus, if you take a 10-year-old child who is dyslexic and perhaps reading at the six- or seven-year-old level, and give him or her a text with a reading level of 10 years, he or she will find this difficult. Any erratic eye movements are a result of the difficulty of the text, not of some primary eye movement problem. In other words, as you learn to read, your eye movements become more fluent, particularly when you are reading a text that is easier than your reading level. Therefore, erratic eye movements simply say that the reader is having difficulty with the text that he or she reading – it is an effect not a cause.

There have, however, been some more recent approaches looking at the role of the visual system, particularly associated with the work of Stein (Stein, 1991; Stein and Talcott, 1999). Essentially, this revolves around speed of processing, especially the rapid processing of visual events, including reading. In particular, the focus is on rapid visual processing via the magnocellular pathway. Here, readers might remind themselves of the visual pathways coming into the brain, as shown in Figure 5.7 (Chapter 5).

Figure 6.8 shows a causal model of dyslexia as a result of the magnocellular abnormality in the biological, cognitive and behavioural terminology used by Frith. In Figure 6.8, we can see that the

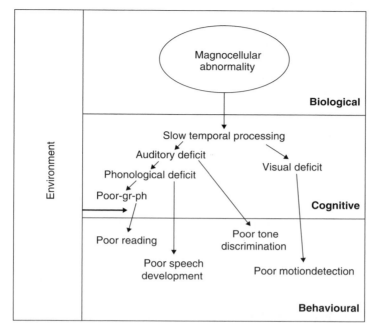

**Figure 6.8** Causal model: a result of magnocellular abnormality. From Frith (1999), Reproduced with permission.
gr-ph, grapheme–phoneme correspondence.

core difficulty is with slow temporal processing. We can now look at the route that visual information takes when going into the cortex, as demonstrated in Figure 6.9.

The first visual input is obviously via the eye to the retina. In the retina, there are cells known as the magnoganglion cells, which have fast links to the lateral geniculate nucleus in the thalamus. From the thalamus, there are routes via the deep magnocellular structures to the primary visual cortex. This is the part of the cerebral hemispheres that deals with visual information. It is here that integration with other signals and visual processing occurs, which include a number of different aspects, particularly the following:

1. What kind of patterns, shapes and forms are seen in the environment (this includes elements of visual acuity and structure)?
2. Where?

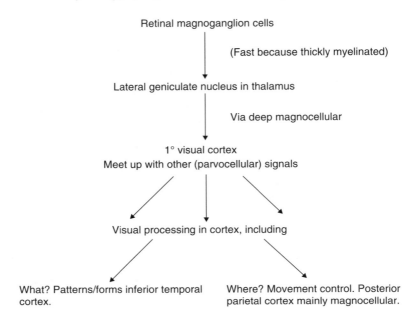

**Figure 6.9** Route of magnoganglion cells to cortex.

Visual processing at this point involves particular elements of movement control. As seen from Figure 6.9, the processing occurs in different parts of what is the temporal cortex. Movement control is in the posterior parietal cortex where magnocellular structures are located.

The magnocellular cortex consists of large neurons that process transient, that is, moving, visual and auditory information. The cells in the optic pathways are split into large and small retinal ganglion cells. The large cells – around 10% – are magnocellular cells and the smaller ones are parvocellular structures. Table 6.4 summarizes the difference between the two types of cell.

Eye movements, binocular control scanning and temporal sequence are crucial elements of the visual transient theories of dyslexia.

Having described the various pathways and briefly the anatomical and functional aspects of the magnocellular system (MCS), we now turn to how it affects reading. Basically, the MCS guides the eyes to the target. Eye movements take place in a series of flicks to

**Table 6.4** Magno- and parvocellular differences.

| Magnocellular | Parvocellular |
| --- | --- |
| Visual transience | Sustained response |
| Illumination change | Continued focus |
| Movement including flicker | Static displays |
| Low light and contrast | Colour |
| Moving targets | Visual acuity (detail) |
| Fast conduction | |
| Eye movements | |
| Binocular control scanning | |
| Temporal sequence | |

the target and, in the case of reading, this gives us the stepwise saccadic movement shown earlier, which is important for developing stable fixations on points to which the eyes move, but it also gives rise to an effect called suppression. This essentially enables us to move our eyes from position to position or to track objects without any blurring of what we are looking at. In other words, our eyes move, not the world. As well as movement, which primarily involves following a reading target as you move across it, the MCS is involved in vergence eye movement (VEM). VEM, as the name suggests, is to do with the mechanism that results in our two eyes focusing and converging on a particular target. Some of the early work of Stein and Fowler (1985) suggested that people with dyslexia had binocular instability, which resulted in difficulties in fixation, but particularly the relationship between tracking a text and fixating a target. Quite clearly, if you are unable to track a target or fixate on the orthography, that is, a particular letter combination at which you are looking, there will be a problem in phoneme–grapheme mapping. Thus, phonemic awareness and grapheme–phoneme mapping skills, which are described as a phonological disorder in people with dyslexia, could equally be the result of a problem in visual fixation of the orthography, as opposed to the relationship between speech-processing systems and phonological representations.

In reading, the MSC also guides the fine detail of the saccades or movement sweeps, for example, the saccade has 30 ms of movement with a 250-ms fixation on average. If we look at the normal eye movement in reading, there are about three letters before and five letters after the central fixation point that are taken in, in a given 'visual chunk' as it were, see the following example:

<u>Let</u> t <u>er</u> <u>and</u>

3   ↓   5

Eye centred

According to research by Stein, people with dyslexia are impaired by flickering stimuli and have problems with low contrast flicker and motion. However, they are normal or perhaps better at colour and fine detail. According to Stein, there is also some evidence that the MSC is smaller and disordered in dyslexics, and he and his colleagues draw attention to the importance of the interrelationship of temporal scanning, visual transience systems, binocular controls and all of these elements in relation to letter–sound mapping systems, which are important in reading, writing and spelling.

Stein, essentially, is arguing that this MCS, particularly in the lateral geniculate nucleus is abnormal, and as a result, movement sensitivity is reduced. Therefore, dyslexics show poor visual recognition, particularly on the left side. Perhaps, the letters they are trying to read appear to move around and cross over each other. According to Stein, this particular theory is not necessarily mutually exclusive from theories we discussed under cerebral dominance and brain functions in general, as the visual system can still coordinate aspects of activation in the phonological areas. Stein went further and proposed that this impaired magnocellular function can result from genetically directed antibody attack and development of the foetus in the uterus, particularly where there is vulnerability to low diets and essential fatty acids. He also went on further, interestingly, to speculate that this weakness in the MCS may result in the emergence of a more efficient parvocellular system. This may result in the reported better 'wholistic' talents of dyslexics and in memorizing of terrain. In other words, other visual systems not involved with linear tracking, would actually be superior.

Some of Stein's work, especially the suggested treatment with eye patching of a nonreferent (dominant) eye, has proved controversial. He suggested that, at the critical age of 6–9 years, it is important that one eye learns to fixate, that is, uniocular control, and that eye patching can be of great help in developing binocular convergence and tracking.

My own particular view is that dyslexia shows a range of difficulties, and there will certainly be some children who do have some problems with aspects of visual processing and other children who have more difficulties in the phonological area. While I would not go as far as saying that they are subtypes of dyslexia, clearly there are different variations within the overall continuum or syndrome of specific learning difficulties.

It is also unfortunate that, as is often the case, the press and others take on complex theoretical notions, which are well documented and researched by people such as Stein, and use them to suggest an immediate 'quick fix' or treatments.

In the case of the cerebellar function, there were some attempts many years ago to prescribe travel sickness pills for people with dyslexia and, in the case of eye patching, I have had children in the past who have been at the school and have had eye patches. One boy in particular lost the eye-patch glasses on the first week and never wore them. When returning to the research centre, it was remarked how well he had done in improving reading and spelling and this was obviously the result of eye patching. In reality, it was the consequence of the hard work that he had done with the teachers. There had been no question about how long he had worn the eye-patch glasses! I have also had individuals who have been diagnosed as dyslexic on the basis of their binocular instability, rather than their reading, writing and spelling performance, which I think is putting the 'cart before the horse'.

Both the cerebellar and visual transient explanations are, however, persuasive because they try to explain many elements of dyslexia, not just reading or aspects of spelling. They are supported by evidence and it would be foolish to ignore them. I do not see that these theories, or others we have or will review, as necessarily mutually exclusive. If we view dyslexia as a syndrome, there may well be children who have more visually oriented problems, or those with more difficulties in the motor area. I have commented previously that I have known children with dyslexia who do not have poor balance, and also those whose binocular instabilities do not seem to feature as important in their own written language development. I could equally comment that I have known children with dyslexia who do well on phonological tests, which would cast doubt on the phonological weakness hypothesis. We are not talking about one sole cause, but a set of contributing factors that may be more important in a given case. We are more likely to discover a 'cause' in an individual – it is when we then generalize to all people with dyslexia that we have problems!

## Further reading

*Dyslexia*, volumes 5.2 and 5.3 (published by John Wiley & Sons, Ltd), for papers on cerebellar and visual transient systems.
Singleton C. (2008) Visual factors in reading. *Education and Child Psychology*, **25** (3); 8–21.

For general reading on biological basis and neuropsychology of dyslexia:
Hulme, C. and Snowling, M. (eds) (1997) Chapters 1–4, in *Biology, Cognition and Intervention*, Whurr Publishers, London.
Pavlides, G. and Fisher, D. (1986) Chapters 4–6, in *Dyslexia, Neuropsychology and Treatment*, John Wiley & Sons, Ltd, Chichester.
Pumfrey, P. and Reason, R. (1991) Chapters 9–11, in *Specific Learning Difficulties*, NFER-Nelson, Windsor.
Robertson, J. (2000) *Dyslexia and Reading: A Neuropsychological Approach*, Whurr Publishers, London.
Stein, J. (1991) *Vision and Visual Dyslexia*, Macmillan, Basingstoke.
Thomson, M.E. (1990) Chapter 3, in *Developmental Dyslexia*, Whurr, London.

# 7

# Models of Reading and Spelling

As I have stated earlier, I look on dyslexia as an individual difference in learning style. One implication of this is that we should look
at the learning task (written language) that we expect children to
acquire so easily at the age of 5 or 6. If we take a kind of 'skills
analysis' approach, we need to examine the written language system
and look at the kinds of skills that are required of a young child
(and indeed a mature reader), before we are able to look at what
might go wrong in the acquisition of written language. It is important for teachers to understand the nature of the reading and spelling process, as well as how it develops in children. There is
surprisingly little of this, in my experience, in teacher training. It
seems fundamental to me that we look at the processes involved in
what we are going to teach, not only to provide us with an understanding of what is required, but also to examine the areas where
some children might find certain skills particularly difficult.

## Written language system

Written language is essentially a form of representation of ideas.
Figure 7.1 illustrates some examples. There are both indirect and
direct ways of accessing an idea that needs to be communicated. In
a picture representation, we see what we observe directly and the
idea is manifest, depending on the observer's world knowledge,
semantic memory or cognitive process. In speech, there is also

*The Psychology of Dyslexia – A Handbook for Teachers,* by Michael Thomson
© 2009 John Wiley & Sons Ltd

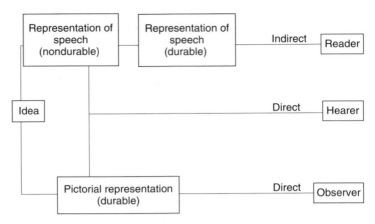

**Figure 7.1** Representation of ideas.

a direct representation by auditory input. This is nondurable, however, and as we listen to speech, we forget what is said, and of course, it is open to interpretation later as a result of our relatively weak memory systems. The development of written language, where speech is represented as a durable and permanent record, has – some writers argue – given rise to modern civilization. However, this is a very indirect representation and the reader has to make a connection between how the speech, or the idea, is represented and how the reading system actually works. As you will see, this indirect representation of the ideas that we wish to communicate can lead to problems in some orthographies.

One problem, particularly in the case of western written language development, has been increasing arbitrariness. Most writers agree that spoken language is the prime symbol system. It appears to be biologically based, or certainly human beings are programmed to acquire spoken language at an early age. People still claim that one of the distinctions between animals and human beings is the fact that humans can use spoken language, and the interrelationship of speech, language and thought was one that gave rise to a great deal of speculation and research in linguistic writings both philosophically and psychologically. What is clear in the context here is that the alphabetical system has been invented by human beings and as such is a secondary symbol system. Many major civilizations in the

**Figure 7.2** Picture and letters representing cup.

world have developed their own written language systems, and as spoken language systems have changed, so the representations of those spoken language systems by the written form have been different. Gradually, however, there has been a move from visual representations, that is, drawing a picture of an idea, for example, a picture of a cat when communicating the idea of the furry feline creature that we keep as a pet. The next stage appears to be the development of pictograms similar to some of the Chinese ideograms. Sometimes, these are developed into syllabaries, where a particular ideogram or picture system represents a syllable in spoken language, and finally into alphabet where individual letters or combinations of letters represent sounds. In English, an example of western orthography, we have 26 symbols which represent over 40 phonemes. A phoneme is, of course, the distinctive sound in a particular spoken language that has a separate entity or meaning. However, for a young child, the individual letters are arbitrary in the first instance; that is, they are meaningless. Furthermore, we combine letter combinations into different orders to give us different words. Figure 7.2 illustrates some of the difficulties this can cause children and is an example I have used before (Thomson, 1990).

In Figure 7.2, we see that letter order and direction are very different from the idea of shape and size constancies. A perceptual constancy is what we learn in the first part of our life, that is, that looking at objects in the environment from different angles does not cause them to become a different object or a different sound or a different element of another object or idea. Thus, looking at a cup from a different angle or from further away gives a different image on our retina, but it is still called a cup. However, with letters, we start to change the labels with slightly different features. A 'b' and a 'd' have different sounds and different phonemic representations in written language. Thus, to represent an object such as a cup with

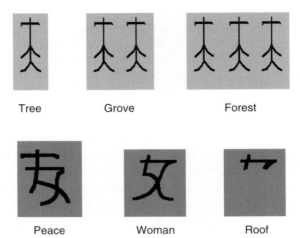

Figure 7.3 Examples of Chinese pictograms.

letters, we have nonsensical pronunciations when looking at the word from a different angle or back to front. This is, of course, something that many children have difficulty with initially, but overcome. The dyslexic child may continue to have problems in this area.

The notion of the difference between a direct or visual route to meaning, as used by something like a Chinese pictogram, and an indirect route to reading via a phonemic or alphabetical system (credited to the Phoenicians) is the key difference seen by many theories in written language development.

One of the key features of a pictogram system, as mentioned, is going straight from meaning to idea. Some examples of Chinese pictograms are given in Figure 7.3.

Some of these have direct written language links, for example, the pictograms from 'tree' to 'grove' to 'forest'. Some are combinations of two components, for example, the symbol for 'woman' and a 'roof' into 'peace' (suggesting that peace is a woman under a roof, with which, of course, we would all agree!).

Even for syllabaries in other language systems, one has difficulties. Discussing dyslexia at Rainbow Academy in Japan, an English Language School, I obtained the following example of syllabaries from Hiragand, which has 52 characters/sounds (Figure 7.4).

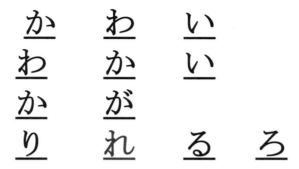

**Figure 7.4** Examples of Japanese syllabary.

I would like the reader now to have a look at these syllabaries. Imagine you are a dyslexic child being asked to read or write these. You will notice that in the first two lines, there are differences in that the first two syllabaries are the same but in a different order. If I told you these were 'ka', 'wa' and 'i' (first line) and 'wa', 'ka' and 'e' (second line), meaning 'cute' and 'young', respectively, you can just see how one is still getting sound order difficulties in different words, even in a language that is only semi-phonemic.

Looking at the next example, (line 3) you may note that the first symbol is the same as it appears in 'cute' and 'young'. This is 'ka'. The second, with just an additional couple of marks is the similar sounding 'ga'. The reason for showing this is just to show how similar they really are, rather like some of the letters in the sounds in English!

The final four are again very similar in looks and these are 'ri', 're', 'ru', 'ro'. You will begin to see the parallels between the difficulties in vowel discrimination and the relationship between letters and letter combinations.

If I was presenting the above at a conference, I would not be telling you the syllabaries and the meanings, but asking you to guess them having told you briefly, as if I was teaching you. This is quite a salutary lesson in realizing how difficult the written language systems can be for the first learner.

Before we look at stage analysis and dual-route theories of reading, it is worth examining some terminology. When reading a word, we can look at it as a whole visual or global system and go

**Table 7.1** Examples of written language units.

| Word | Syllable | Onset and rime | Phoneme |
|---|---|---|---|
| dog | dog | d-og | d-o-g |
| string | string | str-ing | s-t-r-i-n-g |
| magnet | mag'net | m-ag'n-et | m-a-g-n-e-t |

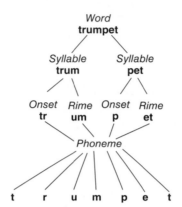

**Figure 7.5** Possible linguistic subdivisions of 'trumpet' .

straight to meaning, for example, *string*, or we could divide it into intrasyllabic units such as *str + ing* or individual grapheme–phoneme relationships such as *s-t-r-i-n-g*, where we have to recognize individual letters given the sound and then blend them together. These phonological skills are a key process in learning to read and use alphabetical systems; we return to them in much more detail when we look at reading and spelling development and the phonological deficit model of dyslexia. Table 7.1 gives some ideas of particular examples of important units within written language. Figure 7.5 shows another way of showing how words can be broken down into different forms, for example, trumpet.

It is worth commenting, in passing, that children find it quite difficult to isolate individual phonemes in words before they are about 7, and onset and rime units and syllable units are much easier to divide. This is a key feature of teaching younger children.

One of the problems in describing theories on the reading and spelling process is that there are so many different levels and tasks to which we can refer to, for example, take the English National Curriculum on this issue. The notion that you can divide written language skills into simply reading, writing and speaking and listening is far too simplistic. As a practical example, we can have a dyslexic child who may be at a very high level in terms of attainment targets when it comes to understanding different genres, being aware of characterization, using description and awareness of poetry. However, his or her mechanical reading skills may be very weak, and therefore, these higher-order skills cannot be accessed, not because of an inability to do them but as a result of problems in letter–sound decoding. Table 7.2 illustrates this problem with reference to reading. Table 7.2 shows reading skills divided into, very broadly, two components: the so-called mechanical, that is, decoding or phonological skills, and lexical or higher-order skills – to do with the word. We can see under each of these the different levels of skill and expertise that might be required. To include all of these different areas in one unified theory of reading and spelling would be very difficult, and most of the reading and spelling theories tend to focus on the process of letter, word and sentence recognition. It is not the purpose here, and it would take up to two or three volumes, to review all of the different reading and spelling models that are current. What I hope to do is to present a skeleton of some examples of approaches that will give the reader an insight into the sorts of skills involved in written language acquisition.

## Routes to reading

A useful approach to the processes involved in reading and spelling is that of stage analysis. Most stage models assume that there is some initial visual processing, followed by decoding visual input into a sound relating to speech and finally into semantic (meaning) and syntactic (grammar) components. The study of language – linguistics – has traditionally been divided into phonology (the sounds involved), syntax (grammar or structure of the language), semantics (the meaning and use of words) and aspects of

**Table 7.2** Mechanical and higher-order skills in reading.

| *Reading skills comments* | |
| --- | --- |
| **Mechanical (decoding/phonological)** | |
| Recognition of 'text' | Includes left/right scanning, recognition of word/line units, top/bottom direction, pages and so on. This simple stage cannot be taken for granted in the dyslexic child. |
| Basic sight vocabulary | High-frequency irregular words read. Able to recognize common vocabulary fluently without sounding out |
| Simple grapheme–phoneme skills | Common word units recognized, for example, consonant blends, vowel–sound combinations |
| Phonic analysis skills | Identification of word units, 'sounding' out skills, blending and syllabification skills |
| Simple punctuation | Recognition of punctuation and its implication in reading aloud |
| **Higher order (lexical)** | |
| What are books, sentences, paragraphs and illustrations? | That books relate to communication, spoken language and can tell stories. Again this cannot be taken for granted |
| Use of context | Being able to follow the gist; expecting the next stage; what that part of the book is about |
| Use of inference | What the book suggests about other things; understand more sophisticated vocabulary, analogy and meaning |
| 'Linguistic' fluency | Using punctuation appropriately; reading aloud with expression; 'skimming' for key meanings |

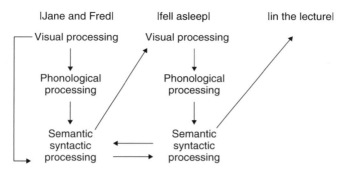

**Figure 7.6** Stage analysis model in reading.

metalinguistics (awareness of your own use of language and also nonverbal communication).

Figure 7.6 presents a simple example of how this is proposed. The lines separating the words, that is, /Jane and Fred/ – /fell asleep/ – /in the lecture/, represent saccades or eye movements, for example, how much visual information can be taken in when reading the text. There is the implication that this has to be decoded, and the line from visual processing to semantic/syntactic processing implies a direct route to reading, whereas going through visual processing to phonological to the final stage implies some kind of indirect route. Semantic and/or syntactical processing can also help in predicting what the next input might be, hence the arrows down to the next chunk of visual processing.

This kind of approach has been formalized into the dual route to reading. It is interesting to note in passing that these models have, to some extent, been developed from observing people with acquired dyslexia, that is, individuals who had a stroke or similar damage to parts of the brain that are responsible for written language learning. It has been observed that patients can produce different kinds of reading and spelling behaviour, for example, some may be able to read irregular words well, whereas others have greater difficulty with nonwords. Being able to read an irregular word implies going directly from input to meaning, whereas reading a nonword implies that we have to go through a grapheme to phoneme, that is, a letter-to-sound correspondence route. The way that people produce differential responses has led to classification

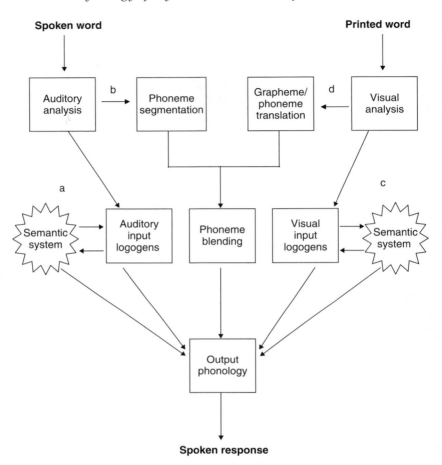

Model of the interface between spoken and written language processing system. (From Snowling (1987) with permission)

**Figure 7.7** Examples of 'dual-route' model of reading. Note: a–d refer to reading 'routes'.

of acquired dyslexias into phonological and surface dyslexias, as a result of differing performance on nonwords, regular words and irregular words. A typical example of dual-route theories to reading is illustrated in Figure 7.7, which presents a model for the understanding of decoding of both the spoken word and the printed word. In both cases, there is a spoken response going through to the box at the bottom called 'output phonology'. Output phonology is essentially the postulated cognitive or brain/thought process involved in putting together the sounds before making a speech utterance. In itself, this is a huge area of psychological interest and research!

In the flow charts going from both the spoken word and the printed word, there is a semantic system. Again, for the purposes of this model, this is just a nebulous and uncharted system that understands words and the context of words, and uses long-term memory and syntactical and semantic–linguistic systems to under- stand the input, whether through the spoken or the printed word, that is, meaning. The two systems depart on the modality in which the words are presented. In the case of the spoken word, there is some preliminary auditory analysis and, in the case of the printed word, some visual analysis. If we focus on the printed word in this context, we can see that after visual analysis, there are two systems labelled 'route c' and 'route d'. Route c is essentially the direct, or so-called Chinese, route to reading. In this, before visual analysis, there is a direct link to the meaning system, involving a mechanism called a visual input logogen. Cognitive psychologists are very fond of developing terms that undertake various tasks, but no one knows the detail of what is going on. In this context, the logogen is simply a mechanism for recognition of visual input; that is, it is someth- ing more than the recognition of what something looks like. For example, we might see the shape of a letter or a word in the abstract but not recognize it as a letter or a word. The visual input logogen recognizes the letters, letter combinations and whole words. There is an access to the meaning system or the so-called internal lexicon. A lexicon is essentially a form of dictionary that is held somewhere in the cognitive system.

From this immediate recognition of the word, the sounds are assembled and the spoken response are made. Thus, looking at a word such as *frog*, the letters are recognized as a whole word and there is access to the notion of a small, green, amphibious creature found in a pond, for example, and the word *frog* is said immedi- ately. This is the way in which most adults, it is postulated, read. We tend to skim, read rapidly and go directly from the visual input to meaning without any indirect or decoding component.

Where we start using an indirect route is where we have difficult words. If we look at 'route d', we see the visual analysis inputs into a box called 'grapheme–phoneme translation'. Essentially, this is the alphabet system, and what we are doing is giving the letters their names or sounds. Sometimes this might be individual letters given individual sounds, such as *f-r-o-g*, or it might be various units, for example, onset and rime like *fr-og* or blend plus vowel as in *fro-g*, and various combinations of these with longer multi-syllabic words. This, therefore, goes through to a box called phoneme blending.

In this instance, the letters that are recognized and held in the short-term memory are blended together, for example, *fr-og* or *f-r-o-g* to *frog* and so on. Finally, the word is spoken, and at this stage the semantic system kicks in, as it were. In other words, the word is now finally recognized as the small, green, amphibious creature found in a pond. This route, it is suggested, is the so-called Phoenician or indirect route and is used in the acquisition of reading. (Phoenicians are credited with inventing the alphabet.) When we come across a word that is not immediately recognized, we can use this grapheme–phoneme translation or the alphabet system route to work out what the word says. At that point, the pronunciation can be matched to our own internal lexicon or semantic system, to see whether the meaning can be understood. Obviously, a nonword such as *spod* could be read through this system. Here, we do not find a semantic or dictionary entry, and therefore, the word has no meaning. On the other hand, we might find a word we read that did not have a dictionary allocation, but was, in fact, a real word that we did not know. Thus, if the word *clan*, which is a relatively simple word to decode, was read by a young child, he or she may not have it in his or her internal lexicon, and therefore would not be able to access its meaning. Nevertheless, it is, of course, a real word. So, one notion is that a child acquires reading in the early stages, when the internal lexicon is not large, by the grapheme–phoneme translation route; similarly, in spelling, we would expect the reverse to occur, that is, a sound to be assembled, put together with a letter combination or grapheme, and then to be spelt in a similar way.

As adults, we might sometimes use this indirect route, for example, I read a lot of fantasy, and occasionally, if I come across

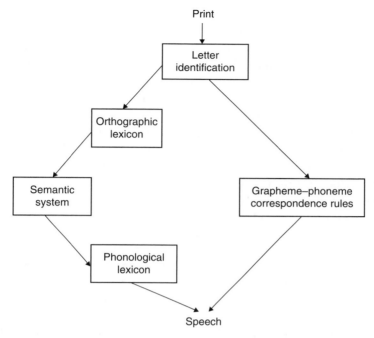

**Figure 7.8** Elaboration of the dual-route theory of reading aloud.

a word such as 'Strakenoris' that I recognize as the Elf Queen, I might not bother to sound it out to myself. However, if I was reading it aloud I would have to pronounce it. Similarly, if reading a fantasy tale set in Celtic times, I might use Celtic pronunciations, if they were given in the book's appendix as 'how to pronounce Celtic orthography'. Here, I would have to use an alphabetical or indirect route to work out what the pronunciations were. Mostly, I might not bother to pronounce it correctly, but just go for the direct route to reading and understand what the word meant in context.

This dual-route theory of reading aloud basically involves three kinds of information from words: their spellings, their pronunciations and their meanings. Another version of Figure 7.7 is given in Figure 7.8, where there is (i) an orthographic analysis (lexicon) representing knowledge about visual forms, (ii) a phonological representation which is a knowledge about the pronunciation of words and (iii) the semantic system, which is information about where the meanings of words are stored. Therefore, the distinction between irregular and regular words becomes quite important. Regular words are those that obey the grapheme–phoneme correspondence in English, like 'rain' or 'cave'. Irregular words do not use these rules like 'said' or 'have'.

Regular words can be read by both lexical and nonlexical reading routes, but irregular words only by the lexical reading route. In nonlexical reading, you will get them wrong. I realize that this second diagram recaps some of what is said earlier – but I feel it is a helpful reformulation!

The mentioned models are sometimes referred to as the 'dual-route cascade' (see Coltheart, 2006, for a review).

The fluency and the interactive component of an adult's written language system have given rise to the development of the stage models into slightly more sophisticated systems. The development of written language models has paralleled with the development of cognitive psychology in other areas, such as memory, which we look at in Chapter 8. Basically, cognitive psychology has moved on from modal or box-like models to more interactive models, based on computer simulations.

Computers reading nonsense words and looking at how they develop their accuracy in recognizing words have also developed 'connectionist' models (see Coltheart, 2006, for a readable review).

Without going into inappropriate detail here, connectionist theory looks at the way in which components of the cognitive system or brain interact. Connectionism is a cognitive model of the reading and spelling process, but it also relates to the way in which the brain works. For example, specializing modules of the brain communicate with each other and there are many connections, which create an information processing matrix. These connections provide feedback loops and support for learning and the brain is essentially a self-teaching system. Once, for example in reading, a word looks right and the correct circuits are in place, the continual reinforcements of these circuits increase the probability of them occurring again; that is, the pattern and the connections are made stronger. The idea is, eventually, the brain no longer requires explicit instruction but begins to read for itself.

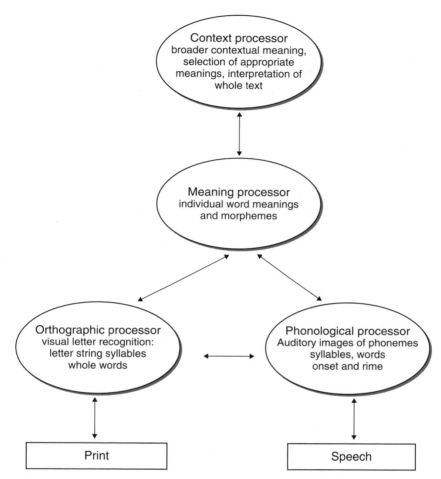

**Figure 7.9** Interactive systems for written language.
Source: Adams (1996).

In the context of written language, there have been developments of the notions of different kinds of processes involved in reading that interact with each other. A good example is given by Adams (1996) and illustrated in Figure 7.9.

The orthographic and phonological processes in Figure 7.9 are, I suppose, similar in many ways to the visual and auditory logogens mentioned earlier, and interact with the meaning processor. This involves both individual word meanings, that is, the internal dictionary, and morphemic units, which would include such things as suffixes – -*ed*, -*ing* – or units of words that have particular meanings. Finally, these three main interactions, that is, orthography, phonology and semantics or meaning, are dependent on the context, and here we have an attempt to extend models into more reality-based systems, including interpretation of the whole text, the context in which the words appear and so on. It also allows two-way interaction.

Those readers who are teachers may notice interesting echoes in some of these models, for example, the notion of a direct route to reading, that is, looking at the orthography (e.g. letters) and accessing the meaning of the word is essentially 'look and say'. Analysing the sounds, whether breaking them down into individual letters and their phonemes or letter combinations or building them up through blending to form the words, is essentially similar to 'phonics'. The notion of reading in context in terms of meaning is associated with the so-called 'real reading'. All of these are particular fashions used in education from time to time, and one of the strengths of being aware of 'models' is that it makes us remember that all aspects are important. Of course, some children will have better skills in some areas and there are whole groups of children who have particular difficulty with aspects of comprehension. For the dyslexic child, the problem is mainly in the alphabetical decoding area. A number of researchers also argue that we cannot get on to the higher-order level recognition of words and their meanings without going through an alphabetical stage, or certainly the use of phonics and awareness of the relationship between the sound structure and the written language system. The Figure 7.9 and similar models are sometimes referred to as the 'triangle model' .

Lexical models would propose that, rather than a word represented as a single unit in the lexicon, there are numerous different systems in brain function. For example, if a nonword is presented, a visual recognition model suggests that all the letters are processed simultaneously. In contrast, the dual-route model, which we looked at earlier, processed letter to sounds, one letter after another from left to right, that is, serially. As learning takes place, the strengths of connections in the reading model and by implication the connections in brain function become progressively more accurate. The dual-route model itself is just a description of the information processing systems that children require, rather than trying to explain the learning process *per se*. We are really getting to a rather more technical discussion than is appropriate for a book of this nature and I would refer you to Coltheart (2006) for a review and, in particular, Vellutino *et al*. (2004) for an overview of the models of the written language system. The latter, in particular, reviews a very complex cognitive process and knowledge-type model.

It is worth making some additional comments on spelling. Spelling skills are not quite a simple difference between word recognition (reading) and production (spelling). They sometimes involve rather different skills. As in reading, spelling becomes lexical, that is, word meaning with semantic and syntactic clues. There will, therefore, be a strong relationship between reading and spelling. On the other hand, we can also spell nonlexically, that is, simply producing a sound, giving it a letter or letter combinations, and writing down nonwords. In this, the focus is on sound–symbol relationships and the phonological and phonemic aspect of written language. Cognitive processing underlies both lexical and non-lexical skills, but there is also the so-called metacognitive, that is, our knowledge about, and regulation of, spelling. To take a specific example in terms of suffix rules: before teaching dyslexic children, I was usually pretty good at spelling words such as 'hopped' or 'hoped', 'dinner' and 'diner' and so on. This was an automatic or implicit skill that I had, but I did not have any orthographic knowledge about the rules involved. Once I began to teach dyslexic children, I soon learned that there was a rule (the doubling rule, which I will not go into here, but see Thomson and Watkins, 1999) to cover this situation. In other words, there was an explicit or metacognitive process that I could apply in working out how to spell words with suffixes and whether or not one doubled consonants. We can spend a good deal of time making the written language system very complex, and Figure 7.10 presents some of the elements involved in the cognitive systems apropos spelling.

At the top of Figure 7.10, we have auditory input. This input can come from outside, if someone is asking us to spell a word and we have to write it down as in a spelling test, or internally if we are trying to create our own spellings. This implies some kind of phonological memory or loop system (see Chapter 8), which enables us

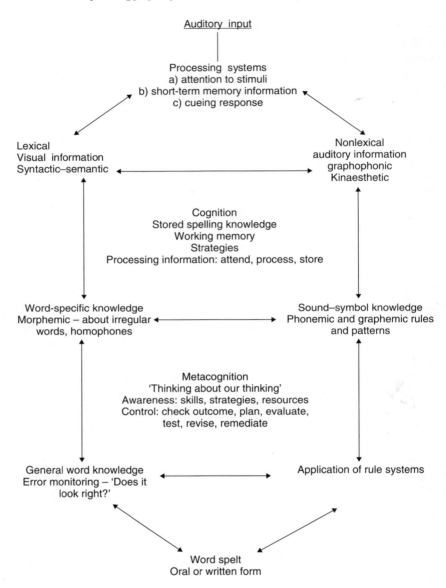

**Figure 7.10** Example of cognitive processes involved in spelling.

to create these sounds internally. The processing system obviously involves short-term (or working) memory and attention to stimuli, as shown in the figure. The auditory input is then broadly divided into lexical and nonlexical systems, that is, words and nonwords if you like. I do not propose to go through the figure in great detail, but it is worth having a look through at all the various interactive (note that the arrows are two-way) aspects. Try to relate the various components to models that we have already discussed and those later in the chapter. You then might like to add your own ideas to make it even more complicated!

This is not supposed to be a complete review, but I hope that it gives the reader some idea of the sorts of approaches involved in developing models of reading and spelling, and also some of the complexities.

## The development of written language

We now turn to some approaches to the development of written language skills. As is often the case in developmental psychology, people try to look at stage developments in children. This essentially follows on from dear old Piaget and tries to place children in the context of their developing learning skills. The implication is that children move from simple to more complex skills, and it is quite interesting to note the parallels between proposed developmental stages in children and the various different stages involved in the models of reading and spelling processes. I am going to start off, unusually, with a summary at the beginning of this section on reading and spelling development so that the reader has a context.

Most developmental stage models of reading and spelling learning have early visual recognition of familiar assembled phonology (sound from speech represented as letters/words) as part of initial learning. This initially implies visual skills in which letter combinations that are learnt are recognized straightaway, but this obviously is a skill that needs to be acquired. The next stage is a letter-to-sound conversion process of some sort, leading to phonological processing. The phonological processing is related to phonemic awareness and has interactive links with short-term memory. Next, there is development of the mental lexicon, that is, a store of sight recognition words. The implication behind this is that there are dual routes with learning sight words via (i) grapheme–phoneme conversion or assembled phonology, that is, letter combinations being put together, or (ii) direct visual recognition and, finally, the relationship between semantic memory (understanding the word) and output phonology (saying the word). There is an assumption that new and unfamiliar words will be recognized by the grapheme–phoneme correspondence route. This will sound familiar, of course, and is essentially what is involved in some of the dual process and aspects of interactive reading processes that we have already looked at. However, let us turn back a bit and look at the development of these systems in written language learning.

One of the most influential and widely quoted stage models has been that of Frith (1985), developed from Marsh *et al.* (1981), who in turn was trying to develop a Piagetian approach to written language learning. It is surprising, in fact, how little research and theoretical modelling has been done on the written language learning process, as opposed to reading and spelling processes in adults. Table 7.3 shows the main elements of Frith's proposed stages.

Broadly, there are three stages: logographic, alphabetical and orthographic. The logographic stage is at the very beginning of learning to recognize text and written material, in which children may recognize whole units, but very much in the context of the environment, for example, a McDonald's sign may be recognized, as might Coca-Cola. There would be no generalization from McDonald's to a word beginning with 'M', or from Coca-Cola to words such as 'cocoa'. Children often read particular words in the environmental context in which they occur. One of the interesting things about Frith's theory is that there is often interaction between one stage and another, that is, reading words logographically can lead on to beginning to spell words, that is, children copying down shapes and symbols that they see in the environment around them. The shapes can then be given names by parents, for example, M for the M in McDonald's, and the letter is spelt. Reading therefore starts off the development of spelling skills. At the logographic stage, particular words can be recognized, remembered, read or spelt, but it is not until the alphabetical stage that the child starts to recognize

**Table 7.3**  Three phases of reading development (Frith, 1985).

Stage 1 Logographic
Associate speech signs with symbols. Read as logograms. Shape
recognition. Memory of environment. Particular words/spoken/written

|  | *Reading* | *Writing* |  |
|---|---|---|---|
| Steps 1a | Logographic 1 | (Symbolic) | Reading logographically |
| 1b | Logographic 2 | Logographic 2 | helps to spell |
|  |  |  | logographically |

Stage 2 Alphabetical
Chunking letter sounds and morpheme identification. Grapheme–
phoneme translation route, sound-to-letter correspondence; requires
phonemic awareness, decoding novel words

|  | *Reading* | *Writing* |  |
|---|---|---|---|
| Steps 2a | Logographic 1 | Alphabetic 1 | Using phonological letter |
| 2b | Alphabetic 2 | Alphabetic 2 | sound approach in |
|  |  |  | spelling creates |
|  |  |  | alphabetical approach in |
|  |  |  | reading? Spelling: |
|  |  |  | 1. Correct sound analysis |
|  |  |  | (within word) |
|  |  |  | 2. Phoneme–grapheme |
|  |  |  | translation |
|  |  |  | 3. Conventionally correct |
|  |  |  | graphemes selected |

Stage 3 Orthographic
Automatic recognition of graphemic clusters: -tion, etc. Access to lexical
representations set up relating to letter-by-letter sequences, use of lexical
analogies

|  | *Reading* | *Writing* |  |
|---|---|---|---|
| Steps 3a | Orthographic 1 | Alphabetical 3 | Uses orthographic code |
| 3b | Orthographic 2 | Orthographic 2 | first in reading then |
|  |  |  | transfers/develops |
|  |  |  | spelling |

new words, generalize and begin to develop implicit knowledge of letter–sound combinations.

In the alphabetical stage, children will start to break down letter sounds into longer units, identify units within words and, crucially, develop grapheme–phoneme translation route skills. In other words, they will be able to recognize individual letters in combination given the appropriate sounds. Underlying this, of course, is the implication that phonemic awareness and phonological skills are required. Table 3.3 (p. 71) shows the sorts of phonological skills involved, as does Table 7.2 (p. 144). Here, developing alphabetical skills begin to feed, from writing or spelling, into the alphabet. As we hear sounds, for example, 'frog', and allocate particular letter combinations to them, that skill can be used in recognizing and decoding novel words in reading, for example, the alphabetic 2 stage in reading.

In spelling, I have added three small stages: correct sound analysis within words, phoneme–grapheme translation, that is, sound to letters, and finally, selecting the conventionally correct graphemes. This is not easy for many children, and at the early stages of spelling can give rise to mistakes such as 'tese', 'cez', 'jes' or 'tz' for 'cheese', all of which are not random representations but approximations to the sound, and also more sophisticated attempts such as 'clend' for 'cleaned', 'jumt' for 'jumped' and so on. Some phonological skills are clearly being used here. Choosing the correct orthography to represent a given sound becomes quite a problem for children with dyslexia, for example, different 13-year-old children with dyslexia in my current teaching group gave the following spellings for 'shield': 'sheild', 'shild', 'shiel', 'sheld', 'sheeld', 'sheeyled', 'cheeld' and 'shiyeld'. Some of these indicate phonological problems, but most are reasonable representations of the word.

The next stage is the so-called orthographic stage. Here, recognition of graphemic clusters becomes much more automatic. There is an implicit, or sometimes explicit, awareness of what sound structures or letter combinations are common in a given language. There is access to lexical representations, that is, word dictionaries, by relating to letter sequences, but also comparing words analogously. This sort of approach has been developed by other theorists such as Goswami (1986, 1988) (see p. 160). In this case, we have the development of reading skills, that is, beginning to recognize and

**Table 7.4** Three stages of sight reading.

| Sight reading (Ehri) | Parallel stages in spelling (Henderson) |
| --- | --- |
| Emergent readers: no sound/symbol, visual aspects of word only[a] | Pre-phonetic |
| Phonetic cue reading: one or two specific cues, individual letters/blends give phonic clues[a] | Semi-phonetic |
| Cipher sight word reading: stored in memory, spelling/phonological associations | Phonetic |

[a]Instruction necessary, that is, letters/phonemic segmentation.

internalize common spelling patterns. Vowel combinations, for example, are fiendish in English /a/ (play, maid, made, eight, great, etc.) and beginning to recognize the most common spellings of the letter sound in reading begins to develop into writing skills.

Frith has given us quite a neat way of examining developmental skills across time and also the interrelationship of spelling and reading. Of course, as Frith would be the first to acknowledge, it is not as simple as a stark three-stage system, but it does give us a clear relationship between the reading and spelling models that we have outlined previously and how they might develop in children. The notion of three stages has been taken on by a number of researchers and other aspects of written language learning have been looked at in more detail, for example, Ehri (1991) examined the development of just sight vocabulary and knowledge of spelling. The stages are presented in Table 7.4.

Ehri proposed three stages in just the sight-reading aspect, although there are parallels between her approach and those of Frith and Henderson. According to Ehri, emergent readers select salient visual cues and associate these with words in memory. The cues bear no relationship to the sound. In the phonetic cue stage, letters that link spelling to word pronunciation are the associations used. Finally, readers learn more conventional ways of symbolizing sounds with letters, enabling readers to retrieve specific pronunciation and meaning as a whole. Cue readers would have problems with similarly spelt words. The spelling mentioned refers to another stage analysis model, that of Henderson (1981). Henderson argued

**Table 7.5** Henderson's five-stage model (Henderson, 1981).

1. Pre-communicative
   Letters at random. Not representing sounds or words

2. Semi-phonetic
   Some awareness. 'R' for 'are'

3. Phonetic
   Representation of sounds, but what sequences are OK in English?
   'ckut' for 'cut'

4. Transitional
   Conventional spelling and meaning. 'Eightee' for 'eighty' (earlier 'ate')

5. Correct
   Fewer errors, knowledge of orthography

that the logographic stage would have to be very brief because there is soon development of phonological skills in spelling. She proposed a five-stage model, shown in Table 7.5, with illustrations of the kinds of mistakes that might be made.

Others, such as Goswami (1988), have argued that children do not develop through discrete stages. She introduced the notion of lexical analogy, and in particular, the development of intrasyllabic skills in children. Goswami emphasized the division between onset and rime, for example, words such as *trap* can be divided into *t-r-a-p* or *tr-ap* or *tra-p* or *t-rap*. Note that 'rime' is vowel plus consonant, for example, -ap in tr'ap. 'Rhyme' is two words that rhyme, not necessarily with the same orthography, for example, pot/lot/yacht. She pointed to the research correlating rhyme detection with reading development, the former being a predictor of reading, and argued that onset and rime awareness appear before reading, for example, during sound and word play. She also emphasized the interrelationship, as we have seen earlier, between chronological development as a consequence of reading and spelling and vice versa, and argued that beginner readers start to use analogies between words, that is, drawing parallels between, for example, *mean* and *heap, bead, beat, peak* and so on.

Again, those who are teachers will begin to recognize the notion of word families among this lexical analogy theory. Without being

**Table 7.6** Stage development: commonalities.

| | |
|---|---|
| Visual recognition | Familiar words/shapes: visualization, recognition |
| Alphabetic component | Phoneme → grapheme rules (phonological coding/short-term memory, phonemic awareness). 'Recognition → recall' |
| Storage of sight words | Mental lexicon, word understanding, orthography (conventional, morphemes, irregular patterns) |

too cynical, in my experience, cognitive and developmental psychologists often reinvent the wheel, or more likely dress up relatively simple classroom concepts in complex cognitive psychology vocabulary!

As in the previous chapters, it is not my purpose to review all the theories of reading and spelling development, but it is worth finishing this section with a slightly more detailed reiteration of the commonalities of stage development theories (Table 7.6).

It may be seen that the three major components – visual recognition, alphabetical and sight word storage – have their echoes in the models of reading and spelling process outlined earlier. Basically, the notion is that children begin to learn to read and spell by recognizing familiar words and shapes, particularly using recognition and so-called visualization skills, that is, what a word looks like and the shapes and visual elements of units. Then comes an alphabetical component involving phoneme-to-grapheme or grapheme-to-phoneme skills (depending on whether one is spelling or reading). The important implication here is that the phonological coding, short-term memory and phonemic awareness skills are all linked, and that there is a difference between recognition (reading) and recall (spelling). The alphabetical component, or phonics, as opposed to the 'look and say' or visual sight vocabulary component, would tend to come later, although of course, there is a good deal of overlap and these stages are not finite or particularly linked to any age group. In my experience, some children with dyslexia may not reach the alphabetical stage until they are 13 or 14 (if at all!), a stage that some five- and six-year-olds will have reached.

Following these decoding skills, we have a storage of sight words and the more contextually meaning-oriented aspects of written language, which come at a later stage. These include the development of a mental lexicon or internal dictionary, understanding words and also the development of orthographic skills. This includes remembering irregular word patterns and also understanding conventional orthography such as -tion.

Another way of conceptionalizing the development of reading and spelling is not through formal theoretical models, but actually observations of what happens. McCormick (2003), for example, analysing spelling errors, proposed various stages ranging from nonphonemic through to orthographic. These examples are given in Table 7.7 and the descriptions are fairly self-explanatory, drawing also on the work of Snowling and Stackhouse (1996).

The teacher's role in the above error analysis is to move the child's spelling skills from right (e.g. nonphonemic) to left (e.g. phonemic) on the table. McCormick's model is well worth further study.

Those teachers experienced in helping dyslexic children or children with specific learning difficulties, using structured phonic programmes, will notice the very broad parallel between how these programmes develop and how reading and spelling are proposed to develop in children. Initially, there is usually some attempt to teach a basic corpus of sight vocabulary. Then the phonic component starts off with simple phoneme–grapheme correspondence rules such as alphabet and consonant blends, and develops into more complicated rules involving phonemic awareness such as vowel combinations. This is followed by syllabification and segmentation skills in teaching multi-syllable regular words, finally building up to spelling rules and use of more complex, irregular words as in the later stages of the stage development models.

We return to phonological skills in more detail when we examine theories of causes of dyslexia, focusing particularly on the core phonological deficit notion (see Chapter 9). However, as a taster for this discussion and to finish off the chapter, Table 7.8 illustrates the relationship between the development in phonological knowledge and how that relates to difficulties in some children with dyslexia.

**Table 7.7** Examples of errors from various spelling stages based on data taken from work at East Court and a mainstream primary school. (McCormick, 2003).

| Target word (standard adult spelling) | Orthographic | Phonemic | Semi-phonemic | Metaphonemic | Nonphonemic |
|---|---|---|---|---|---|
| Fish | Phish | Fis | Fit/firch | Filts | S |
| Puppy | Pupy | Pupe | Pup | Puet | Bcpns |
| Tulip | Tullip | Cholip | Choop | Tup | Stuncds |
| Polish | Pollish | Pullish | Posh | Pch | Nutbe |
| Refreshment | Reafreshment | Rfeshmet | Refrsmt | Ffmet | Lletp |
| Instructed | Instruckted | Instudid | Insrud | Isd | Tents |
| | Evident within this set of spellings is the emergence of orthographic spelling rules. Patterns transcend the one sound–one letter relationship of the alphabetic stage and show more complex relations and use of morphemes. | The phonemic stage is shown by the representation of a one-to-one correspondence between sounds and letters. A key feature of this stage is the representation of stressed vowel segments. | These spellings show a growing awareness of the salient sounds within words – some vowel sounds are indicated; initial and final sounds are marked, with the occasional medial consonant. | These spellings demonstrate the emergence of metaphonological awareness. The early stages of sound–letter correspondences can be seen in the correct transcription of the initial sound of the word. | These letter strings bear no discernible relationship to the target word and are categorized as nonphonemic responses. |

**Table 7.8** Phonological knowledge.

| Development | Some dyslexic children |
|---|---|
| Names of objects/events | Difficulties in naming, syllable omission, juxtaposition, substitution |
| Sound patterns → sounds in words | Vowel confusions within words, following speech difficulties |
| Segmentation → onset/rime → blend string into words | Sound-blending difficulties |
| Phonological recoding → link sounds/letters | Grapheme–phoneme correspondence |
| Orthographic knowledge (phonemic awareness) <br> • automaticity <br> • self-teaching, analogies <br> • similarities | Short-term memory problems <br> Lack of phonemic awareness |

# Further reading

More detailed descriptions of models and written language process can be found in:

Perfetti, C. (1985) *Reading Ability*, Oxford University Press, New York.

Detail and/or sources for the development of written language and relevance to dyslexia can be found in:

Goswami, U. and Bryant, P.J. (1990) *Phonological Skills and Learning to Read*, Lawrence Erlbaum, Hillsdale, NJ.

Hulme, C. and Snowling, M.J. (eds) (1997) Chapters 8, 4 and 11, in *Dyslexia: Biology, Cognition and Intervention*, Whurr Publishers, London.

Snowling, M.J. (1987, 2001) *Dyslexia: A Cognitive Perspective*, Blackwell, Oxford.

Snowling, M.J. and Thomson, M.E. (1992) Chapters 5–8, in *Dyslexia: Integrating Theory and Practice*, Whurr Publishers, London.

# 8

# Models of Memory

As well as obvious problems with reading and spelling, one of the key features of the dyslexic learner is problems with aspects of memory. In particular, these centre around short-term memory, in its relationship both to classroom instructions and organization and in particular, to aspects of written language learning. Obviously, a failure to internalize or remember grapheme–phoneme rules or sound–symbol correspondence is a key feature of learning to read and part of the memory system. However, in addition, we need to look at the naming problems that people with dyslexia manifest and their use of phonetic or phonological codes in short-term memory systems, and an overview of aspects of current thinking about human memory is essential if we are to understand the totality of the dyslexia syndrome. It is also on the syllabus of all the courses that deal with dyslexia, from certificate through diploma and post-graduate masters degrees! Inevitably, as in other cases of reviewing the psychology underlying dyslexia, we need to be selective. There is a mountain of psychological research, many books on memory (see Further reading). The focus will be primarily on working memory (a way of conceptualizing short-term memory), but I make a brief reference to other aspects of memory systems. We shall briefly review some of the more recent ideas in describing memory, but most have their roots in the idea of a modal memory system. This describes memory in terms of a series of stages, and a typical example is given in Figure 8.1.

*The Psychology of Dyslexia – A Handbook for Teachers,* by Michael Thomson
© 2009 John Wiley & Sons Ltd

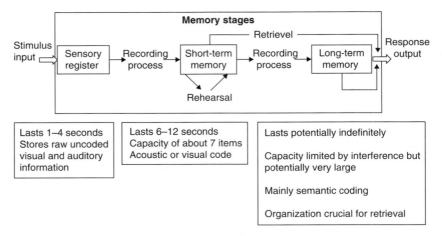

**Figure 8.1** Multi-store or modal model of memory.

Memory systems are very broadly divided into three areas, sometimes referred to as the sensory register, short-term or working memory, and long-term memory. The sensory register is essentially a very brief store of uncoded visual and auditory information. There are, of course, sensory registers for other modalities, including kinaesthetic and all of our five senses, but there has been much less research and focus on these in the psychological literature. Basically, a sensory register decays rapidly but has quite a large capacity. A typical experiment demonstrating a visual sensory register (sometimes known as iconic memory) is a tachistoscopic task (Table 8.1): an array is presented very briefly (50 ms) in a tachistoscope (a box-like machine where stimuli are presented for someone to look at through a viewer). Subjects are asked to report what they remember once the light has been turned off. On average, they remember about four to five items before their memory of the numbers decays. However, if the subjects are asked to read off the top, bottom or middle line, that is, their memory is cued by a high, medium or low tone, they are usually able to remember three to four of any line cued (despite not knowing which line was going to be cued). The implication for this is that the whole array is available very briefly in our sensory register or iconic memory, but because it decays so rapidly, we are only able to remember a few of the numbers unless

**Table 8.1** Array of 12 digits presented by a tachistoscope.

| | | | |
|---|---|---|---|
| 3 | 1 | 8 | 4 |
| 2 | 6 | 5 | 2 |
| 9 | 4 | 7 | 9 |

we are cued specifically to focus on one or two areas. If we do this, we are able to read these off quite happily, while the others decay.

When we look at the relationship between memory and dyslexia, we see that there is some evidence for problems in certain aspects of the sensory register, particularly naming, but in general terms, this is not now a primary area of research into dyslexia and its relationship to reading difficulties.

The modal model shows a short-term memory system that involves recoding material, both for input and output in short-term memory, and there is a need for rehearsal. The capacity in short-term memory systems is very limited. Acoustic or visual (and other) codes are used, and as Figure 8.1 illustrates, this lasts about 6–12 s. Finally, there is a long-term memory system that potentially has a very large capacity. One of the main problems concerns the retrieval of information from the long-term memory stores.

Traditionally, short-term memory has seemed to be mainly an acoustic or visual storage system, whereas the long-term memory system is mainly semantic. Also, originally, there were proposals that the short-term memory system was essentially an electrical feedback system, that is, material was kept in the short-term memory by electrical activity or traces in the central nervous system, in particular the brain, whereas the long-term memory was seen to be a more permanent store. This was postulated to be the result of bio-chemical changes in the ribonucleic acid in the cells of the brain's neurons. It is beyond the scope of this book to pursue these ideas further; instead, I would like to present a more up-to-date picture of memory systems, and then we can focus in particular on working memory.

Figure 8.2 is an expanded, slightly different version of the modal memory system. We see in this that there is still a sensory memory,

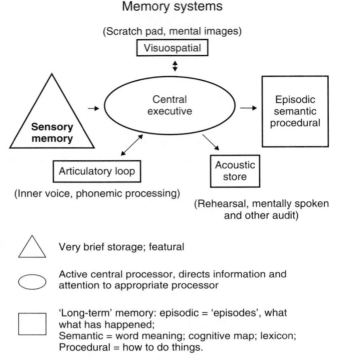

**Figure 8.2** Memory systems.

which involves very brief storage and looks at the features of input coming to us from the environment. We then have the working memory system that consists of a central executive. This is an active central processor, to make a computer analogy, and directs information to other processors and also into the memory system. You can see that there are interactive loops between the central executive and the articulatory loop, the visuospatial processor and the acoustic store. These involve, respectively, the so-called inner voice or phonemic processing, a visuospatial 'scratch pad' dealing with mental images and an acoustic store dealing with rehearsal and mentally spoken and other auditory materials. We return to these areas in more detail later.

Finally, there is the long-term memory. This is broadly agreed to be divided into at least three components. One is the episodic which, as the name implies, is essentially what has happened in the past and the 'episodes' in one's life, for example, what happened when you went to the fair in Bognor! Semantic memory deals with word meaning. It is related to what is sometimes known as the cognitive map, that is, our awareness of the world around us, its structure, assumed and common memories, and knowledge. In addition, semantic memory deals with the lexicon, that is, our internal dictionary. There are obviously important components of accessing the lexicon in both reading and spelling, as well as our language work, and this is an area that has some impact on dyslexic difficulties. Thirdly, there is procedural memory, that is, how to do things or procedures. This might be things such as boiling an egg, changing the carburettor on the car and so on. It is interesting to note that procedural memory can consist of a string of small items or just one overall procedure, depending on how one codes and memorizes, for example, the procedure to 'boil an egg' is essentially just one unit of memory for myself and most readers. On the other hand, for a young person away from home for the first time, 'boil an egg' is not one procedure – it is a whole series of different ones: find a saucepan, put water in it, put it on to boil, place egg in saucepan, time egg and so on!

We now look in more detail at working memory, which is the system that is most relevant to dyslexia. Working memory is essentially what we might call the 'desktop' of the brain. It keeps track of what we do moment by moment and organizes and directs our attention. It has a number of features. The first is its relatively limited capacity, that is, it deals with an immediate past experience. Although all senses input information into the working memory system, there is also a selection and attentional component here, as a result of the limited capacity. In addition, it is a temporary system. The purpose of this seems to be to avoid 'crowding'. Obviously, if we were unable to forget information coming in to us at any particular moment, we would have difficulty dealing with everyday events. An example that illustrates dyslexic difficulties came from a boy I taught recently. Although very severely dyslexic, he was able, given time, to undertake multi-syllable words. However, with a simpler example such as *magnet*, if I gave him another word before he had finished processing the first, it was almost as though he was unable to use selective attention or avoid the second word crowding

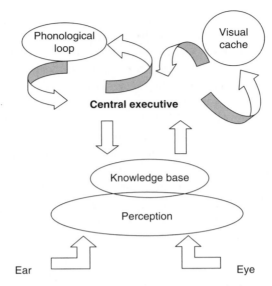

**Figure 8.3** Representation of working memory.

out the first. Thus, he would get very frustrated and annoyed with me if I gave another word before he had finished processing the first one, and sometimes the second one would interfere with the first, so that he might write *mag-fem* if the second word given was *poem*. To return to the working memory, it is also an active system, that is, material must be combined, manipulated and interpreted by the central executive.

Figure 8.3 illustrates a slightly different way of conceptualizing working memory. It may be seen, for the purposes of illustration here, that the input is just auditory and visual. The phonological loop is connected with speech and sounds, and the visual cache with writing output. The central executive also has the function of allocating inputs and directing operations. There is a connection between what is referred to as a knowledge base. This can also refer to information from long-term memory and semantic and lexical systems, as well as procedures and episodes. Figure 8.4 breaks these elements down into further detail, with some additional notes.

The central executive is seen to be modality free, whereas the phonological loop and the visuospatial scratch pad are linked to

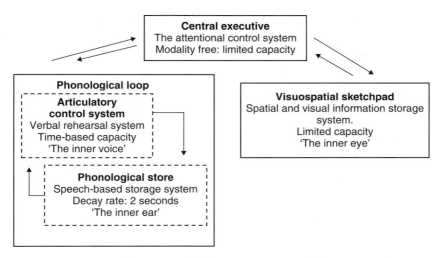

**Figure 8.4** Working memory model.

auditory and visual information, respectively. Again, we use various terminologies here – visual cache, visuospatial scratch pad and so on. The visual cache appears to have a number of different functions. One is concerned with visual appearance and location. If you imagine shutting your eyes and then picking up an object in front of you, this is essentially an aspect of visual imagery. You are remembering where the object is and can put your hands on it without looking. Similarly, the sort of memory required to describe a scene that you have looked at is involved in this aspect of working memory. Information is held and new information is also generated from a knowledge base, that is, having seen a double-decker bus when looking at a scene, but also your knowledge of double-decker buses, the fact that they tend to be red and so on, all help in the description of the scene.

Visual cache is also involved in the so-called mental discovery. You might want to imagine some shapes or, if you are given some shapes, you can recombine them in different ways to produce something else. This form of mental imagery may also transfer to the phonological loop if you are naming something. You might want to try using a large rectangle, a triangle and three smaller rectangles of the same size. If you recombine these using the triangle as a roof, the large rectangle as walls and the three smaller rectangles as a door and two windows, we now have a new object that we can label 'house'. The phonological loop is of particular interest to us because it has relationships with language, reading and dyslexia, in particular. It is generally divided into articulatory control and a phonological store. The articulatory control system is described as the so-called 'inner voice'. This is essentially a verbal rehearsal system, which is linked to some vocal activities. Importantly, it is a serial and temporal system; that is, it maintains things in order and concerns time-based decay. These are key features of some difficulties that dyslexics have.

The phonological store, on the other hand, is a speech-based storage system. The so-called 'inner ear' is less involved with articulatory rehearsal. It decays quite rapidly, but as indicated in Figure 8.4, it can be recycled through the articulatory control system. The phonological loop is quite clearly linked to our speech system, and indeed to language. There is also an additional assumed coding system within the phonological loop. Phonological coding can involve two elements. One is the loudness and acoustic pitch of auditory stimuli coming in and the second, importantly as far as written language is concerned, is phonemic speech sounds; that is, what are the important, significant sounds in a given language and, in the case of reading, how do these relate to the graphemes used to represent them. Phonological coding is quite clearly related to aspects of phonemic awareness and phonological skills that we have described in assessment procedures and in the nature of written language systems (see Chapter 7).

# Recent models of working memory

I make no apology for the fact that including recent models of working memory will include some overlap with previous models. These concepts are not easy for readers who do not have a psychological background and I certainly find rereading and recapping by looking at the different diagrams very helpful!

The working memory systems were always seen to be somewhat independent of long-term memory. For example, Vallar and Baddeley (1984) showed that phonological working memory

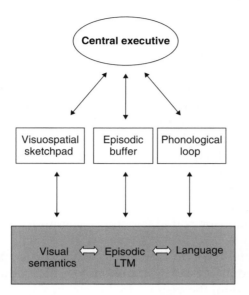

**Figure 8.5** Recent model of working memory after Baddeley (2002). LTM, long term memory.

difficulties can occur independently of normal language and verbal long-term memory. Baddeley (2002) proposed a further system, however, which is needed to integrate information from long-term memory that allows active maintenance and manipulation of information. Therefore, a fourth component to memory, the episodic buffer was proposed. This is a storage system using many different modalities, for example, visual or auditory, and is episodic in the sense that it holds scenes or 'episodes' and provides a limited capacity for an interface between the systems that use different kinds of codes. The idea of this is that there is retrieval from the buffer through conscious awareness. The central executive is purely attentional, whereas the buffer would be a new storage system. A figure representing these more recent versions of the current models is illustrated in Figure 8.5.

It may be seen from this that there is an explicit link between the two memory systems. The flow of information between what is described as fluid and crystallized systems is bidirectional, that is, between the subsidiary systems feeding the relevant areas of long-term memory and also, crucially, in this view, the episodic buffer combining information from long-term memory and that of the other systems. There is some evidence that these systems do have neuropsychological or other anatomic basis (Prabhakaran *et al.*, 2000).

In this additional model, a crystallized system indicates the accumulation of long-term knowledge, such as language and meaning, whereas fluid systems or capacities are those that are unchanged by learning, other than indirectly by the crystallized systems – such as attention and temporary storage. (The concept of fluid versus crystallized cognitive skills in relation to intelligence is also discussed in Chapter 3.) Thus, a memory trace in phonological store might stem either from a direct auditory input or from a subvocal articulation or sound/symbol recognition, such as a letter knowledge.

We, therefore, have an attentional controller (central executive) and two subsidiary systems – the phonological loop holding speech-based information, the visuospatial sketchpad providing a similar function for visual information and a 'buffer' providing a storage interface between long-term memory and other systems. These themselves form active stores capable of combining information from sensory input and from the central executive.

There are some quite interesting relationships between the so-called span tasks and language in the phonological loop, for example, there is a good correlation between speech rate and digit span. Many dyslexics have problems with digit span, and it is also interesting to note that a good deal of research has shown that remembering a sequence of longer words is more difficult than remembering a sequence of shorter words in general. This appears to be linked with the memory capacities involved in the articulatory control system. The longer the words, the more the system is being stretched in its capacity. We can see the resonance with dyslexia – if there are short-term memory weaknesses, it is not surprising that long words can present difficulties and that dyslexics can have segmentation problems.

There are also some quite interesting effects that can occur in laboratory-based tasks, one of which is the so-called 'articulatory suppression'. Try counting a simple number sequence in your head – say 1–10 or 10–20. This is an easy task, but if at the same time you repeat the word 'the' – 'the' – 'the' out loud, you will find that the task becomes much more difficult! This illustrates quite nicely the limited capacity of some of these systems, and perhaps may give an insight into what could be happening with dyslexic children. Perhaps asking a person with dyslexia to spell is equivalent to giving him or her an articulatory suppression task. Obviously, articulatory control, the phonological code and the phonological store are all aspects required in written language learning. Segmentation and pronunciation tasks are linked to articulatory control; giving a grapheme a sound code is phonological coding and remembering that link is the phonological store.

One suggestion is that the phonological loop is a key element of learning to read, but perhaps when reading becomes difficult, it is also a system back-up. There is evidence to suggest that when reading becomes difficult, there are subvocalized larynx movements in individuals, and articulatory suppression tasks decrease comprehension. In general, an articulatory suppression task enables us to remember the gist of what we have read if we are fluent readers, but the exact wording suffers.

There have also been attempts to link the categorizations from experimental psychology of working memory to research in neuropsychology, for example, in brain imaging techniques using the cerebral blood flow, we can find evidence for different neuropsychological systems. These imaging techniques rely on an increase in blood flow to areas of the brain that are excited or fired up when particular tasks are being performed. We examined some examples of research in Chapter 6, but in this case using positron emission tomography, that is, looking at blood flow and getting colour-coded brain maps, we find evidence for a phonological loop being divided into a memory store and a rehearsal system (phonological store and articulatory rehearsal, respectively). In addition, mental rehearsal of letters seems to fire up Broca's area, which is involved in speech production, whereas letter memory is related to the supramarginal gyrus (see Chapters 5 and 6).

There are, of course, other models of human memory systems. There is no space to examine these, but it may be worth just mentioning a couple so that interested readers can follow this up from further reading later. Two slightly different approaches to memory are the adaptive control of thought (ACT) system and the parallel distributive processing (PDP) system linked to neural networks.

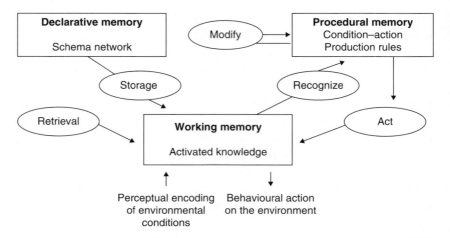

**Figure 8.6** A general framework for the adaptive control of thought system, identifying the major structural components and their interlinking processes.

The ACT system can be summarized in terms of its general framework (Figure 8.6). The main elements are particularly associated with long-term memory and look at a number of processes, including encoding, storage, retrieval, recognition, action, performance and modification, which are seen as interlinking processes.

The PDP approach looks at the development of neural networking ideas in neuropsychology, as well as in cognitive psychology. Basically, the idea is that, as neurons seem to have multi-connections with each other and build up networks, perhaps our memory system works in similar kinds of ways. PDP research gets quite complicated and builds up mathematical models of the extent and way in which neurons are weighted. The idea is that our experience and things that we learn will result in the neural nets in our brain learning. The way this is done is by the activation traces between neurons being easier to excite because of previous experience and excitations. This results in certain input patterns that are weighted, so information from minimal cues can give rise to memories. The advantage of this kind of approach is that it explains how much of our brain is redundant – the notion of 'redundant encoding' is an important component of the PDP approach. It also takes into account the so-called graceful degradation, that is, that our memory systems do not suddenly stop, but we can gradually forget things over time.

As far as the relationship between PDP and written language is concerned, there are some quite interesting research approaches coming out. Indeed, the following discussion could equally be in Chapter 7. The most influential model is that of Seidenberg and McClelland (1989), although a review by Snowling (1998) is the most relevant to dyslexia. In their connectionist or PDP model, multi-level processing assigns weights to the representation of words. Two representational units are proposed – orthographic and phonological units. An orthographic unit is the coding of letters in printed words and the phonological unit is the coding of word pronunciation. The former is seen to be an input unit and the latter output, both connected via intermediate or hidden units.

Research looking at the recognition of triple strings in a given word, for example, -ma, mak, ake and ke-, has examined the sequence of features that activates the unit. It has been found that the brain responds to many different input triples, that is, recognition of orthographic units. These can then access phonological, that is, pronunciation or output, units each of which will specify a triplet of phonetic features. Researchers have constructed computer networks, based on the above principles, that behave in similar ways to human subjects undertaking the same task. In particular, computer models, after training, in recognizing specific triplets, can generalize to words that have not been explicitly taught. The above model looks purely at word recognition and it is recognized that semantic information is also used during reading; later models have incorporated this.

Snowling (1998) stated that such models can be a useful metaphor for the reading process because they are sensitive to the irregularities of the English language and, as they are explicit, can be easily tested. Thus, the observation that children use rime as opposed to phonemes (i.e. fr-og rather than f-r-o-g) more easily in English is predicted by the connectionist model because more 'transparent' languages, that is, those with more regular sound–symbol correspondence, are more easily learnt at the phoneme level.

As far as dyslexia is concerned, we have the possibility of problems in either or both orthographic or phonological units.

Computer modelling of coarse coding of output units can be shown to learn less effectively or generalize less well. So, we not only have specific deficits at verbal short-term memory that link to the phonological theories of dyslexia, but also leave open some of the perceptual or visual processing difficulties that might operate in some people with dyslexia.

We have not touched on many other aspects of memory, including schemas, semantic memory, everyday memory, including eye witness accounts, meta-memory and so on. These are really beyond the scope of this book, and the interested reader is referred to Further reading. The purpose of this chapter has been to provide an outline of those concepts that are needed to understand memory and phonological difficulties in dyslexia.

## Further reading

Baddeley, A. (1990) *Human Memory: Theory and Practice*, Lawrence Erlbaum, Basingstoke.
Baddeley, A. (1999) *Essentials of Human Memory*, Psychology Press, Hove.
Cohen, G., Kiss, G. and Le-Voi, M. (1993) *Memory: Current Issues*, Open University Press, Buckingham.

# 9

# Phonological and Memory Deficits in Dyslexia

## A core phonological deficit

In this chapter, we turn to the cognitive level of dyslexia, examining, in particular, the notion of a phonological deficit and its overlap with verbal short-term memory difficulties in children with dyslexia. Figure 9.1 shows a typical causal model of dyslexia resulting from phonological deficit, as put forward by Frith (1999).

In Figure 9.1, unspecified assumptions about the biological basis are made, for example, left hemisphere disconnection or difference in processing (see Chapter 6). However, the notion of a left hemisphere disconnection has become much more specific as we have seen from the recent magnetic resonance imaging scans and other research that are underlined and outlined in Chapter 6. Again, as mentioned earlier, a differential processing in the brain does not mean that we cannot overcome those difficulties. Differences in neurological processing give rise to a phonological deficit, which can result in poor grapheme–phoneme (G–P) knowledge, that is, difficulties in learning the alphabet. Of course, there will be an environmental part to play here because, if you do not get taught letter–sound correspondence, you are not going to have that knowledge. This component is acknowledged in Figure 9.1. Also included are the type of orthography, for example, the difficulty of English against, say, more regular spelling in Spanish or a pictograph system in Chinese. This phonological deficit gives rise to some of the things that you observe in children with dyslexia. In Figure 9.1, particular

*The Psychology of Dyslexia – A Handbook for Teachers,* by Michael Thomson
© 2009 John Wiley & Sons Ltd

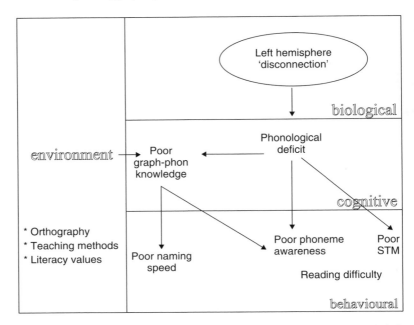

**Figure 9.1** A casual model of dyslexia as a result of a phonological deficit. Adapted from Frith (1999) graph-phon, grapheme-phoneme; STM, short-term (working) memory.

examples of poor phonemic awareness and naming speed and short-term memory as a result of a phonological deficit are given. The directionality of this particular relationship is something that we discuss in more detail later in the chapter. Also of note are literacy values, that is, expectations of learning from home or at school, which are all important elements associated with school learning and its relationship to written language learning.

An important element of this model, which we have discussed elsewhere as well is the differential cause or roots of phonological difficulty. One can see that a phonological deficit can give rise to poor phonemic awareness, poor working memory and naming speed difficulties, as well as poor G–P knowledge. Poor G–P knowledge is just another way of explaining alphabetical decoding

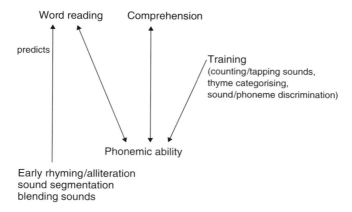

**Figure 9.2** Phonological knowledge and literacy.

difficulties in dyslexia and you can see that the environment impinges on that. Of course, if you have never been taught that /c/ /ă/ /t/ represents the sounds used in speech or you have not been given any information about developing reading skills, in terms of being taught, you will also have weak G–P knowledge. You have seen, particularly in our discussions of discrepancy models and elsewhere, that there could be a number of other reasons or barriers to learning, which could affect a child's G–P correspondence and, by inference, a child's decoding and reading skills. What we are discussing in this chapter is the notion of a core phonological deficit, which is seen to be causing the weakness in this area.

Before we look at an overview of the evidence for a phonological deficit in children with dyslexia, it is worth examining one or two methodological issues. At this point, it is also worth reminding readers that they should be familiar with the earlier chapters on the development of written language learning in children, as well as models of reading, writing and spelling process. A good deal of research has pinpointed the relationship between early rhyming skills and future reading, and Figure 9.2 illustrates elements of this.

Just to remind the reader – language can consist of grammar or syntax, semantics or meaning, the pragmatics or communicative interaction including nonverbal elements as well as phonology or

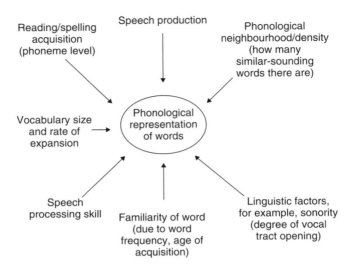

**Figure 9.3** Factors affecting phonological representation. (Adapted from Goswami, 2000.)

the sound component. Speech input processes give rise to phonological representation. This phonological representation of words is affected by many different factors including vocabulary size, size and structure of the words themselves, as well as the frequency the particular language the person is using and the ages of that acquisition of words, as well as speech process (see Figure 9.3).

According to Goswami (2000), the child's phonological representations become increasingly segmented as they start to sound out within words, whether by syllables or individual phonemes. As vocabulary grows, the phonological representations are restructured, so that smaller elements of sounds are represented.

More recently, Snowling and Hulme (2006) provided a good deal of evidence in their review that phonological difficulties predict future reading performance and there are two causal foundations for reading. This is shown in Figure 9.4. Here, it may be seen that phonemic skills and letter knowledge are both good predictors of early reading.

There is an interaction between pre-reading letter knowledge, giving rise to phonemic awareness and phonemic awareness to

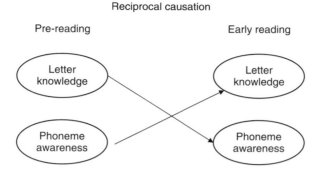

**Figure 9.4** Relationship between letter knowledge and phoneme awareness (after Snowling and Hulme, 2006).

letter knowledge. Another way of expressing this reciprocal causation is that letter–sound knowledge and phoneme awareness are related in the sense that 'each promotes and in turn is promoted by the other.'

The ability to blend sounds together or to segment or separate sound units, and the use of alliteration and rhyming skills are all good predictors of later reading skills. Phonemic ability, which again is associated with the relationship between speech and the sound, and also syllabification skills, sounding out words, separating them into sound units, are also important for word reading. There is an interaction here, that is, the better you are at reading, the better you are at phonemic skills. Conversely, the better you are at phonemic skills, the better your reading is likely to be. This inter-relationship is, of course, one of the problems in aspects of dyslexia research, particularly when looking at control groups. Phonemic ability, which to some extent is interactive, dependent on and gives rise to good word reading, is also linked to comprehension. Training, that is, teaching by categorizing sounds, phoneme discrimination and other such skills, can improve phonemic ability, which underlies both word reading and comprehension; this in turn can give rise to improved phonemic ability. It sounds rather complex and full of circularities, but it is important to understand this inter-activity and 'networking' of the learning process.

Research suggests that, if a child has good skills in the area that predicts reading at age 4 or 5 years, he or she will become a good reader at 6 or 7 years, and a number of longitudinal studies have supported this (e.g. Bryant and Bradley, 1985). However, there is a two-way relationship between word reading and phonemic ability. As we develop our reading skills, for example, alphabetical skills, we would expect phonemic abilities to develop, particularly those in letter–sound or G–P correspondence; if we look at Frith's premise that early alphabetical skills are derived from spelling, the notion of mapping letters on to their sound units is also a phonemic ability relating to reading. We thus have the problem that an individual who shows poor phonemic abilities may show those resulting from their poor reading skills, rather than poor reading being caused by poor phonemic ability.

One very useful representation that looks at the relationship between comprehension and phonemic ability is discussed by Snowling and Hulme (2006). If we look at two dimensions, phonology or phonological process and wider language difficulties, one can place these as right angles as shown in Figure 9.5.

Obviously, there are many other dimensions that readers might want to propose, but here is a quite good conceptualization that helps us in reviewing children's teaching programmes. The classic dyslexic has good wider language skills by and large, and therefore, as we saw earlier, typical tests like the Neale Analysis, where comprehension can be tested following words given to a child, might

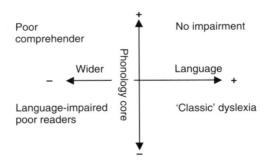

**Figure 9.5** Spectrum of reading difficulties.

be rather better. In general terms, their comprehension skills are good and these children form part of the bottom-right quadrant. Children with good phonology and good wider language skills showed no impairment at all (top right-hand quadrant). Those who show poor performance in both, at the bottom left-hand side of the quadrant, are language-impaired poor readers, that would include some dyslexics, but also might include the so-called common or garden reader or the slower learner. Finally, a very specific kind of learning difficulty, which is receiving increasing attention now, is those children who are good phonologically. Their word reading may be good and their nonword reading may be excellent, but they do not understand what they read and there may be a specific problem in that area. It is interesting to note, however, that this is also independent of intelligence as you might get some intelligent children who have specific comprehension weaknesses, but also some children of low ability, who can read very well, but might fall in to the top left-hand quadrant in this particular model.

Another way of conceptualizing this is by looking at the diagram on Chapter 7 – Figure 7.5 on interaction systems for written language. We can see here that if you put deficits in, for example, the phonological processor, you might find the typical dyslexic child. If you put deficits in the meaning processor, you might find meaning or comprehension difficulties and so on.

There is also a relationship between phonemic abilities and comprehension. Obviously, the better you are in reading, the more your comprehension skills will develop; there is also the relationship between specific training of phonemic ability skills, which will develop phonemic ability. We therefore have at least three different aspects – word reading, comprehension and specific teaching – that will develop phonological abilities. (Note that the term phonological skills or phonemic ability is used very widely here and the reader is referred to Tables 3.2 and 7.7 for a description for some of these subskills.)

This interrelationship between cognitive skills, as measured in the laboratory or by psychometrics, and the reading, writing and spelling process is a problematic one. Let us take, for example, a typically early experiment looking at the ability of children to blend sounds together. The test, that is, dependent variable, might be the

**Table 9.1** Control groups used in a hypothetical study.

|  | Chronological age (years) | Reading age (years) |
|---|---|---|
| Dyslexic children | 10 | 7 |
| Control group 1 | 10 | 10 |
| Control group 2 | 7 | 7 |

score out of 10 for a child's ability to put /c/–/a/–/t/ together to make a word along with nine other examples. Table 9.1 shows typical control groups that might be used.

One method of examining the relationship between sound blending and dyslexia would be using children with dyslexia and control group 1. Typically, the dyslexic children might have an average chronological age of 10 and be reading 3 years behind with an average reading age of 7. However, children in the control group would be reading at their chronological age. If, for example, the dyslexics were found to be weaker at sound blending than the controls, one could say that sound-blending difficulties are a cause of dyslexia. However, we could argue that the sound-blending difficulties of children with dyslexia are not a result of the underlying phonological deficit but a result of their reading ability. Perhaps the skills of reading from the level of a seven-year-old through to the level of a 10-year-old require more phonemic awareness and alphabetical skills, which develop sound blending. An analogy might be the skill of swimming. If we took a group of good, highly trained swimmers and a group of nonswimmers, we might find that the trained swimmers would have larger pectoral muscles. We could conclude that having large pectoral muscles meant that you became a good swimmer. However, a much more likely explanation is that, as you learn to swim, become a better swimmer and train often, so your pectoral muscles develop. Having large pectoral muscles is a result of swimming. Thus, good sound blending could be a result of better reading.

In an attempt to sort out this chicken and egg argument, most recent research looking at aspects of cognitive development that are linked to reading and spelling development uses a similar control group to control group 2 shown in Table 9.1. Here, we have children who are at the same reading level as children with dyslexia – they, of course, need to be younger children so that they are 'normal' and do not have reading and spelling difficulties. However, this means that, if you find that the younger control group who are reading at the same level as the older children with dyslexia are better, in this example, at sound blending, we can be more confident about the assertion that weak sound-blending ability in dyslexic children shows a causal relationship to their weakness in reading. This is the result of the fact that, despite having the same reading level as (younger) nondyslexic children, they have a weaker sound-blending ability. Of course, there are also difficulties in interpretation. The fact is that the control group are developmentally younger, and making generalizations comparing this with an older group may be fraught with difficulties. Furthermore, some researchers argue that the very point is that the children with dyslexia, despite being exposed to the same teaching experience and reading material as other children, are not acquiring reading and spelling (and sound-blending skills) and this itself is of significant interest.

As we can see, these issues are complex; heated debates occur at scientific conferences, with people taking particular views. Fortunately, with my teacher's, as opposed to my psychologist's, hat on, I can say that it will not affect very much how I actually teach the children; I am interested in results rather than the underlying theory. The theory does guide the way that I teach and the principles I use. However, the specific features of a child, which I have gleaned from assessment and observed in my teaching, are probably more important in guiding the detail of my teaching. What is quite clear to me is that children with dyslexia show a wide variety of different behaviours under the general umbrella of the syndrome of dyslexia, which would include aspects of visual processing, motor development and other approaches that we examined in earlier chapters.

To return to the phonological deficit notion, however, it is worth commenting that this has become a central plank for many researchers, almost to the level that it has become an accepted assumption that children with dyslexia have phonological weaknesses. Part of the Orton Society's definition of dyslexia reads '…characterized by difficulties in single word decoding, usually reflecting insufficient phonological processing abilities'. The implication is that the main weakness of a person with dyslexia will be with phonological processing abilities, resulting in single-word decoding problems.

We can be more specific about the phonological weaknesses shown by children with dyslexia. The reader might want to refer to Table 3.3 (p. 71) for different skills tapped under 'phonological' and Table 7.8 (p. 164) for general comments on phonological development and dyslexia. However, Table 9.2 summarizes some specific research findings. (See also an earlier review by Snowling, 1987, 2000.)

The results expressed in Table 9.2 (p. 189) can be subsumed under the notion that children with dyslexia are weak at the explicit analysis of phonemic or perhaps acoustic information needed for accurate reading and spelling, and the notion of 'fuzzy representations' has been put forward by those examining the relationship between speech development and written language development. Basically, the idea is that poorly specified phonological representations prevent the precise learning of phoneme–grapheme mapping. In other words, if you cannot follow speech sounds very well, this prevents you from relating that particular sound to the particular letter combinations representing that sound. Obviously, the difficulties in phonemic mapping, that is, which particular aspects of the sounds are represented by which particular part of the word, are implicated here; the reader may remember that this could be at the phonemic level, for example, f-r-o-g, onset and rime level, for example, fr-og, or syllable level, for example, mag-net.

All of these have been suggested as being weak at one point or another in children with dyslexia and, if there are no stable representations of these elements, there will be no sublexical developments. This implies that there will be no ability to build up parts of words and therefore no generalization to new words using alphabetical skills, in learning new words to read. We have therefore some quite strong evidence that phonological processing skills are certainly intimately tied up with dyslexic learning difficulties. We have already seen that recent neuropsychological evidence (see Chapter 6) highlights the speech-to-phonemic awareness to written language link as being weak in people with dyslexia. One suggestion is that, although the 'normal' brain is processing one sound at a time, people perceive/combine the letters as a whole word. In good readers, this process is so fast that, although they read whole words, in fact they are converting letters on the written page to sounds. Therefore, to read the word 'cat', the reader initially must

**Table 9.2** Examples of studies on phonological deficits in dyslexia.

| Findings | Examples of researchers |
| --- | --- |
| Weak sound blending good predictor of dyslexia (poor phonemic awareness/segmentation skills). Also found weak auditory and visual short-term memory good predictors | Newton and Thomson (1976) |
| Dyslexic children weaker at naming tasks, for example, pictures, colours, letters. As good as controls for visual recognition itself (poor phonological/verbal coding) | Denckla and Rudel (1976) Liberman et al. (1977) Ellis and Miles (1978) Swan and Goswami (1997) |
| Dyslexic children weaker reading and repeating nonwords (poor phonological representation/sublexical components) | Snowling (1981) Bruck and Treiman (1998) Castles and Coltheart (1993) |
| At-risk (for reading) children weaker on vocabulary, phonological awareness, letter knowledge | Scarborough (1990) Snowling and Nation (1997) |
| Poor rhyming and alliteration are good predictors of later reading failure (poor sound categorization skills) | Bradley and Bryant (1983) |
| Brain imaging differential activation of left hemisphere in phonological tasks in dyslexics | Paulesu *et al.* (1996) Shaywitz, Shaywitz and Pugh (1998) |
| Weak phonological segmentation (and naming/short-term memory) | Ellis and Large (1988) |
| Dyslexic children weaker on word generating on the basis of phoneme, but equal on categories (weak alphabetical skills) | Frith, Landerl and Frith (1995) |
| Dyslexic children weak on grapheme–phoneme tasks, specifically on sound coding. Good on visual coding | Mark *et al.* (1977) Snowling (1980) Hick (1981) |
| Dyslexic children poor at segmenting syllables into phonemes | Fox and Routh (1980) |
| General phonological awareness difficulties | Blachman (2000) Share and Stanovich (1995) Stanovich and Siegel (1994) Torgesen, Wagner and Rashotte (1994) Griffiths and Snowling (2002) |

parse, or segment, the word into its underlying phonological elements. Once the word is in its phonological form, it can be identified and understood. In dyslexia, an inefficient phonological module produces representations that are less clear and hence difficult to bring into awareness. Chapter 6 gives examples of explicit parts of the brain that process phonological information differently in dyslexics.

It is worth commenting at this point on the distinction between two levels of the so-called lexical access or word reading. One is the phonological lexicon or a permanent storage for word forms and another is the so-called sublexical phonological representation, which is the short term store for whatever can be represented in phonological forms. This could be words, nonsense sequences of phonemes, nonwords, bit of words, rhymes and so on and so forth. One notion of the phonological deficit model of dyslexia is that the representations of phonemes or strings of phonemes at the sublexical level are sparser or have insufficient resolution. Another notion is that the features of a given phoneme are unspecified, in other words, in the awareness of a sound structure, whether it is voiced, unvoiced – where different aspects of its phonology are not clear or possibly that representations are defined, but they compete with each other.

One of the ways that I conceptualize this confusion is by thinking of the written language system. In English and most western orthographies that different sounds can be spelt in different ways and also the same letters or orthographic combinations have different sound representations (e.g. great, meat, meet). You can imagine a whole array of possible sounds connecting to a whole array of possible orthographies (letter combinations) representing those sounds! The sounds and letters are trying to be matched by the brain, as it were, seeking what possible representations of sounds are available and vice versa and connecting. Sometimes, these connect correctly; so /wāt/ is spelt 'wait' or /sěd/ is spelt 'said'. At other times, they are connected incorrectly; so we have 'wayt' or 'wate' or 'sed' or 'ced'. That sort of model does explain some of the more phonetic errors that children have problems with. When you look, however, at the more nonphonemic errors that children produce, then it becomes more difficult. If you look at the errors given in Table 7.7 in Chapter 7, you can see examples of nonphonemic attempts. For example 'bcpns' for 'puppy' and other examples. Here, the notion of confused choice of phonemic representation does not perhaps hold so well, and one has to look at problems with actual representation of the sounds in the first instance.

It is, of course, argued that if there are difficulties in phonological and alphabetical mapping, which give rise to difficulties in word decoding, this will prevent proper comprehension of reading developing as well. Vellutino *et al.* (2004) argued that there is an asymmetry such that difficulties in word decoding or identification are much greater determinants of future comprehension than reading comprehension affecting the early stages of reading development; that is, word decoding affects comprehension more than the other way around. Furthermore, that sublexical knowledge, such as phonological awareness, application of letter–sound correspondence, spelling ability, name retrieval, verbal memory or word identification are the at-risk areas rather than higher-order lexical components such as vocabulary and general knowledge.

The notion of 'poorly specified phonological representations' (Griffiths and Snowling, 2002) might be due to the difficulties in storing and retrieving printed words, in particular distinct orthography representations, as well as difficulties in processing information in working memory. Difficulties in name storage and retrieval could impair reader's ability to establish connections between spoken and graphic counterparts of printed words, which in turn, prevent the reader's ability to store good representations of word spellings and, therefore, prevent them from acquiring fluency in word identification. This is, of course, as we have discussed, critically important as a prerequisite for good reading comprehension.

Another idea is 'mappings'. Mappings reflect a child's organization and understanding of how the sounds of language 'fit' onto letters. Dyslexic children are seen as having deficits at the level of phonological representations which compromise their ability to set up mappings between orthography and phonology. Many dyslexic children are insensitive to such phonological connections and treat each word as if it is unique; they therefore have no schema for organizing and generalizing.

At this stage, the reader can see that it is not exactly possible to decide whether the detail is in a difference in phonemic representation, in memory bonding or inter-phonetic boundaries. What we can say is that there is certainly a very heavy component of phonological awareness, phonological coding and working memory included in the cognitive aetiology of dyslexia!

Before we briefly evaluate the phonological deficit approach in dyslexia, it is worth making a comment on the so-called 'double-deficit hypothesis.' There is a good deal of research showing that dyslexics have difficulties in naming. Wolf, Bowers and Biddle (2000) argued that the speed of naming is a combination of perception, attention, articulation and word-retrieval processes.

They suggested that there are three subtypes of reading difficulty. The first is the deficit in phonological awareness and letter sign coding problem. The second is slow naming speed, which particularly disrupts orthographic processing and fluency. The third type of deficit, known as the double deficit, is the most severe form of difficulty combining both phonological and rapid naming skill deficiencies. There is certainly plenty of evidence to show that dyslexics do have naming difficulties, even with simple naming of colours at speed, but the issue is how to interpret this. Wolf and her coworkers postulated that poor naming is due to timing mechanisms in integrating the sound and visual components of printed words. In other words, the letters cannot be identified quickly and there will not be a process close enough in time to relate the second to orthography. There is, therefore, an impairment in the storage of representations of spellings. Vellutino *et al.* criticized this particular approach as they say that the timing mechanism is too vague and assumes serial processing of visual information in word or letter components, which is not related to current reading theory. Also, they argued that phonological deficits have not been controlled, and these essentially are what naming components are about. There are quite complex theoretical and methodological arguments to take into account here, and it is certainly possible that rapid letter or digit naming may simply be a method of reading speed, as opposed to component process. However, these esoteric arguments are beyond the scope of this book – the interested reader is referred to the review by Schatschneider *et al.* (2002).

A further suggestion on specific mechanisms is that dyslexics' phonological storage is coarser grained. In other words, their phonological categories are broader and less well separated. For example, according to Mody, Studdert-Kennedy and Brady (1997), dyslexic children made errors on 'ba'–'da' and 'da'–'ga' syllable identification, whereas they made no errors on 'ba'–'sa' and 'da'–'sa', which have wider differences phonologically.

There are, however, a number of question marks about the full acceptance of a phonological deficit as a total explanation of dyslexia. The first of these is what one might term the 'syndrome of dyslexia', that is, examining what dyslexic children actually do. One of the key features is that many dyslexics have problems with organization. One might almost argue that weak organizational skills underlie many problems of children with dyslexia, including things that we might describe as being concerned with short-term memory, for example, remembering instructions and events during the day, as well as longer verbal memory tasks, such as days of the week, months of the year and tables. Some children with dyslexia have problems in motor development (see Chapter 6), and others have apparent visual difficulties (see also Chapter 6). So, we cannot just accept phonological deficit as the only answer because there are other models and theories of aetiology.

A second problem is the extent of the phonological weakness and why it does not extend to other aspects of language. Many dyslexics with dyslexia have very good speaking and comprehension skills, whether measured psychometrically or by talking to dyslexic children. In reading itself, a good deal of research (see Thomson, 1990) shows that dyslexic children are much better at comprehension skills; indeed, Stanovich (1994) argued that one definition of dyslexia could be the discrepancy between word reading and comprehension skills (see Chapter 4). If we accept that specific phonological skills may be weak in children with dyslexia, surely that would affect other aspects of verbal reasoning, vocabulary development and so on. Phonological weakness could affect the metacognitive, that is, the conscious segmentation of alphabet, or what Galaburda (1999) elegantly calls 'parsing the phonetic stream'. Another problem is the relationship between phonological deficits and intelligence. We have examined this in relation to the discrepancy models in Chapter 4, but if we look at Figure 9.6, taken from Frith (1999), we can see another proposed relationship between tests that tap G–P knowledge, phonological processes and so-called 'g' or general ability.

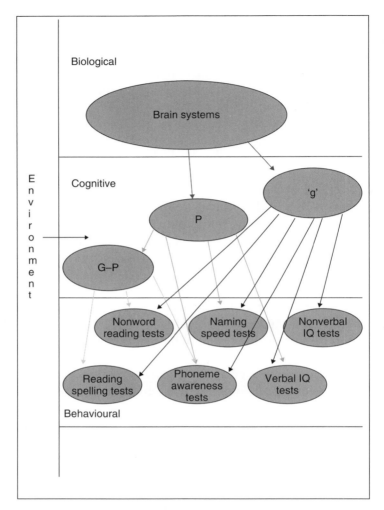

**Figure 9.6** A sketch of the hypothetical relationships between tests tapping grapheme–phoneme (G–P) knowledge, phonological processes (P) and general ability (g).

One problem here is that weak phonological processing can give rise to problems in verbal IQ, as well as G–P knowledge and other behavioural skills. However, children with dyslexia do not, in general, have a weaker verbal than nonverbal IQ. This is particularly the case with the WISC-IV as weak subtests for dyslexics are no longer used to compute verbal IQ (WISC-III used Arithmetic, Information and sometimes Digit Span to compute verbal IQ; all of which could be weak in dyslexics).

Another problem is that, if G–P knowledge is linked to environment, that is, teaching methods, then specific weaknesses in these areas will be very much affected by received teaching. Some of the research I have undertaken with students at East Court has shown that dyslexic children who have been given help in their reading, writing and spelling also develop their phonological skills. Using the Phonological Abilities Battery (see Chapter 3), it was found that dyslexic children who had made good progress in reading performed well on the test. Basically, if one assumes that phonological abilities are causal, one might expect them still to remain weak even though children's reading, writing and spelling develop. However, training can develop these skills so we come back to cause-and-effect interpretations.

A third problem is the overlap and direction of explanation of phonological deficits and short-term memory. There have been a number of attempts to claim that phonological deficits are a core feature, and therefore, we can reject the notions of short-term memory weaknesses. This has been the result of differences between the notion of 'short-term memory' and 'working memory'. The latter enables a more detailed analysis of the processes involved (see Chapter 8). I believe that there is really not much distinction between the phonological loop in working memory and phonological deficits. These seem to be all part of the same weak process in people with dyslexia; the next section looks in more detail at research into memory and dyslexia.

## Memory difficulties in dyslexia

As well as phonological process, there is also a long history of research into memory difficulties in dyslexia. Table 9.3 summarizes examples of these. Some of the results can clearly be interpreted as phonological or verbal coding, but others seem to suggest other factors in memory. Specific phonemic skills include remembering phoneme–grapheme correspondence rules in order to produce the correct output of letters in spelling; remembering letter-by-letter

**Table 9.3** Examples of studies on dyslexia and memory.

| | |
|---|---|
| Poor performance on 'span' or capacity tasks (weaker information processing) | Bakker (1972) |
| | Miles and Ellis (1981) |
| | Naidoo (1972) |
| | Thomson and Wilsher (1979) |
| | Cohen and Netley (1981) |
| Memory for verbal tasks weaker (poor verbal coding) | Vellutino (1979) |
| | Vellutino *et al.* (1975) |
| | Shankweiler *et al.* (1979) |
| | Mann, Liberman and Shankweiler (1980) |
| | Jorm (1979) |
| | Rack (1985) |
| Weak short-term memory, normal long-term memory (early coding problems in memory) | Nelson and Warrington (1980) |
| | Jorm (1979) |
| | Vellutino *et al.* (1975) |
| Sequential memory (weak sequencing skills) | Thomson and Newton (1979) |
| | Zurif and Carson (1970) |
| | Bakker (1972); Bakker and Schroots (1981) |
| | Thomson (1977) |
| Difficulties in storing and retrieving printed words linked to weak phonological coding and working memory processing | Borstrom and Elbro (1997) |
| | Torgesen *et al.* (1994) |
| | Wagner *et al.* (1997) |

sounds; remembering sounds long enough to blend these in forming words (e.g. c-a-t = cat); being able to correct spelling errors by remembering what the whole word or letter combination looks; being able to copy spellings from the blackboard without having constantly to look up every 2 s or so; and maintaining an auditory or visual image of a spelling or reading pattern long enough for it to be internalized and transferred into other memory systems.

More recent studies have shown a very close connection between working memory skills and performance, for example, as predictors as to whether children would have high or low scores in English (Gathercole, Knight and Stegmann, 2004) and also specifically those children with severe working memory difficulties having problems with literacy and mathematics (Alloway *et al.*, 2004).

If we look specifically at the proposed working memory system outlined in Chapter 8, we see that the skills described in our models of reading and spelling process are part of the phonological loop. Thus, speech-to-reading difficulties are accounted for by problems in the articulating control system and G–P correspondence problems by the phonological store. In addition, the 'inner voice' or articulatory control system is a serial and temporal system that might account for the sequencing and capacity findings outlined earlier.

We can build up more explicit links to the alphabet weaknesses proposed as the core phonological deficit. To build up their vocabulary and read new words, children typically begin to exploit an alphabetical strategy. This approach facilitates the decoding of unfamiliar letter sequences by applying the associations between letters and their sounds. Forming long-term representations of novel phonological material is a key component of written language development, especially at the alphabetical stage; for example, Gathercole and Baddeley (1989) stated that 'phonological memory appears to make a critical contribution to reading development at the point at which relationships between letter groups and sounds are being acquired.' It seems that it is the phonological loop component of 'working memory' that facilitates the learning of new words. They viewed this ability to generate long-lasting representations of brief and novel speech events as a fundamental human capacity and believed that it is this predisposition for vocabulary development that provides the basis for literacy. Indeed, the successful building of an internal store of words, or lexicon, is thought by some to be the main determinant of a child's eventual educational attainment (Sternberg, 1987). Baddeley, Gathercole and Papagno (1998) cited a number of studies that have found that performance on verbal short-term memory tasks, subserved by the phonological loop, correlates with good vocabulary knowledge (e.g. Gathercole and Adams, 1993; Michas and Henry, 1994). According to Gathercole and Baddeley (1989), the function of the phonological loop is to provide temporary storage of novel phonological stimuli while more permanent memory representations are being formed. In their view, some children have a memory deficit that reflects an impairment in the ability to store phonological material in 'working memory', thus interfering with the acquisition of long-term phonological memories. The exact nature of this impairment, they thought, has still to be determined but they put forward a number of possibilities, for example, a 'noisy' system could result in phonological traces being less easily discriminated at retrieval. Alternatively, the capacity to store brief phonological representations may be less in these individuals, leading to fewer items being stored or items being inadequately represented. Another possibility is that the phonological trace decays more rapidly in people with dyslexia.

Of course, there are links between theories of working memory and the psychometric measurement of that. A number of studies, as we have seen in Chapter 3, (e.g. Thomson, 2001) found that dyslexics tend to score less well on the working memory component of the Wechsler Scales. The relevance of this to teaching can be seen in a quote from one of the assessments given on the CD-ROM:

> X's performance is characterized by a very low score on the letter–number sequencing task where he was asked to remember, manipulate and then repeat back a series of digits and letters. The letter–number sequencing task is essentially a measure of the so-called executive function, which is manipulating and holding information in store, while one is undertaking a task, for example, subtraction or other mental arithmetic task. X's performance was a little higher on a second task, digit span, requiring him to repeat back an increasing string of numbers, but the score remained below average. The digit span task is predominately a test of phonological memory, often associated with difficulties with spelling and also following instructions and other auditory processing tasks, which occur in a general school day. X's difficulties in the area of working memory will mean that he will find classroom activities such as remembering, carrying out a list of instructions or taking notes while the teacher is talking, far less easy than his peers. Working memory weaknesses are also related to problems with remembering spelling patterns and phonological decoding, and as a result, reading and spelling attainments are delayed.

More details on what one might suggest about how to cope with such working memory difficulties as a teacher can be found in the attachments to examples, given in the reports in the CD-ROM, under the section entitled 'Some pointers and strategies for short-term memory and working memory difficulties to children'. This illustrates the important relationship between working memory aspects of classroom behaviour and learning.

So, there are very specific parallels between phonological skills in general and working memory models. However, if we look at other aspects of the memory models, we find some useful pointers on other aspects of dyslexia, for example, attentional focus problems. The 'but I taught you this yesterday' and the 'but didn't you hear me say page 8–10 for your homework' and similar comments could be part of the phonological loop, but does have 'central executive' implications (see Chapter 8).

The central executive has a number of functions including the following:

- strategy
- monitoring and planning
- attentional control
- initiation, sustaining, shifting, inhibition, stopping.

Attention is by its nature selective, whether to an internal event, such as an image of a spelling pattern, or external to a teacher, classmate, worksheet or blackboard. The direction and focus of attention are thus selective and will involve attention shifting. Thus, the sequence of events attended to and the process of 'engage'/ 'disengage' are all elements of the central executive. A further element of attention is accuracy over an extended period of time, that is, sustained attention.

The reader who is experienced in working with children with dyslexia will note the resonance of these features. Many dyslexic children with dyslexia find it difficult to keep engaged and will often switch focus. The maintenance of attention, particularly to written language that is difficult for them, is also problematic. (How often do we as adults keep our focus on something that we find difficult?)

There has been little work on examining the role of the central executive in children with dyslexia, but what we can say is that the problems in phonology, written language and attention are all elements of working memory systems. Individual differences in working memory organization explains specific dyslexic features

**Table 9.4** Research and teaching-oriented approaches to specific learning difficulties.

| Research psychologist | Experienced teacher |
|---|---|
| **Difficulties with:** | |
| Grapheme–phoneme links | Problems learning the letters of the alphabet |
| Grapheme–phoneme conversion rules | Weak decoding skills |
| Grapheme–phoneme mapping | Forgets which letter(s) to use for the sound |
| Phonemic awareness | Confuses sounds in words |
| Systematic simplifications of vowels | Confuses vowel sounds in words |
| Metaphonological skills | Problems in following speech and applying to spelling |
| Visual orthographic processing | Weak proofreading – problems remembering what a word looks like |
| Phonological coding | Problems with phonics (yes, but specifically where?) |
| Phonological segmentation skills | Cannot beat out syllables in words |
| Phonological recombination skills | Cannot blend sounds |
| Lexical access | Cannot remember whole word spelling or meaning |
| **Teach by:** | |
| Visualization of orthographic patterns | Look and say |
| Explicit phoneme–grapheme mapping | Phonics |
| Lexical analogy | Word families |
| Multi-sensory simultaneous oral spelling | Hearing, saying letters, writing or tracing, saying, reading |
| Orthographic conventions | Spelling rules |
| Onset and rime | Split words into consonant blend unit plus vowel/consonant unit |
| Systematic simplification of phonological segmentation process | Syllable analysis |

(e.g. digit span, lack of attention to enable encoding into phonological loop space), as well as the phonological deficits that are more directly related to written language systems.

Dyslexia is from the failure to acquire phonological awareness and skills in alphabetic decoding. These may be due to poorly specified phonological representations, due to weak phonological coding. These may underlie some of the other difficulties in memory as in storing or retrieving printed words or remembering distinctive orthographic representations as well as general processing information of the working memory. It further suggests that the difficulties in name storage and retrieval also impair connective bonds between spoken and graphic outputs of printed words. These impair the reader's ability to store appropriate representations of word spellings.

However, all of this is still the subject of ongoing research and I am afraid I still cannot say to the reader 'this is the proven cause of dyslexia'. It is a syndrome of related difficulties. As we have seen, core elements are differential processing of phonological material in the left hemisphere. This gives rise to the core phonological/working memory deficits at a cognitive level. However, we still need to take into account the motor and visual systems mentioned in Chapter 6. All of these points have been discussed in earlier chapters.

The final comment really is a slightly tongue-in-cheek one, because I feel that there is a great deal of what one might term 'academic jargon' in relation to phonological deficit. Some of the early researchers talked about specific weaknesses in G–P correspondence. This is nothing less than saying that children with dyslexia have problems in learning letter–sound links, hardly a revelation and really a description of their difficulties! Table 9.4 shows some descriptions by research psychologists against those of teachers and various other ways of describing processes. These might help the reader to 'decode the jargon'!

# Further reading

Hulme, C. and Snowling, M.J. (1994) Chapters 1–6, in *Reading Development and Dyslexia*, Whurr, London.

Miles, T.R. and Miles, E. (1999) Chapters 4–7, in *Dyslexia or Hundred Years On*, Open University Press, Milton Keynes.

Pumfrey, P. and Reason, R. (1991) Chapter 5, in *Specific Learning Difficulties*, NFER–Nelson, Windsor.

Snowling, M.J. (1987, 2000) *Dyslexia: A Cognitive Development Perspective*, Blackwell, Oxford.

Snowling, M.J. and Stackhouse, J. (eds) (1996) Chapters 3 and 4, in *Dyslexia, Speech and Language*, Whurr, London.

Thomson, M.E. (1990) Chapter 3, in *Developmental Dyslexia*, Whurr, London.

# 10

# The Social Psychology of Dyslexia

This is a completely new chapter in this second edition book as it was suggested by many people that ignoring the social aspect of dyslexia does not give a rounded picture of dyslexia. The majority of the book does come from a cognitive psychology background, but this chapter will reduce the balance a little.

## Social context

According to Whitehead (2008), $\frac{3}{4}$ of the British public understand very little about dyslexia and those that do know about dyslexia think it is just about getting letters back to front or that dyslexics need to work harder.

As we have seen, dyslexia does not represent a general learning difficulty. Indeed, according to Hurry (1999), there has been a steady rise in literacy standards over the years, and comments about climbing standards recently are explained by the increase at the lower end of the distribution, that is, the poor attainers progressing. Unfortunately, any reported improvement do not prevent current surveys by organizations such as Dyslexia Action or the British Dyslexia Association from quoting large numbers of dyslexics in the population clearly not being given appropriate help.

In addition, dyslexia is an international problem, and indeed, whenever there is an alphabetical type orthography – there are difficulties. The effects of this lead to substantial loss of skills of society,

*The Psychology of Dyslexia – A Handbook for Teachers,* by Michael Thomson
© 2009 John Wiley & Sons Ltd

let alone the individual problems suffered by those who cannot learn to read in a literate society.

It is surprising, however, how different countries have taken on board the identification and help with dyslexics. According to Malofeef and Kukushkina (2000), Russian children are evaluated soon after their first oral language. There is a multidisciplinary team and their aim is to remediate dyslexics by the age of 10 years old. Chile also has the same scheme running. The whole of the United States identifies so-called 'learning disabilities', which is equivalent to specific learning difficulties in the United Kingdom. However, it was only really from 1986 onwards that the true extent of national dyslexia emerged in the United States (McKinney and Feagans, 1987).

In India, in areas where there is a means to identify dyslexia from other general literacy difficulties, the numbers concerned are staggering. If one takes an estimate of 5% of the population being dyslexic, there must be around 5 million dyslexic children in India alone. Probably a further 15 million adults are dyslexic, although this is complicated by the hundreds of different languages and dialects throughout the subcontinent. Some cultures, of course, are less willing to identify learning difficulties in general and sometimes problems with reading are considered to be unacceptable or even shameful. For example, according to Yamada (2000), research suggests a figure of over 6% to be dyslexic in Japan, whereas the official Education Department estimate is 1%. It is also noticeable that the International Dyslexia Association grew from 28 members in 1949 to 12000 in 50 countries in 1997.

Of course, there are huge swaths of the population of the world, where dyslexia is not that relevant in relation to literacy difficulties. By that I mean, that there is no universal literacy expected, or there is no education for much of the population – there are few schools and there may be many other priorities in the educational development of literacy.

In addition, the social context needs to take into account the specific language that a child is learning. Technically, the term transparency is used to identify languages, which are either very or not very regular. In European languages, for example, Finnish, Greek, Italian and Spanish are more regular and are more 'transparent'

(ā)

| |
|---|
| make *rain* play great<br>*vein* *eight* reign<br>baby the*y* |

**Figure 10.1** Phoneme chart for (ā) taken from East Court School indicating possible alternative spellings of sounds.

with 'shallow orthography'. English is one of the least transparent where there are, for example, many irregular words and different ways of spelling sounds. For example, the sound 'ā' can be spelt in many different ways as shown in Figure 10.1.

Here, it can be seen that the same sound has different spellings and the same spellings may have different sounds. No wonder there is confusion!

See also page 141 for some examples of Japanese syllabaries illustrating how language can be confused. We have seen in this book all the various 'deficits' that dyslexic children have. Of course, this is only part of the story because the difficulties that the person has with reading and writing are in the context of a social landscape. My experience and many others working in dyslexia is that, contrary to the notion that labelling is harmful, calling a person dyslexic is actually incredibly helpful. Many are so relieved to have a label for their odd problems that it simply becomes associated with relieve from stress. They have not been dropped on their heads when they were 2 years old! More seriously, the adjectives such as stupid, thick, spastic, maladjusted, retarded, disturbed, brain injured, handicapped and backward that have been thrown at them (surely much more destructive labels than 'dyslexic') can no longer be applied by them to themselves. This sense of relief for families and for the individuals is tremendous.

Many dyslexics, therefore, do not see themselves labelled as having 'disabilities', as Whitehead (op. cit.) commented, dyslexia is essentially a difference in thinking style and it can be empowering to help them make educational decisions for themselves. This is a comment I heartily agree with.

There is also the cultural and ethnic context to take into account. It is so very often assumed that if a child comes from a home background that is socially disadvantaged, or that their first language is not English, that their problems are essentially to do with that background. According to Morgan and Klein (2000), very few nonwhite, working class or bilingual speakers were diagnosed as dyslexic at school because of the low expectations surrounding the children, which concealed the dyslexia that was subsequently recognized.

Indeed, they found that all 'ethnic group' dyslexics felt that their learning problems, rather than class or race, were the most significant aspects of the learning and social contexts in which they existed.

Another aspect of the social situation in which dyslexics find themselves, is what Scott (2004) calls 'isolation'. She argued that dyslexics can become isolated because:

- their outward communication is faulty, in terms of their language processing difficulties;
- dyslexics can find difficulty with incoming information, that is, inward communication is faulty, obviously reading and spelling but also language processing;
- perhaps more importantly, poor literacy means that a dyslexic child is separated within the class and withdrawn for remedial work and fails to integrate properly within their age group.

This can make dyslexics anxious and depressed, and frequently, relationship problems can be linked to isolation and have their roots in peer problems at school. We shall look in the next section on various aspects of peer rejection, as a result of being dyslexic. Scott (2004) not only talked about a number of different aspects of isolation, as a result of cognitive processing difficulties but, significantly, also talks about 'learnt helplessness'. This is where one is so used to not being able to do something such as reading, writing and spelling, that it generates a general feeling that you cannot do anything. This can be very important in the social context.

Finally, in this section, it is worth drawing attention to the surprising lack of politicization among dyslexics. In this country, if we take a conservative estimate of 4% of children who are dyslexic, there will be two dyslexic children in a class of 25, 10 or more in a primary school of 250 and in a comprehensive school of 1500, around 60 children. That is over 390 000 dyslexic children in the United Kingdom alone, and we have seen how those figures stack up in a larger population. If you look at all of these children as they become adults, you can see that there is a huge part of the population that is dyslexic. Scott (2004) made the point that if this minority ever became organized, their effect would be significant. Many of the current literacy problems and the associated waste of potential in dyslexics will be solved, within a very short time. Scott commented that the number of dyslexics in any one constituency must be larger than the overall majority of most MPs! According to Whitehead (2008) over 200 million adult dyslexics worldwide are not even aware that they are dyslexic either!

## Dyslexia at home and school

*Home*

There are two aspects to the importance of the home for dyslexics that I want to briefly examine. One is what happens when the child is identified as being dyslexic and the importance of that identification, and secondly, the effect that this can have on family dynamics.

The first stages are, of course, the slow recognition that there is a difficulty with the child. As has been implied throughout this book, the difficulty is really a result of the written language system that the child has to confront. A happy and cheerful child going to school, full of enthusiasm and bright-eyed with excitement to learn, comes up against the reality of relating their, possibly, good vocabulary and language use to the written language system. The general failure to remember instructions perhaps, or odd speech patterns may have been put down to immaturity, but soon the child may not be able to write their names as quickly as others. Perhaps, they are not being given a book to read because they are not recognizing key flash cards, or perhaps their ability to remember sounds and letters are weak. There begins to be a little bit of a worry and a concern among parents that something is not quite right. There will be implicit comparisons with other children, who are apparently of equal ability and doing well at school and, perhaps, siblings who show themselves to be further ahead in written language despite being younger. As well as this lack of progress, there may be regressions to other forms of behaviour, such as bed-wetting and even emotional disturbances, like temper tantrums or aggression. This general stress, not only comes from school experiences, but also begins to infiltrate the home.

Parents often comment how their child has completely changed and I must say, with my other hat on, one of the wonderful things about running a school for dyslexic children is how parents will make comments such as 'I have got my child back', when they are getting the appropriate help.

The next stage is, hopefully, an assessment and recognition of the child's learning difficulty. As I have intimated at the beginning of this chapter, this is a tremendous relief for all concerned. Parents and children may have a huge layer, sometimes even years, of humiliation, of guilt with a child's difficulties because they thought they put them in the wrong school or it was because he or she was not loved enough; perhaps there was a fear that there was some brain damage or severe neurological problem, which would never be helped. The children may be concerned that they are, as they always suspected, stupid, or despite the fact that they have been trying hard, no one understands them and just calls them lazy.

My experience is that this understanding of the specific learning difficulty called dyslexia is a very important element in getting a child on the road to overcoming all these secondary emotional reactions that are linked to learning difficulties. Table 10.1 illustrates some of the secondary emotional reactions that can result from having a primary learning difficulty.

These characteristics, of course, overlap with other aspects of the school and I am sure that readers will recognize some of these characters. The child who tries to do anything to avoid having to do the task (of course, dyslexic children have to do the very thing they find the most difficult and have no choice in the matter), or tries to distract the teacher from the task of literacy. This includes off-task behaviour and making jokes, and also, there is the child that will not accept that there is a difficulty and just has a false image of what they can do. This is sometimes linked to both parents and teachers not being congruent. By this counselling term, I mean that

**Table 10.1** Secondary reactions in dyslexic children.

| | |
|---|---|
| 'Overreaction' | • Classroom joker<br>• I am alright/brilliant<br>• Everyone else's fault<br>• Aggression<br>• Work refusal<br>• Sibling rivalry |
| 'Under-reaction' | • Anxiety<br>• Work avoidance<br>• Timidity/victim<br>• Psychosomatic illness<br>• School refusal |
| Underlying loss of confidence | [Suicidal feelings] |

General observed reactions of dyslexics to their learning difficulties.

they are often giving false praise for things which the child knows very well is not good, for example, spelling or reading ability. The 'everyone else's fault' and aggression can quite often be linked. Of course, the notion of work refusal and work avoidance in the under-reaction section are very closely linked.

The general misery that is caused by anxiety and stress in dyslexic children is very much what is reflected at home and extreme reactions being suicidal feelings and feeling that life is not worth living.

Another important element of the home is to understand that while parents and, indeed, siblings want to help the dyslexic child in the home, there are all kinds of implications. One of these is the organizational skills required, which relate to the other aspects of dyslexia, such as losing books, clothes, forgetting messages and appointments, confusing the days of the week, incomplete followings of instructions, inability to read what the homework requires and general disorganization. Parents need strategies such as check-lists, details of lunch money, reading books, pencil cases, materials, schedules worked out and put in appropriate places, bullet boards to be organized, back-up strategies for telephone numbers and many other different planning demands. It would not be very surprising that many parents sometimes resent rather than enjoy these extra routines!

Scott (2004) write eloquently on this and other aspects, particularly the effect of having a child with a learning difficulty in the family. She describes the reactions of both dyslexic and nondyslexic parents as follows:

|  | *Mother* | *Father* |
|---|---|---|
| Dyslexic (parent) | Own anxieties/ separation | Wants help for child as he never got help; sees own failure and helplessness |
| Nondyslexic (parent) | 'Tiger' mode Overprotective Mum – infantilization of the dyslexic – safe to be young | Lazy/stupid child? Hostile and critical Dad – jealous of all the attention |

In the case of the *dyslexic* mothers and fathers, they are both very anxious about their son/daughter having the same difficulties they have. According to Scott and, indeed, in my own experiences, this can result in mothers having even more separation anxiety about a child going to school than normal. A father can see his own failure and helplessness much more clearly which, perhaps, had not been acknowledged before.

In the case of the *nondyslexic* mothers, they go into 'tiger mode', that is, trying to protect their young and fighting tooth and nail for them. The number of dyslexia associations and organizations, both nationally and locally that were originally set up by mothers wanting to get help for their children is a good case in point. Fathers, in my experience, tend to be, perhaps, a little bit less understanding than they might be and can label of their children as being lazy and not trying or perhaps deeply fear that their child is not particularly intelligent.

One of the important elements of this is both from either dyslexic or nondyslexic mothers is that they can be very overprotective. This can result in an infantilization of dyslexic children. It is safe to be young because you do not have to read or spell that well when you are 6 or 7 years old, whereas when you are 12 or 13 years old, you are expected to perform! Similarly, if you want to cling on to your children because you are worried that they will not be successful in the world, this becomes an important issue.

Ironically, this can sometimes have a counterproductive effect on the fathers. The dyslexic child is getting all the attention (this also affects siblings as we shall see later) and sometimes fathers can be rather jealous of the attention. All of these have important implications for the family dynamics and, indeed, the relationship between the parents.

Another important element is, of course, siblings. There is obviously the case that if you have an older dyslexic child who is struggling with reading and spelling and then you have a younger child who is reading and spelling well, this can lead to some bullying, particularly if the dyslexic is being bullied at school. The relationship between dyslexic and nondyslexic siblings can be even more challenging than with ordinary siblings where aggression can rear its head. The relationship between parents and siblings and patterns of conflict is explored by Scott (2004).

All of this need not be too negative, however, as a lot of these issues can be resolved by assessments, giving reasons and accepting dyslexia. Crucially, the child learning and becoming literate, the parents being self-aware and not living out their own difficulties throughout their own children, and, very importantly, telling it how it is, or being congruent, that is, not trying to keep the child younger.

## School

This situation can appear to be even more fraught with difficulties when we turn to the social context of school. Schools can be hostile places for many children, but if you are unable to read, write and spell, it does become a place where, according to Donaldson (1978), the levels of human stress and wasted effort are too high to bear. Edwards (1994), following in-depth interviews with dyslexics, found that many had been neglected and bullied by both their peers and staff, with barely adequate help from their teachers. Later, there was discrimination, humiliation and sometimes violence. Dyslexics

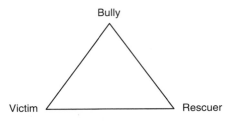

**Figure 10.2** 'Bullying triangle'.

lacked confidence, were sensitive to criticism and experienced disabling behaviours, including truancy, psychosomatic pains, isolation, alienation from peers and a breakdown of family communication.

It is interesting to note that while we are on this topic of victim and aggressive behaviour, that when we did a survey at the school a few years ago, we found that 85% of our children had been bullied. This is not just physical bullying from other children, but also name calling, being made fun of and sarcasm from teachers and so on. There is a 'bullying triangle' (see Figure 10.2), whereby the bullied can become a victim and almost invite bullying or could even slip into becoming a bully, almost as a kind of revenge or that 'this is the way people behave'. There is also then the rescuer, who very often can be the parents, particularly mothers, or perhaps a teacher or friend. We look at bullying again later in this chapter.

*Some factors important in dyslexics and the school situation*   Of course, the major element in dyslexia is the failure in literacy. The important aspect here is that this is very much a public failure. This failure is experienced every time dyslexics are asked to undertake any literacy, which happens many times at school. Dyslexics often talk about the daily terror surrounding these events with a general feeling of not succeeding during many aspects of their school life. However, it is not just literacy, as we have seen, but organization, copying off the board, losing possessions, forgetting lessons and instructions, tripping, dropping things and difficulty with processing of information. All of these can make it difficult to make friends, particularly in the fast language processing in the playground or being chosen to take part in the soccer or netball team.

Schools also, obviously, vary tremendously in terms of the amount of support that is given. Many local education authorities are still slow to recognize dyslexic children and some refuse to statement or even assess them.

Obviously, running a specialist school, I will be accused of bias, but I do think that there is a too ready an expectation that schools should be organized for total inclusion of all special educational needs (SENs). There is certainly a place in schools for units and dyslexia support in the classroom, and this is something that all organizations hope for. Nevertheless, there are still those children that have severe difficulties that require much more intensive specialist help, and it is disappointing that the government and even organizations like the National Association for Special Educational Needs are obsessed with inclusion, without considering how children feel about it themselves.

Individual teachers have tremendous power and importance to any child. Van der Oord and Rispens (1999) found that psychosocial adjustments of children were much more affected by an individual teacher than the school as a whole. The class regulates peer reaction, and a teacher that never gives up and expects good performance of children is very important.

## Psychosocial effects of dyslexia

We have seen on Table 10.1 how behaviours can be internalized and externalized. Looking at those external factors a little bit more, there is some evidence that conduct disorders and even criminality can be associated with dyslexia. My own view is that this is very much a function of literacy skills. The acquisition of literacy can be an effective antidote to re-offending among prisoners. There is a very high incidence of illiteracy among prison populations, some of whom, of course, will be dyslexic. I am more concerned here, however, with the effects of dyslexia within a child and these are really quite marked. Although I have listed these under various headings for convenience, they are interlinked.

## Anxiety

There is a good deal of evidence that anxiety disorders among older pupils are more common in dyslexics, and of course, if you are expected to go to school to read, write and spell and you cannot, then this is not surprising. Anxiety, however, can be presented in many different ways including irritability, restlessness and poor concentration as well as the physical symptoms including dizziness, faintness, sweating, tremor, nausea, shortness of breath, diarrhoea, hyperventilation and many more symptoms. I have observed many dyslexic children with panic attacks, which are the most tremendously fearful thing to happen to anybody. Of course, one should be careful not to make too great a generalization between a dyslexic child who is anxious and the normal anxieties of childhood. However, learning a written language is primarily associated with school, and it is these anxieties that can lead to worries about reading and even lead to school phobia. Of course school phobia as a recognized psychiatric condition may be linked to other causes such as separation anxiety, social phobias and depression as well as dyslexia.

The notion of maternal overprotection can be linked to separation anxiety, as well as the worries and fears about going to school. The provision of 'safe' and 'unsafe' environments are also important. 'Safe' means being able to learn and not be bullied. One of the important aspects of treatment is enforced return to school; but in my experience, this is only helpful if the school is able and willing to meet a child's specific learning difficulties, success in academic matters, support from the social group and praise from the teachers can have a miraculous affect on children who are school phobic because of their dyslexia. The Division of Educational and Child Psychology report on dyslexia by the British Psychological Society (1999) even goes so far as to suggest that emotional behaviour problems linked to dyslexia can be an aspect of the diagnosis, particularly in relation to school absence.

## Stress

Stress can, of course, be linked to anxiety and also correlated with dyslexia. Stress and anxiety are direct and indirect responses, according to Scott (2004), of 'actual and anticipated failure, fear, frustration, suppressed anger and erosion of confidence.' She propose that some dyslexics show aspects of post-traumatic stress disorders (PTSD) and also suffer from the notion of 'daily hassles'. The sudden exclusion from the peer group, the intense anger of a teacher or parent and physical thumps from the bully give rise to the realization that something identifiable is terribly wrong in the relation to the world.

The behavioural effects of PTSD include depression, general anxiety disorder and panic attacks. Perhaps the most relevant form of PTSD is in relation to those who endured years of bullying by teachers, parents, peers or siblings. There is also evidence that physical effects of PTSD can result in inability to make decisions and becoming paralysed with anxiety as adults.

The notion of 'hassles' is really about the daily inconveniences, for example, missing buses, going to the wrong place at the wrong time, being ridiculed in class, forgetting things in class or at home due to problems in short-term memory and so on. These gradually build up, and those dyslexics who have particularly weak short-term memory or processing speed are the most vulnerable. This can also link to stress and illness as well as the debilitating effects of PTSD.

As with all things in children, we should bear in mind research limitations, for example, the assumption of a 'directional hypothesis'. For example, 25% of dyslexics meet the criteria for a serious anxiety disorder, yet other research indicates that 20% of teenage children show severe anxiety disorders; therefore, is that difference between dyslexics and nondyslexics a significant one?

## Bullying

We have already touched on the effects that school can have on dyslexic children, and of course, bullying is a very important aspect of that. We also looked at the bullying triangle, and our own survey at East Court found that 85% of the children had been bullied prior to arrival at the school. McDougall (2001), however, found only 10% in a nondyslexic group who had been bullied. This sort of finding is common to a number of children with SENs, particularly those with dyspraxia or clumsiness problems. Of course, if you are bullied, there can also be the bullying-victim relationship as described earlier, and going to a new school can result in getting your retaliation in first, as it were. Unfortunately, in this day of inclusion, bullying occurs much more in mainstream schools where SEN children join large classes; for example, Whitney, Smith and Thompson (1994) found SEN children more vulnerable to bullying, (see also Euade 1999)

There is the obvious effect of bullying that consists of calling people stupid, lazy, thick, spastic and so on. This can make the victim feel ill, anxious, depressed, angry, resentful or withdrawing and can destroy self-esteem and confidence tremendously. Some of the ways dyslexics can be bullied – hit, pinched, burnt, kicked, having their work destroyed and their possessions stolen – and some of the events that are described by Scott (2004) are truly shocking. Being bullied frequently (and a third of our survey suggested at least three times every week) can lead to worries about school, and severe and long-term bullying can induce PTSD, which can have very significant long-term effects.

Unfortunately, as Parsonage (2002) reported, sometimes children do not tell others about their bullying. Teachers often underestimate the amount of bullying that actually goes on around the school or feel it is helpful to ignore the bullies. The teachers can also be seen as bullies in terms of their lack of understanding or inappropriate labelling. The relationship between literacy and bullying is also particularly acute as it starts to affect dyslexics at around 8–10 years old when the effects of poor literacy are becoming more obvious. This is a peak age for unhelpful behaviour among children, particularly boys (Terwogt, 2002). This age, which a dyslexic child is in most need of dyslexic support, is the age he or she is likely to be bullied. This can also affect aspects of social isolation. While it is true that victims of bullying also demonstrate poor social skills and social cognition, there are sometimes not too great a difference between bullies and being bullied. In general, social bullying is the most common, which involves both physical and verbal abuse. This may involve attacks, or helping the others bully, laughing, watching and also relationship bullying, which is an attempt to destroy friendships or isolate individuals from close friends.

Rigby (2002) also provided more detail on this important aspect of children's development. Here, we have just touched on to how it relates to dyslexia.

## Further reading

Miles, T. and Varmar, V. (eds) (1995) *Dyslexia & Stress*, Whurr (now John Wiley & Sons, Ltd), London.

However, the major source of material for this chapter, a highly readable and thoroughly researched book is:
Scott, R. (2004) *Dyslexia and Counselling*, Whurr (now John Wiley & Sons, Ltd), London.

# References

Adams, M.J. (1996) *Beginning to Read, Thinking and Learning about Print*, MIT Press, Cambridge, MA.

Alloway, T.P., Gathercole, S.E., Adams, A.M. and Willis, C. (2004) Working memory and cognitive skills as predictors of progress towards early learning goals at school entry. *British Journal of Developmental Psychology*, **23**, 417–26.

Annett, M. (1991) Laterality and cerebral dominance. *Journal of Child Psychology and Psychiatry*, **32**, 219–32.

Aylward, E.H., Richards, T.L., Berninger, W. *et al.* (2003) Instructional treatment associated with changes in brain activation in children with dyslexia. *Neuropsychology*, **61**, 212–9.

Baddeley, A. (2002) Is working memory still working? *European Psychologists*, **7** (2), 85–97.

Baddeley, A., Gathercole, S. and Papagno, C. (1998) The phonological loop as a language learning device. *Psychological Review*, **105** (1), 35ff.

Bakker, D.J. (1972) Temporal order in normal and disturbed reading, in *Developmental and Neuropsychological Aspects in Normal and Reading-Retarded Children* (eds D. Bakker and R. Satz), Rotterdam University Press, Rotterdam.

Bakker, D.J. and Schroots, H.J. (1981) Temporal order in normal and disturbed reading, in *Dyslexia Research and Its Applications to Education* (eds G. Pavlides and T. Miles), John Wiley & Sons, Ltd, Chichester.

Bakwin, H. (1973) Reading disability in twins. *Developmental Medicine and Child Neurology*, **15**, 184–7.

Beaumont, J.G., Thomson, M.E. and Rugg, M. (1981) An intrahemispheric integration deficit in dyslexia. *Current Psychology Research*, **1**, 185–9.

*The Psychology of Dyslexia – A Handbook for Teachers*, by Michael Thomson
© 2009 John Wiley & Sons Ltd

Bech-Nielsen, N. (2008) Updated WISC VI profile and index scores on example of dyslexic children. East Court School, Ramsgate. Unpublished paper.

Blachman, B. (2000) Phonological awareness, in *Handbook of Reading Research*, Vol. 3 (eds M. Kamil, P. Mosenthal, P.D. Pearson and R. Barr), Longman, New York.

Blakemore, S.J. and Frith, U. (2005) *The Learning Brain, Lessons for Education*, Blackwell Publishing, Oxford.

Borstrom, I. and Elbro, C. (1997) Prevention of dyslexia in kindergarten: effect of phoneme awareness training with children of dyslexic parents, in *Dyslexia: Biology and Cognitive and Intervention* (eds C. Hulme and M. Snowling), John Wiley & Sons, Ltd, London, pp. 235–53.

Boyle, J. and Fisher, S. (2007) *Educational Testing: A Competence-Based Approach*, BPS Blackwell.

Bradley, L. and Bryant, P.E. (1983) Categorising sounds and learning to read – a causal connection. *Nature*, **301**, 419–21.

British Psychological Society (1999) Working Party of Division of Educational and Child Psychology of the BPS. *Dyslexia, Literacy and Psychological Assessment*, BPS, Leicester.

Brown, K. and Rack, J. (2004) Specific learning difficulties – summaries of information and guidance. *Dyslexia Review*, **15** (3), 10–4.

Bruck, M. and Treiman, R. (1998) Phonological awareness and spelling in normal children and dyslexics: the case of initial consonant clusters. *Journal of Experimental Child Psychology*, **50**, 156–78.

Bryant, P. and Bradley, L. (1985) *Children's Reading Problems*, Blackwell, Oxford.

Cardon, L.R., DeFries, J.C., Fulker, D.W. *et al.* (1994) Quantitative trait locus for reading disability on chromosome 6. *Science*, **265**, 276–9.

Castles, A. and Coltheart, M. (1993) Varieties of developmental dyslexia. *Cognition*, **47**, 149–80.

Cattell, R.B. (1963) Theory of fluid and crystallized intelligence: a critical experiment. *Journal of Educational Psychology*, **54**, 1–22.

Cohen, R.L. and Netley, C. (1981) Short term memory deficits in reading disabled children, in the absence of opportunity for rehearsal strategies. *Intelligence*, **5**, 69–76.

Coltheart, M. (2006) Dual route and connectionist models of reading: an overview. *London Review of Education*, **4**, 5–17.

Coltheart, M. and Jackson, N.E. (1998) Forum on dyslexia. *Child Psychology and Psychiatry Review*, **3** (1), 12–6.

Connors, C.K. (1970) Cortical visual evoked response in children with learning disorders. *Psychophysiology*, **7**, 418–78.

Connors, C.K., Bouin, A.G., Winglee, M. *et al.* (1984) Piracetum and event-related potentials in dyslexic children. *Psychopharmacology Bulletin*, **20**, 667–73.

DeFries, J.C. (1985) Colorado reading project, in *Biobehavioural Measures of Dyslexia* (eds D.B. Gray and J.F. Kavanagh), York Press, Parkton, MD, pp. 107–22.

DeFries, J.C. (1991) Genetics and dyslexia: an overview, in *Dyslexia: Integrating Theory and Practice* (eds M.J. Snowling and M.E. Thomson), Whurr Publishers, London.

DeFries, J.C. and Decker, S.N. (1982) Genetic aspects of reading disability: the Colorado Family Reading Study, in *Reading Disability: Varieties and Treatments* (eds R.N. Malatesha and P.G. Aaron), Academic Press, New York, pp. 255–79.

DeFries, J.C., Gillis, J.J. and Wadsworth, S.J. (1990) Genes and genders: a twin study of reading disability, in *The Extraordinary Brain: Neurobiologic Issues in Developmental Dyslexia* (ed. A.M. Galaburda), MIT Press, Cambridge, MA.

Denckla, M.B. and Rudel, R. (1976) Naming of pictured objects by dyslexic and other learning disabled children. *Brain Language*, **3**, 1–15.

Donaldson, M. (1978) *Children's Minds*, Fontana, London.

Duff F.J. (2008) Defusing reading disorder and evaluating reading intervention. *Journal of Education and Child Psychology*, **25** (3), 31–5.

Dunn, L.I.M., Dunn, L.M., Whetton, C. and Burley, J. (1997) *British Picture Vocabulary Scale*, 2nd edn (BPVS-II), NFER–Nelson, Windsor, Berks.

East Court School (1983, 2000) *Dyslexia and Your Child*, East Court School, Ramsgate.

Edwards, M. (1994) *The Scars of Dyslexia*, Continuum, London.

Ehri, L. (1991) The development of reading and spelling in children; an overview, in *Dyslexia: Integrating Theory and Practice* (eds M. Snowling and M.E. Thomson), Whurr Publishers, London.

Eisenberg, L. (1966) The epidemiology of reading retardation and a program for preventive intervention, in *The Disabled Reader: Education of the Dyslexic Child* (ed. J. Money), Johns Hopkins University Press, Baltimore, MD.

Elliott, J. (2005) The dyslexia debate continues – response. *The Psychologist*, **18** (12); Channel 4 Documentary – The Myth of Dyslexia, September 2005.

Ellis, N. and Large, B. (1988) The early stages of reading: a longitudinal study. *Applied Cognitive Psychology*, **2**, 47–76.

Ellis, N. and Miles, T. (1978) Visual information processing in dyslexic children, in *Practical Aspects of Memory* (eds M. Gruneberg, P. Morris and R. Sykes), Academic Press, London.

Euade, T. (1999) *Learning Difficulties: Dyslexia, Bullying and Other Issues*, Letts Educational, London.

Finucci, J.M., Guthrie, J.T. and Childs, A.L. *et al.* (1976) The genetics of specific reading disability. *Annals of Human Genetics*, **40**, 1–23.

Fisher, S.E., Marlow, A.J. and Lamb, J. (1999) A quantitative-trait locus on chromosome 6p influence different aspects of developmental dyslexia. *American Journal of Human Genetics*, **64**, 146–56.

Fox, B. and Routh, D. (1980) Phonemic analysis and reading disability in children. *Journal of Psycholinguistic Research*, **9** (2), 115–9.

Frederickson, N., Frith, U. and Reason, R. (1997) *Phonological Assessment Battery (PhAB)*, NFER–Nelson, Windsor, Berkshire.

Frith, U. (1985) Beneath the surface of developmental dyslexia, *in Surface Dyslexia in Adults and Children* (eds J.C. Marshall, K.E. Patterson and M. Colheart), Routledge & Kegan Paul, London.

Frith, U. (1992) Model for developmental disorders. *The Psychologist*, Jan issue.

Frith, U. (1999) Paradoxes in the definition of dyslexia. *Dyslexia*, **5** (4), 192–215.

Frith, U. (2008) One to one interview with psychologists. *The Psychologist*, **21** (1), 88.

Frith, U., Landerl, K. and Frith, C. (1995) Dyslexia and verbal fluency: more evidence for a phonological deficit. *Dyslexia*, **1**, 2–11.

Galaburda, A.M. (1989) Ordinary and extraordinary brain development. Anatomical variation in developmental dyslexia. *Annals of Dyslexia*, **39**, 67–80.

Galaburda, A.M. (1999) Developmental dyslexia: a multi-level syndrome. *Dyslexia*, **5** (4), 183–91.

Galaburda, A.M., Signoret, J.C. and Ronthal, M. (1985) Left posterior angiomatous anomaly and developmental dyslexia: report of five cases. *Neurology* **35** (suppl. 6), 198.

Gathercole, S.E. and Adams, A. (1993) Phonological working memory in very young children. *Developmental Psychology*, **29**, 770–8.

Gathercole, S.E. and Alloway, T.P. (2008) *Working Memory and Learning – A Practical Guide for Teachers*, Sage Publications Ltd, London.

Gathercole, S.E. and Baddeley, A.D. (1989) Evaluation of the role of phonological STM in the development of vocabulary in children: a longitudinal study. *Journal of Memory and Language*, **28**, 200–13.

Gathercole, S.E., Knight, C. and Stegmann, Z. (2004) Working memory skills and educational attainment – evidence from National Curriculum assessments at 7 and 14 years of age. *Cognitive Psychology*, **18**, 16.

Gayan, J., Smith, S.D., Cherny, S.S. and Cardon, L.R. (1999) Quantitative trait locus for specific language and reading deficits on chromosome 6p. *American Journal of Human Genetics*, **64**, 157–64.

Goswami, U. (1986) Children's use of analogy in learning to read: a developmental study. *Journal of Experimental Child Psychology*, **42**, 72–83.

Goswami, U. (1988) Children's use of analogy in learning to spell. *British Journal of Developmental Psychology*, **6**, 21–33.

Goswami, U. (2000) *Inset Lecture to East Court School*, Ramsgate.

Goswami, U. and Bryant, P. (1990) *Phonological Skills and Learning to Read*, Erlbaum, Hove, Sussex.

Griffiths, Y.M. and Snowling, M.J. (2002) Predictors of exception word and non-word reading in dyslexic children: the severity hypothesis. *Journal of Educational Psychology*, **94** (1), 34–43.

Grigorenko, E.L., Wood, F.B., Meyer, M.S. (1997) Susceptibility loci for distinct components of developmental dyslexia on chromosome 6 and 15. *American Journal of Human Genetics*, **60**, 27–39.

Habib, M. (2003) Re-wiring the dyslexic brain. *Trends in Cognitive Sciences*, **7** (8), 330–2.

Hallgren, B. (1950) Specific dyslexia ('congenital word blindness'): a clinical and genetic study. *Acta Psychiatrica et Neurologica Scandinavica Supplementum, 65*.

Hedderly, R.G. (1995) The assessment of SpLD pupils for examination arrangements. *Dyslexia Review*, **7** (2), 12–6.

Henderson, E.H. (1981) *Teaching Children to Read and Spell*, Northern Illinois Press, Chicago, IL.

Hick, C. (1981) B/D confusions in dyslexia. *Journal of Research in Reading*, **4**, 21–8.

Hinshelwood, J. (1900) Congenital word blindness. *Lancet*, **I**, 1506–8.

Horn, J.L. (1967) Intelligence – why it grows, why it declines. *Trans-action*, **5**, 31.

Hurry, J. (1999) Annotation: children's reading levels. *Journal of Child Psychology and Psychiatry*, **14** (2), 143–50.

Johnston, R.S. and Morrison, M. (2007) Toward a resolution of inconsistencies in the phonological deficit of reading disorders: phonological reading difficulties are more severe in high – IQ poor readers. *Journal of Learning Disabilities*, **40**, 66–79.

Jorm, A.F. (1979) The cognitive and neurological basis of developmental dyslexia: a theoretical framework and review. *Cognition*, **7**, 19–33.

Liberman, I.Y., Shankweiler, D., Liberman, A.M. *et al.* (1977) Phonetic segmentation and recoding in the beginning reader, in *Towards a Psychology of Reading. The Proceedings of the CUNY Conferences* (eds

A.S. Reber and D. Scarborough), Lawrence Erlbaum Associates, Hillsdale, NJ.

Malofeef, N. and Kukushkina, O. (2000) Advances in diagnosis and treatment of dyslexia in Russia. *Perspectives*, **26** (1), 14.

Mann, V.A., Liberman, I.Y. and Shankweiler, D. (1980) Children's memory for sentences and word strings in relation to reading ability. *Memory Cognition*, **8**, 329–35.

Mark, L.S., Shankweiler, D., Liberman, I.Y. and Fowler, C.A. (1977) Phonetic recoding and reading difficulty in beginning readers. *Memory Cognition*, **5**, 623–9.

Marsh, G., Friedman, M., Welch, V. and Desbery, P. (1981) A cognitive developmental theory of reading acquisition, in *Reading Records: Advancing in Theory and Practice*, Vol. 3 (eds G.E. Mackinson and T.G. Waller), Academic Press, New York, pp. 199–221.

McCormick, M. (2003) Consonants and vowels – an evidenced-based approach to dyslexia, in *Dyslexia Included a Whole School Approach* (ed. M.E. Thomson), David Fulton.

McDougall, S. (2001) Experiences of dyslexia – social and emotional factors associated with living with dyslexia, *Dyslexia Review*, **12** (2), 7–9.

McKinney, J. and Feagans, A.L. (1987) Current issues in research and services for learning disabled children in the United States. *Paedoverasse*, **1** (1), 91–107.

Michas, I.C. and Henry, L.A. (1994) The link between phonological memory and vocabulary acquisition. *British Journal of Developmental Psychology*, **12**, 147–63.

Miles, T. (1974) *Understanding Dyslexia*, Priory Press, London.

Miles, T. and Ellis, N. (1981) A lexical encoding deficiency 1 and 11. Experimental evidence and classical observations, in *Dyslexia Research and Its Application to Education* (eds G. Pavlidis and T. Miles), John Wiley & Sons, Ltd, Chichester.

Miles, T.R. and Varma, V. (1995) *Dyslexia & Stress*, John Wiley & Sons, Ltd, London.

Milne, D. (2005) *Teaching the Brain to Read*, S.K. Publishing, Auckland, New Zealand, Hungerford, Berkshire.

Mody, M., Studdert-Kennedy, M. and Brady, S. (1997) Speech perception deficits in poor readers: auditory processing or phonological coding? *Journal of Experimental Child Psychology*, **64**, 199–231.

Morgan, E. and Klein, C. (2000) *The Dyslexic Adult in a Non-Dyslexic World*, Whurr, London.

Morgan, W.P. (1896) A case of congenital word blindness. *British Medical Journal*, **II**, 378.

Muter, V. (1997) Phonological assessment of dyslexics. Workshop/paper at BDA Conference, York.

Naglieri, J.A. (1985) *Matrix Analogies Test (Short Form)*, Charles Merrill, Columbus, OH.

Naidoo, S. (1972) *Specific Dyslexia*, Pitman, London.

Neale, M.D. (1997) *Neale Analysis of Reading Ability – Revised* (NARA-II; 2nd revised British edn), NFER–Nelson, Windsor.

Neisser, U., Boodoo, B., Bouchrhard, T.J. *et al.* (1996) A type of intelligence – knowns and unknowns. *American Psychologists*, **51**, 70–101.

Nelson, H.E. and Warrington, E.K. (1980) An investigation of memory functions in dyslexic children. *British Journal of Psychology*, **71**, 487–503.

Newton, M. (1970) A neuro-psychological investigation into dyslexia, in *Assessment and Teaching of Dyslexia in Children* (eds A.W. Franklin and S. Naidoo), ICAP, London.

Newton, M.J. and Thomson, M.E. (1976) *The Aston Index: A Screening Procedure for Written Language Difficulties*, Learning Development Aids, Wisbech.

Nicolson, R.I. and Fawcett, A.J. (1999) Developmental dyslexia. The role of the cerebellum. *Dyslexia*, **5** (3), 53–177.

Orton, S.T. (1937) *Reading, Writing and Speech Problems in Children*, Chapman & Hall, London.

Ott, P. (2007) *Teaching Children with Dyslexia: A Practical Guide*, Routledge, Oxford.

Owen, F.W. (1979) Dyslexia – genetic aspects, in *Dyslexia: An Appraisal of Current Knowledge* (eds A.L. Benton and D. Pearl), Oxford University Press, New York.

Owen, F.W., Adams, P.A., Forrest, T. *et al.* (1971) Learning disorders in children: sibling studies. *Monographs of the Society for Research in Child Development*, **36**.

Parsonage, M. (2002) Social effects of dyslexia. Unpublished Master Thesis, Primary Communication.

Paulesu, E., Frith, U., Snowling, M. *et al.* (1996) Is developmental dyslexia a disconnection syndrome? Evidence from PET scanning. *Brain*, **119**, 143–57.

Pavlides, G.T.H. (1981) Sequencing, eye movements and the early objective diagnosis of dyslexia, in *Dyslexia: Research and Its Applications to Dyslexia* (eds G.T.H. Pavlides and T. Miles), John Wiley & Sons, Ltd, Chichester.

Pennington, B.F. (1999) Toward an integrated understanding of dyslexia: genetic, neurological, and cognitive mechanisms. *Development and Psychopathology*, **11**, 629–54.

Pennington, B.F. and Lefly, D.L. (2001) Early reading development in children at family risk for dyslexia. *Child Development*, **72**, 816–33.

Petersson, K., Reisa Askelof, S., Castro-Caldas, A. and Ingvar, M. (2000) Language processing modulated by literacy and network analysis of verbal repetition in literate and illiterate subjects. *Journal of Cognitive and Neuroscience*, **12** (3), 364–82.

Prabhakaran, V., Narayana, K., Zhao, Z. and Gabrielli, J.D.E. (2000) Integration of diverse information of working memory in phonically lobe. *Nature Neuroscience*, **3**, 85–90.

Proctor, B. and Prevatt, F. (2003) Agreement among 4 models used for diagnosing learning disabilities. *Journal of Learning Disabilities*, **36**, 459–66.

Rack, J. (1985) Orthographic and phonetic encoding in normal and dyslexic readers. *British Journal of Psychology*, **76**, 325–40.

Ralford, S., Weiss, L., Rolfus, E. *et al.* (2006) *WISC IV General Abilty Index*, Harcourt Assessment, UK.

Riddick, B. (1996) *Living the Dyslexia, The Social & Emotional Consequences with Specific Learning Difficulties*, Routledge, London.

Rigby, K. (2002) *New Prospectives on Bullying*, Jessica Kingsley, London.

Rutter, M., Tizard, J. and Whitmore, K. (1970) *Education, Health and Behaviour*, Longman, London.

Salvia, J. and Ysseldyke, J.E. (2004) *Assessment in Special Inclusive Education*, 9th edn, Houghton & Miffoin Company, Boston.

Scarborough, H.S. (1990) Very early language deficits in dyslexic children. *Child Development*, **61**, 1728–43.

Schatschneider, C., Carlson, C.D., Francis, D.J. *et al.* (2002) Relationships of rapid automatized naming and phonological awareness in early reading development: implications for the double-deficit hypothesis. *Journal of Learning Disabilities*, **35**, 245–56.

Scott, R. (2004) *Dyslexia & Counselling*, Whurr (now John Wiley & Sons, Ltd), Chichester.

Seidenberg, M. and McClelland, J. (1989) A distributed, developmental model of word recognition and naming. *Psychological Review*, **96**, 523–68.

Shankweiler, D., Libermann, I.Y., Mark, L.S. *et al.* (1979) The speech code and learning to read. *Journal of Experimental Psychology: Human Learning Memory*, **5**, 531–45.

Share, D.L. and Stanovich, K.E. (1995) Cognitive processes in early reading development: accommodation individual differences into a model of acquisition. *Issues in Education: Contributions from Educational Psychology*, **1**, 1–57.

Shaywitz, B.A., Shaywitz, S.E., Pugh, K.R. *et al.* (2002) Disruption of a neuro-circuitry for reading in children with developmental dyslexia. *Biological Psychiatry*, **52**, 101–10.

Shaywitz, S.E., Shaywitz, B.A. and Pugh, K.R. (1998) Functional disruption in the organisation of the brain for reading in dyslexia. *Proceedings of the National Academy of Sciences of the United States of America*, **95**, 2636–41.

Siegal, L.S. (1989) IQ is irrelevant to the definition of learning disabilities. *Journal of Learning Disabilities*, **22**, 469–78, 486.

Silani, G., Frith, U., Demonet, J.F. *et al.* (2005) Brain abnormalities underlining altered activation in dyslexia – a voxel-based morphometry study. *Brain*, **128**, 2453–61.

Simos, P.G., Fletcher, J.M., Bergiman, E. *et al.* (2002) Dyslexia specific brain activation profile becomes normal following successful medium training. *Neurology*, **58**, 1203–13.

Singleton C. (2008) Visual faction in reading. *Journal of Education and Child Psychology*, **25** (3), 8–21.

Sladen, B.K. (1971) Inheritance of dyslexia. *Bulletin of the Orton Society*, **31**, 30–9.

Smith, S.D., Kimberling, W.J., Pennington, B.A. and Lubs, H.A. (1982) Specific reading disability: identification of an inherited form through linkage analysis. *Science*, **219**, 1345–7.

Snowling, M. (1998) Dyslexia as a phonological deficit: evidence and implications. *Child Psychology and Psychiatry Review*, **3** (1), 4–11.

Snowling, M.J. (1980) The development of grapheme-phoneme correspondences in normal and dyslexic readers. *Journal of Experimental Child Psychology*, **29**, 294–305.

Snowling, M.J. (1981) Phonemic deficits in developmental dyslexia. *Psychological Research*, **43**, 219–35.

Snowling, M.J. (1987, 2002 2nd edition) *Dyslexia: A Cognitive Developmental Perspective*, Blackwell, Oxford.

Snowling, M.J. (2005) There are myths about dyslexia, but dyslexia is not a myth. Personal Communication and Press Release, University of York.

Snowling, M.J. and Hulme, C. (2006) Language skills, learning to read and reading intervention. *London Review of Education*, **4**, 63–76.

Snowling, M.J., Muter, V. and Carroll, J. (2007) Children at family risk of dyslexia – a follow-up of early adolescence. *Journal of Child Psychology and Psychiatry*, **48**, 6, 609–18.

Snowling, M.J. and Nation, K.A. (1997) Language, phonology and learning to read, in *Dyslexia: Biology, Cognition and Intervention* (eds C. Hulme and M. Snowling), Whurr Publishers, London.

Snowling, M.J., Stothard, S.E. and Maclean, J. (1996) *Graded Nonword Reading Test*, Thames Valley Trust Co., Bury St Edmunds.

Stanovich, K.E. (1988) "Explaining the differences between the dyslexic and the garden-variety poor reader: the phonological-core variable". *Journal of Learning Disabilities*, **21** (10), 590–604.

Stanovich, K.E. (1994) Annotation: does dyslexia exist? *Journal of Child Psychology and Psychiatry*, **35**, 579–95.

Stanovich, K.E. (1996) Towards a more conclusive definition of dyslexia. *Dyslexia*, **2** (3), 154–66.

Stanovich, K.E. and Siegel, L.S. (1994) Phenotypic performance profile of children with reading disabilities: a regression-based test of the phonological-core variable-difference model. *Journal of Educational Psychology*, **86**, 24–53.

Stein, J. (2001) The magnocellular theory of developmental dyslexia. *Dyslexia*, **7**, 12–36.

Stein, J. and Fowler, S. (1985) Effects of monocular occlusion on visuomotor perception and reading in dyslexic children. *The Lancet*, **2** (8446), 69–73.

Stein, J. and Talcott, J. (1999) Impaired neuronal timing in developmental dyslexia – the magnocellular hypothesis. *Dyslexia*, **5** (2), 59–77.

Sternberg, R. (1987) Most vocabulary is learned from context, in *The Nature of Vocabulary Acquisition* (eds M. McKeown and M. Curtis), Lawrence Erlbaum Associates Inc., Hillsdale, NJ, pp. 89–106.

Stevens A. and Bech-Nielson N. (in press) Sub-test profiles of dyslexics in the WISC-IV and WAIS III. *Dyslexia, Innovation and Insights*.

Stevenson, J., Graham, P., Fredman, G. and McLaughun, V. (1987) A twin study of genetic influences on reading and spelling ability and disability. *Journal of Child Psychology and Psychiatry*, **28**, 229–47.

Swan, D. and Goswami, U. (1997) Phonological awareness deficits in developmental dyslexia and the phonological representations hypothesis. *Journal of Experimental Child Psychology*, **66**, 18–41.

Terwogt, M. (2002) Emotional study in self and others as motives for helping in 10-year-old children. *British Journal of Developmental Psychology*, **20** (1), 131–47.

Thomson, M.E. (1975) Laterality and reading: a research note. *The British Journal of Educational Psychology*, **45**, 313–21.

Thomson, M.E. (1976) Laterality effects in dyslexics and controls using verbal dichotic listening tasks. *Neuropsychologia*, **14**, 243–6.

Thomson, M.E. (1977) Individual differences in the acquisition of written language: an integrated model and its implications for dyslexia. University of Aston. PhD Thesis.

Thomson, M.E. (1979) The nature of written language, in *Readings in Dyslexia: A Study Text to Accompany the Aston Index* (eds M.J. Newton,

M.E. Thomson and I.R. Richards), Learning Development Aids, Wisbech.

Thomson, M.E. (1990) *Developmental Dyslexia*, 3rd edn, John Wiley & Sons, Ltd, London.

Thomson, M.E. (2001) *The Psychology of Dyslexia: A Guide for Teachers*, John Wiley & Sons, Ltd, London.

Thomson, M.E. (2003) Monitoring dyslexics intelligence and attainments – a follow-up study. *Dyslexia*, **9**, 3–17.

Thomson, M.E. and Newton, M.J. (1979) A concurrent validity study of the Aston Index, in *Readings in Dyslexia: A Study Text to Accompany the Aston Index* (eds M.J. Newton, M.E. Thomson and I.R. Richards), Learning Development Aids, Wisbech.

Thomson, M.E. and Watkins, E.J. (1999) *Dyslexia: A Teaching Handbook*, 2nd edn, Whurr Publishers, London.

Thomson, M.E. and Wilsher, C. (1979) Some aspects of memory in dyslexics and controls, in *Practical Aspects of Memory* (eds M. Gruneberg, P. Morris and R. Sykes), Academic Press, London.

Tizard Report, Department of Education and Science (1972) *Report of the Advisory Committee on Handicapped Children*, HMSO, London.

Torgesen, J.K., Wagner, R.J. and Rashotte, C.A. (1994) Longitudinal studies of phonological processing and reading. *Journal of Learning Disabilities*, **27**, 276–86.

Turner M. (2006) The Athlete and the Triage Nurse. *Dyslexia Review 18*, **1**, 8–11.

Vallar, G. and Baddeley, A. (1984) Fractionation of working memory neuro-psychological evidence for a phonological short-term store. *Journal of Verbal Learning and Verbal Behaviour*, **23**, 151–61.

Van der Oord, E. and Rispens, J. (1999) Differences between school classes in pre-schools' psychosocial adjustment. Evidence for the importance of children's interpersonal relationships. *Journal of Child Psychology and Psychiatry*, **40** (3), 417–30.

Vellutino, F.R. (1979) *Dyslexia – Theory and Research*, The MIT Press, Cambridge, MA.

Vellutino, F.R., Fletcher, J.M., Snowling, M.J. and Scanlon, D.M. (2004) Specific reading ability/dyslexia – what have we learnt in the past four decades? *Journal of Child Psychology and Psychiatry*, **45**, 1–40.

Vellutino, F.R., Steger, J.A., Desetto, L. and Phillips, F. (1975) Immediate and delayed recognition of visual stimuli in poor and normal readers. *Journal of Experimental Child Psychology*, **19**, 223–32.

Waddington, C.H. (1957) *The Strategy of Genes*, George Allen & Unwin, London.

Wagner, R.K., Torgesen, J.K., Rashotte, C.A. *et al.* (1997) Changing relations between phonological processing abilities and word-level reading as children develop from beginning to skilled readers: a 5-year longitudinal study. *Developmental Psychology*, **33**, 468–79.

*Wechsler Objective Reading Dimensions* (1993) Psychological Corporation, Sidcup.

Whitehead, R. (2008) Dyslexia socially misunderstood S.E.N. *Journal for Educational Needs*, **32**, 26–7.

Whitney, I., Smith, V. and Thompson, D. (1994) Bullying and children with special educational needs, in *School Bullying Insights and Prospectives* (eds P. Smith and S. Sharp), Routledge, London.

Wilkinson, G.S. (1993) *The Wide Range Achievement Test*, 3rd edn (WRAT-3), Wide Range, Wilmington, DE.

Wolf, M., Bowers, P. and Biddle, K. (2000) Naming speed processes, timing and reading – a conceptual review. *Journal of Learning Dissabilities*, **33**, 387–407.

Yamada, J. (2000) The myth of absence of dyslexia in Japan. *Perspectives*, **26** (1), 22.

Yule, W. (1967) Predicting reading ages on Neale Analysis of Reading Ability. *The British Journal of Educational Psychology*, **37**, 252–5.

Yule, W., Rutter, M., Berger, M. and Thomson, J. (1974) Over and under achievement in reading: distribution in the general population. *The British Journal of Educational Psychology*, **44**, 1–12.

Zurif, E.F. and Carson, G. (1970) Dyslexia in relation to cerebral dominance and temporal analysis. *Neuropsychologia*, **8**, 351–61.

# Index

*The Psychology of Dyslexia – A Handbook for Teachers,* by Michael Thomson
© 2009 John Wiley & Sons Ltd